# A SUMMIT READER

## ESSAYS AND LECTURES IN HONOR OF DAVID NOEBEL'S 70TH BIRTHDAY

EDITED BY
MICHAEL BAUMAN AND FRANCIS BECKWITH

Summit Press
P.O. Box 207
Manitou Springs, CO 80829
(719) 685-9103
www.summit.org

**A Summit Reader**

Edited by Michael Bauman and Frank Beckwith

**ISBN 0-936163-39-9**

Cover Design by Micah Wierenga

# Table of Contents

# Preface

Known universally and affectionately as "Doc," David Noebel has touched the lives of tens of thousands of students at Summit Ministries, in Colorado, over which he has presided for well more than 40 extraordinary years. Under his leadership, that ministry has grown both nationally and internationally. Doc has witnessed first hand how his efforts have flowered among and across three generations of students. Many of those he taught in the 1960s later sent their children to him, and those children are now doing the same with their own, fully confident that the invaluable training they received at his hands will set their own progeny in good stead, no matter what challenges they might face well into the 21st century.

Of course, Doc's influence reaches not only to his students, but also to his faculty and staff, who together have worked to pay tribute to him in the production of this volume. Every one of us, without exception, has benefited from his insight, his knowledge, his good will, his loyalty, and his generosity more times than we can remember. We know by personal experience that Doc Noebel is a wonderful leader, a widely informed and diligent scholar, and a colleague and friend without compare. We intend this book to be a token of the esteem and affection with which we shall always regard him, especially now as he reaches the Biblical milestone of "three score and ten." In more ways than even we ourselves can recount, Doc has taught us better how to "understand the times."

We are sad, but honored, to include in this volume one of the last published works of Dr. Ronald Nash, our late and lamented friend, himself a man of inspiring strength, acumen, and achievement.

      The Editors,
      Michael Bauman and Francis Beckwith

# Noebel Cause
## A Brief History of Summit Ministries

Jobe Martin & Don Baker

---

The God of the Bible knows all, is all powerful, and is good (Psalm 86:15, 89:1)!

An old hotel in Manitou Springs, Colorado, was in the sovereign plan of the Lord Jesus Christ to be used as a leadership training center for the Christian youth of America. The Grand View Hotel was the perfect place to teach teens and young adults how to defend the biblical Christian Faith in relationship to their family, their country, and the faithfulness of their living and loving Redeemer and Heavenly Father. With the overarching purpose of equipping young people to understand their times and to know what they should do about it (1 Chronicles 12:32), Summit Ministries was birthed.

An 1890's advertisement stated:

Manitou Springs, 6527 feet above sea level, is nestled
at the very foot of Pike's Peak, and is beyond question the greatest *Health, Pleasure and Scenic* resort
in the world. It is located in the heart of all the chief
scenic attractions of the Rocky Mountain region,
and its mineral springs make it justly famous as the
Saratoga of the West. Manitou's climate is unsur-
passed in both winter and summer.

Manitou Springs was famous as a health resort in the
late 1800s. The history of the Summit Hotel, originally
known as the Grand View Hotel, began with a German
emigrant couple and their children more than 100 years
ago. The couple was William D. and Margaret (Deterling)
Paulson, born in 1852 and 1855 respectively. The young
couple sailed to the United States in 1869 and settled in
Brooklyn, New York, where William became a wholesale
produce grocer and father of four children.

In 1888, due to Margaret's ill health, the Paulsons
and their children, William, John, Adolph and Dorothy,
migrated westward to the new health resort of Manitou
Springs, Colorado. In May of 1889, the Paulsons purchased,
for $5,000.00, a large house on Osage Avenue from Charles
Pollen. The Paulson's new home sat high above downtown
Manitou, giving them a grand view which reached from the
Ute pass on the west to the Garden of the Gods on the east.

Once her health was regained, industrious Margaret
converted their home into a boarding house for the resort's
year around health-seeking visitors. The Paulsons were
very popular and gained an outstanding reputation for the
home-comfort of their boarding house. Over the next thirty
years this popularity enabled them to enlarge the facility
several times.

The Paulson's kept the hotel in the family for many
years. Shortly after World War 1, William and Margaret's
son, John B. Paulson and his wife, Anna, took over the
active management of the hotel. Under the second genera-

tion of Paulsons, the Grand View hotel continued its prosperity, welcoming guests year around through the roaring 20s, the depression years of the 30s and the war years of the 40s. John served two terms as mayor of Manitou Springs. In 1949 the third generation, John Jr. and his wife, Mary, assumed the active management of the hotel. John and Mary Paulson continued the family tradition of a fine resort hotel until the last guest checked out in September, 1961.

The original Queen Anne style Victorian Grand View Hotel was built sometime prior to 1889. Sitting in the foothills of Pikes Peak and high above Manitou Avenue, at what today is 935 Osage Avenue, it commanded a grand view of the valley below. At least three major additions and several renovations were made to the hotel building by William and Margaret Paulson between 1890 and 1902. The large East Annex was built onto the hotel in 1913 at a cost of $30,000.00, bringing the total guest rooms to sixty-eight. The third floor dining room seated one-hundred twenty-five. The grand opening of the Grand View was held on May 16, 1891 and the hotel was owned and operated by the Paulson family for the next seventy-two years.

(Most of the historical information in this chapter is derived from personal interviews and from John F. McClenahan's *The Grand View Hotel, Manitou Springs, Colorado, 1891-1961,* which he compiled in 1995 for the Manitou Springs Historical Society.)

The following is a newspaper report of the opening of the Grand View Hotel:

### The New Grand View Hotel

The Grand View, William Paulson's new hotel on Osage Avenue, will be opened May 16 [1891]. This is an entirely new addition to the hotel accommodations of Manitou. It is situated on a high eminence just south of the soda springs park and commands unequalled views both of the plains, of the mountains, of the town of Manitou and the adjacent canyons. The Grand View contains twenty-five rooms, elegantly furnished. The dining room is large and well lighted and commands fine views. The building is two stories in height with a high basement, and so stands against the rising ground in the rear that the top floor is only a little higher than the ground, making exit in case of fire easy as well as facilitating the transfer of baggage. The office is large and nicely furnished, with an open fire place and comfortable lounges and chairs. It is Mr. Paulson's intention to run the hotel in a thoroughly first-class manner. His rates will be $2.50 a day with a reduction to permanent guests and families.

In the June 1, 1893 *Manitou Springs Journal,* the hotel was described as being "electrically lighted and heated throughout. The dining room is artistically frescoed and finished in oak. The bedrooms are finished in oak and cherry and carpeted with Moquette and Axminster rugs." The hotel building is a frame construction with beautiful Manitou Greenstone fireplaces in the lobby and ballroom. Many afternoon tea dances with live orchestras in the mezzanine at the back of the ballroom were enjoyed in the beautiful Grand Ballroom on the front ground level.

The original Grand View property extended from the nine-stall garage on the south side of Prospect Place, down one block to Osage Avenue (where the hotel stands), then continued north down the hill to Manitou Avenue. The hotel's private access road (later known as Manitou Place) ran from Osage down to where the stone steps are located, now at 923 Manitou Avenue. A one-story trolley waiting pavilion was also built next to the steps. The hill ascending from Manitou Avenue to the Grand View Hotel is so steep that when the 1920 addition was being built, the Crissey-Fowler lumber trucks could not make the grade, so six-team wagons were used to carry the building materials to the construction site.

Fires were a major problem in the early days of Manitou Springs, but God had a plan for the old Grand View and no fire ever harmed it. The fate of all the other hotels rose and fell with the town's rise and decline as a health resort. Most of the hotels would close for the winter and try to make ends meet by opening only for the summer season. As many of the hotels fell victim to fires, or, as the cost of taxes, maintenance, and insurance escalated, they were converted into low-income apartments. However, the Grand View continued unhindered! The Lord Jesus Christ in His infinite wisdom was protecting this special place for His future use. *"Ah Lord God! Behold Thou hast made the heaven and the earth by Thy great power and stretched out arm, and there is nothing too hard for Thee"* (Jeremiah 32:17).

One noteworthy event happened in the late 1930s. At this time, William Southern, publisher of the Independence Missouri *Examiner,* was staying at the Grand View. One afternoon he was visited by an old friend and United States Senator from back home—Harry S. Truman. They spent the afternoon rocking and visiting on the hotel's veranda, while enjoying the "grand view" of Manitou Springs.

In 1962 the Paulson family sold the well preserved hotel to the Christian Crusade Summer College, now known as Summit Ministries. God's plan was beginning to sprout!

Remember the former things of old: for I am God, and there is none else; I am God, and there is none like me, Declaring the end from the beginning, and from ancient times the things that are not yet done, saying, My counsel shall stand, and I will do all my pleasure (Isaiah 46:9, 10, emphasis added).

On May 5, 1962, the headlines of the *Pikes Peak Journal* of Manitou Springs, Colorado read: "Grand View Hotel Sold; To Be Anti-Red College." Then on Friday, June 1, 1962 the newspaper reported:

The 1963 sessions of the Christian Crusade Anti-Communist Summer College will comprise five terms of two weeks each, and will be under the supervision of accredited college and university professors, teachers in the fields of religion, Constitutional government, economics, Communist theory, practice and subversion, and international relations....Certificates of completion will be issued to those students who qualify at the end of each two-week course.

June 22, 1962: Billy James Hargis of Tulsa, Oklahoma, founder of the Christian Anti-Communist Crusade, announced that the newly purchased Grand View Hotel would be renamed The Summit Hotel and would be used as an "anti-communist youth university." In Jeremiah 29:11 the God of the Bible says, *"For I know the thoughts that I think toward you, saith the Lord, thoughts of peace, and not of evil, to give you an expected end."* The Lord had been preparing hearts, minds and a building to begin to accomplish a specific and intended end in the hearts, minds, and lives of thousands of future young Christian leaders of America.

In order to understand the importance of the founding of Summit Ministries, an understanding of the times in which it was born is necessary. The 1960s were turbulent times. The United States was involved in two undeclared wars; the Cold War and the Vietnam War. A third undeclared war had just ended in a stalemate in Korea at the 38th parallel. The McCarthy censuring by the U.S. Senate had left the country in a quandary. Conservative anti-Communists were trying to awaken the citizens of the USA to the deadly threat of Communism. But others in the USA considered anti-Communists to be trouble-makers and extremists, who spread fear and defamed good people.

For the most part, the church viewed the wars and Communism as political and did not get involved, except as an opportunity for various programs of evangelism. During these confusing times, several organizations arose to warn the American people of the peril, from atheistic Communism. One such organization was the John Birch Society. This Society was established in 1958 with the purpose of educating and warning America of the dangerous penetrations of Communism into the United Nations, the media, government, churches and schools. The Birch

Society advocated that the USA should get out of the United Nations and that the U.N. should get out of the USA.

The U.S. House of Representatives Committee on Un-American Activities held a conference May 29, 1957 with Dr. Fred Schwarz. According to the *Congressional Record*, Mr. Richard Arens asked Dr. Schwarz the following question: "How would you characterize or describe the ideology and morality of communism, and how in, your judgment, can that ideology and morality be countered or met in this world struggle?

**Dr. Schwarz:** The ideology of communism is applied Godless materialism. The problem that perplexes many people is the overwhelming appeal that communism apparently exercises for the student mind.

**Mr. Arens:** What is the nature of that appeal, Dr.?

**Dr. Schwarz:** The nature of that appeal is a promise that the student can achieve two things by association with the communist party. He can participate in the conquest of the world and, following the conquest of the world, he can then participate in a program to change human nature, perfect human character, and populate the entire earth with a new quality of personality infinitely superior to any that history has ever known. The appeal that attracts the young student is almost a religious appeal that his life can be utilized for the regeneration of all mankind.

**Mr. Arens:** Would you care to elaborate on that theme?

**Dr. Schwarz:** When you ask the communists a simple question: "How are you going to change human nature?" They would answer with one word, and that word is *science.* "We are scientists. Science has changed the material world. Science has changed the world of agriculture. Science has changed the world of animal husbandry. We can use science to change human nature itself."

This sounds very appealing. You can understand how this sounds to a young student infatuated with the techniques of science. To participate in using science for its greatest achievement is a seductive vision.

However, to be scientific you must follow scientific laws, and communism then proceeds to give it three scientific laws. These laws are as follows:

The first one is: "There is no God." They are proudly, unashamedly atheistic in theory and in practice. When they deny God, they simultaneously deny every virtue and every value that originates with God. They deny moral law. They deny absolute standards of truth and righteousness. An entire civilized code of moral and ethical values is destroyed so that they are free to erect in their place new moral and ethical standards as the occasion demands.

The second law of communism is that man is a material machine. He is matter in motion and nothing more. Man is a body, and he is completely describable in terms of the laws of chemistry and physics. Man has no soul, no spirit, no significant individual value, no continuity of life. He is entirely an evolutionary product, the specie Homo sapiens, and subject to modification, adaptation, and transformation by the applied, established laws of animal husbandry.

William Z. Foster, chairman of the American Communist Party, expresses it in his book, *The Twilight of World Capitalism*, which he wrote in 1949. In the last chapter, "The Advent of the Socialist Man," he writes: "Henceforth, the evolution of the human species must be done artificially by the conscious action of man himself." Their second law, therefore, is the material animal nature of man.

The third law of communism is economic determinism. It states that the qualities of human intel-

ligence, personality, emotional and religious life
merely reflect the economic environment; that in
the last analysis what we think, what we feel, what
we believe, whom we love, and whom we worship is
simply an expression of the environment in which we
are raised, and since that environment is primarily
concerned with economic forces, in the final analysis,
man is a determined economic being....

Communism rests on a class concept. They
believe the proletariat class is the progressive class
of history and that the capitalist classes, the degenerate classes, are discarded by history and must be
destroyed. To them this is the law of historical development. To argue on a bourgeois moral basis merely
reflects degenerate class origin.

Economic determinism is the third law of
communism.

When Russia sent up the first man into space (Sputnik),
suddenly the people of America began to wake up to the
threats around us. Educators and politicians began calling
for additional science programs in our schools and universities. President Kennedy gave his famous speech, "Ask not
what your country can do for you, but what you can do for
your country."

In the midst of the uncertainty and confusion of the
times, the play, *Inherit the Wind*, was running on Broadway.
Its theme was based on the "Scopes Monkey Trial" of 1925
(classified as the trial of the century). The play, and then
the movie which followed, presented Christianity as ridicu-
lous and the Bible as untrustworthy.

Before the Scopes Trial, Tennessee had passed a law,
the "Butler Act," which outlawed the teaching of evolution
in the public schools. Fifteen other states had similar laws
or had bills pending in their legislatures. The American Civil
Liberties Union, observably anti-Christian, advertised in
Tennessee for a teacher to challenge the law against teaching evolution. John Scopes agreed to challenge the law even
though he probably never had taught evolution.

An aberrant trial procedure took place when the lawyers, Clarence Darrow, an atheist, and William Jennings Bryan, a Christian, agreed to cross-examine each other. Bryan took the witness stand first and Darrow questioned. Darrow's objective was to embarrass Bryan, a noted Christian. William Jennings Bryan was a prominent political figure who had run for president of the USA three times. He was also a great orator and well-known Christian who spoke out against teaching evolution in the public schools.

When Bryan could not biblically defend where Cain got his wife, if the days of Genesis 1 were 24-hour days, or how old the earth was, Darrow had accomplished his goal and demonstrated to the world that there was doubt about the trustworthyness of the Bible. Newsmen from every continent were at the trial and spread the news around the world. All but two of the states with laws or pending legislation against teaching evolution rescinded them and the church became reluctant to defend the literal history in the Genesis narrative.

Following the Scopes trial, the Humanists published *Humanist Manifesto I.* This is the statement of faith of the Humanist worldview. It is a philosophy of life that excludes God, and is intended to be a secular replacement for Christianity. Atheistic Humanist, Madalyn Murray O'Hair (who had ties with Communism) initiated a lawsuit in 1963 which ultimately traveled to the Supreme Court making prayer in the public schools illegal. No Christian organization filed a brief in favor of school prayer. Where was the godly Christian leadership? *"And I sought for a man among them, that should make up the hedge, and stand in the gap before me for the land, that I should not destroy it: but I found none"* (Ezekiel 22:30).

Reflecting on the infamous 1960s brings multiple images into focus. Castro was allowed to communize Cuba in 1959. This laid the ground work for the Bay of Pigs disaster of 1961 and the Cuban Missile Crisis of 1962, when America confronted the Soviet Union and their installation of missiles capable of reaching the mainland of the United States. President Kennedy was assassinated

November 11, 1963. *Mad Magazine* and Johnny Carson had American laughing at things never laughed at before—there was nothing sacred. A certain sense of modesty, decorum, manners, and duty to God, family, and country were being broken down, and few even noticed. Frank Sinatra was singing, "I Did It My Way," and Debbie Boone crooned "How Can It Be Wrong, When It Feels So Right." School children were required to memorize *Invictus*, by Henley, which cemented into their minds the lines: "I am the master of my fate. I am the captain of my soul." The parents and grandparents of the "It's All About Me" generation were being indoctrinated and developed. Prayer was removed from our public schools in 1962. Bible reading in the schools of "Christian America" was banned in 1963. The Barry Goldwater/Lyndon Johnson presidential campaign of 1964 brought many issues to the forefront of our nation, issues of conservatism versus liberalism (with its socialistic and communistic tendencies), and it appeared that socialistic liberalism was winning. Enter Martin Luther King and the national tensions of the Civil Rights movement, culminating in King's death on April 3, 1968 and then the Washington, D.C. riots.

Into this climate of the sixties with its anti-Vietnam war riots and demonstrations, Cold War nuclear holocaust fears, Russians in space, Martin Luther King riots and marches, overwhelming preponderance of evolutionary indoctrination in the schools and universities (after the Supreme Court removed the God of the Bible from public education), and the flower-power of the Hippy revolution, Summit was born! The climate of the age needed to be changed. It was time to convert the Christian "thermometers" sitting placidly in their churches to Christian activist "thermostats." The climate was prepared for change and the Summit was ready for the task.

Nineteen-sixty-two brought David and Alice Noebel to Manitou Springs, Colorado, with a vision—train up a generation of anti-communist, conservative Christian young people to understand the worldviews of their times and to know what they should do about it. There were many Christian youth camps in America in the 1960s, but Summit was the first to warn of the danger of the Communist threat. The purpose was and is to equip a generation of Christian youth for the leadership of our nation in the years to come. Leadership was encouraged, not just in politics, but also in theology, ethics, philosophy, biology, economics, law, sociology, history, art, and music.

Dr. Noebel chose 1 Chronicles 12:32 as one of the theme Bible verses for Summit. *"And of the children of Issachar, which were men that had understanding of the times, to know what Israel ought to do; the heads of them were two hundred; and all their brethren were at their commandment."* The men of the tribe of Issachar understood their times and knew what they should do about it. Israel drew its leaders from this little tribe exactly because these men understood their times and knew what needed to be done. Summit's longstanding goal is to train young people in the understanding of our times and to help them discover the best and most efficient ways of doing what needs to be done to stop the downward spiral into the attractive, but false, worldviews penetrating and destroying Western Civilization.

Dr. Noebel aimed Summit at presenting the trends and events of the day with a biblical critique and perspective. The original curriculum included an hour of Bible lecture each day pointing out major people, places, and doctrines from Genesis to Revelation. From the earliest days of Summit a Bible test (with a passing grade) was required for graduation. The summer of 1962 forty students graduated. This summer (2005) more than 1500 will graduate.

*"I have given them Thy word; and the world hath hated them, because they are not of the world, even as I am not of the world. I pray not that Thou shouldest take them out of the world, but that Thou shouldest keep them from the evil. They are not of the world, even as I am not of the world. Sanctify them through Thy truth:* Thy word is truth" (John 17:14-17, emphasis added). The Christian youth of America must know, understand, and be able to practice the truth of the Bible in order to stand against the erroneous worldviews of their generation. Marxist Communism, Humanism,

New Age Occultism, Postmodernism, Islam, morality, government, nutrition, leadership, economics, history, and evolution are some of the subjects introduced to the students. They are taught how to spot deceptive ideas and combat them both intellectually and biblically. *"But he that doeth truth cometh to the light, that his deeds may be made manifest, that they are wrought in God"* (John 3:21).

Another verse that Dr. Noebel incorporated into the Summit curriculum is Colossians 2:8, *"Beware lest any man spoil you through philosophy and vain deceit, after the tradition of men, after the rudiments of the world, and not after Christ."* Dr. Noebel has always wanted the students to be aware of what they are facing in the secular universities and to know their Christian worldview well enough to be able to stand up against the secularism of the day with biblical and intellectual truth.

In the early days of Summit, Dr. David Noebel spent many hours lecturing about the harmful lifestyle practices generated by Rock 'n Roll music. The Beatles were attracting millions of teens to their hypnotic beat, long hair, and immoral lifestyles. The *Gazette Telegraph* published an article about Summit Ministries on July 1, 1990, and quoted Dr. Noebel as saying, "What does rock 'n roll mean? Sexual intercourse....What is Christian rock 'n roll? Christian sexual intercourse." Noebel is not one to mince words. The challenge to young people is clear: *"If ye continue in My word, then are ye My disciples indeed; And ye shall know the truth, and the truth shall make you free"* (John 8:31b-32). By 1974 Dr, Noebel had published a 346 page book about rock music entitled *The Marxist Minstrels: A Handbook On Communist Subversion Of Music.*

One evening that has been especially important to each Summit session is the last Thursday night of the second week. This is the evening aimed at evangelism and the encouragement of the saints. There have been many young people who have come to a saving knowledge of the Lord Jesus Christ during a Summit session, and often it happens on evangelism night. The staff look forward to this night, but no one lived for it more than Brent Noebel, Dr.

Noebel's son. Dr. Noebel would ask certain staffers or friends of Summit to share their testimonies, and then Brent would close the evening with his testimony. The students always were challenged and encouraged through Brent's words. Brent would ask Scott Myers, brother of Jeff Myers, to play the piano and sing. Two of his favorites that Scotty would play were "Elijah" and "The Lifeboat."

The evening always included a presentation of the Gospel through the testimonies that are shared. The students are told that *"all have sinned and come short of the glory of God"* (Romans 3:23). It is explained to them that *"God commendeth His love toward us in that while we were yet sinners, Christ died for us"* (Romans 5:8). *"For the wages of sin is death; but the gift of God is eternal life through Jesus Christ our Lord"* (Romans 6:23). *"That if thou shalt confess with thy mouth the Lord Jesus, and shalt believe in thine heart that God hath raised Him from the dead, thou shalt be saved"* (Romans 10:9). *"For whosoever shall call upon the name of the Lord shall be saved"* (Romans 10:13). *"For God so loved the world that He gave His only begotten Son, that whosoever believeth in Him should not perish, but have everlasting life"* (John 3:16). After the testimonies, Dr. Noebel has the students think about the account of the Apostle Peter being released from prison by the angel of the Lord as recorded in Acts 12:6-11. He reminds the students that Peter needed to put on his own sandals and walk out on his own. God, however, is the One who released him from the chains that bound him and opened the prison doors. The point is there are some things that only God can do, but then there are some things that man is responsible to take the step to do on his own. Each student has the responsibility to either receive or reject the gift of salvation.

Those who work at Summit desire that no staff member, student, or patron will spend eternity in the Lake of Fire. *"And whosoever was not found written in the book of life was cast into the lake of fire"* (Revelation 20:15). On evangelism night, scores of Summit students have come to realize the fact that they are sinners according to God's Law, and have received Jesus Christ as their Lord and Savior.

Lasting commitments are made during each Summit session. In 1987, a young lady made the commitment to her Lord and Savior that she would do everything she could to bring honor and glory to His name at her university. One day during her sophomore year one of her professors came to class with a project. He announced to the class that the students were going to play the lifeboat game. A ship had hit an iceberg and was sinking and there was not enough space in the lifeboat for everyone to fit, so the students were going to have to choose who would be left behind to drown. The Summit graduate raised her hand and said, "I am sorry Professor, but I cannot do this exercise. I believe that my Lord Jesus is in charge of who lives and who dies, not me. I think this would offend Him." The professor replied, "You will either participate in this exercise or you will fail my course." The young lady politely responded, "I am sorry Professor, but I cannot do this. I believe that my Lord Jesus Christ is in charge of who lives and who dies, not me. I think that this would offend Him." "Then get out of my class and don't come back!" the professor exploded. The sophomore got up and walked out of the classroom in front of 350 stone silent fellow students.

The next day she came back to class. The professor noticed her and walked back to her seat. Standing over her he said, "Young lady, I have been investigating your scholastic record and discovered that you have a four point average. Is that true?" "Yes, Sir," she answered. The professor then said, "Young lady, are you telling me that you will sacrifice a straight 'A' average because of this little exercise that you think would offend your God?" "Yes, Sir." "Anyone who thinks that highly of their God we deserve to hear from. Young lady, I am giving you today's lecture period to tell us about your God." And the young Summit graduate had fifty minutes, with no preparation time, to get up and defend the faith! Our God is an awesome God Who prepares the way and fights for His children. *"But sanctify the Lord God in your hearts: and be ready always to give an answer to every man that asketh you a reason of the hope that is in you with meekness and fear"* (1 Peter 3:15). *"But when they deliver you up, take no thought how or what ye shall speak: for it shall given you in that same hour what ye shall speak. For it is not ye that speak, but the Spirit of your Father which speaketh in you"* (Matthew 10:19-20).

Summit grew slowly in the 60s and 70s. The classes of students fit comfortably on the main dance floor (now the lecture auditorium) of the old hotel. Guests and parents were seated in the orchestra mezzanine. Then in the 1980s, the explosion occurred. It was most probably ignited as a result of one particular student who went home excited about his Summit experience. His name was Ryan Dobson. His father, Dr. James Dobson, saw the godly influence the Summit experience had had on his son and so he promoted the Summit on his *Focus on the Family* radio show, resulting in approximately 14,000 new student applications.

Almost overnight the main auditorium was filled with students, even jamming the mezzanine and displacing the guests and parents to the hotel lobby to observe via closed circuit TV. *"I will praise Thee, O Lord, with my whole heart; I will show forth all Thy marvelous works"* (Psalm 9:1).

As Summit grew, it needed more space. Across the street are the VanHorne cottages. These 27 cottages and one house/office originally housed tuberculosis patients. The cottages were built with many windows to allow the circulation of clean, mountain air. Summit was able to purchase the cottages in December of 1989. The cottages needed a lot of work to up-date them. God then brought the Rich Honken family to Summit with all their construction skills. In the 1990's, with the help of Suresh, they were able to upgrade most of the VanHorne cabins. The Honkens proceeded also to modernize the kitchen of the old hotel and remodel various rooms, bathrooms, and nearby houses.

A few miles west of Manitou Springs, off highway 24, are the 36 Acres owned by Summit Ministries. It became the ideal paintball battle ground for both the staff and the students. Dr. Noebel also allowed the staff to have staff picnics and bonfires on the property. Many meaningful moments between staff members and our Lord Jesus Christ have been enjoyed around the 36 Acres camp fire.

Over the years, the idea of turning Summit into a year-round university was considered. This idea attracted faculty such as Jay Butler, Wayne Lutton, Jeff Baldwin, Clark Bowers, and Jeff Meyers. Ultimately, Jeff Meyers would join the faculty of Bryan College in Tennessee and establish the first Summit Extension—a two-week Summit Ministries camp on the Bryan College campus. The Bryan College Summit became very popular in the late 90s and is prospering into the twenty-first century, now with two sessions. The popularity of Summit Ministries keeps growing. The summer of 2005 will welcome yet another location for the two week summer training: Cedarville University in Ohio.

At this point, it is important to remember that history always involves people. There have been many that have given of their time, treasure and talents to help the Summit be a place most useful to the work of the ministry. These are people who not only have a desire to share the vision that the Noebels started, but also share the same love for the students. These are the people who will always be remembered as part of the Summit "family." Sadly, not everyone can be cited in this limited space.

The most important family in the history of Summit Ministries is, of course, the Noebels themselves. Dr. and Mrs. Noebel's vision and purpose for the ministry has already been mentioned. Now it is important to note their direct physical involvement in the success of Summit. Just as service is the mark of any great leader, so it is with the Noebels. In the beginning years of the ministry, students could see Dr. Noebel, hammer or screwdriver in hand, ready to take care of any maintenance situation. No doubt he helped Alice in the kitchen whenever the need arose, as she would often be the sole cook for the whole group of students and guests. As the years progressed, God brought in many more to help, but Mrs. Noebel still does the grocery shopping for the Summit kitchen.

The students have always been enamored with Dr. Noebel and by the end of the session start calling him "Doc," just as the staff do. During meals, Doc's table will always be full of students eager to discuss issues with him or ask him questions. The students love it when Doc nicknames one of them "Tiger." They also love it when he challenges them to tennis matches, sometimes with Dr. James Bowers or David Akridge as his tennis partner. Usually the students are thoroughly defeated.

The students enjoy Dr. Noebel in the classroom also, as many of them state that Dr. Noebel was their favorite speaker. One thing that Dr. Noebel thought was important to the curriculum was to incorporate a thought and a Bible verse for the day. Each day he gives the students something to think about. On graduation night, the students will give Dr. Noebel a standing ovation. Truly God has blessed Dr. Noebel with the personality and intelligence needed to get the attention of youth. God gifted him with a vision and a love for these students.

Dr. Noebel's son, Brent, and daughter, Joy, were also greatly involved in the ministry. Joy used her talents to help in the interior design. Brent came on strong in the late 90s and early 2000s with his campaign to get Bibles, the *Jesus* film, and Christian flags into the Sudan. Brent collected donations from the Summit students and passed the money on to missionary Peter Hammond, who delivered the goods deep into the Sudan, at great personal risk, reaching even into area of the Nuba mountains. Brent, although blind, left a great legacy at the Summit and in the Sudan. He was an inspiration to countless young adults as they saw him pressing toward the mark in spite of his painful and weakening physical condition due to diabetes. There were times that Brent was so weak he had to be carried to the auditorium. But he never wanted to miss evangelism night.

Because the Summit hosted nearly 200 young people every two weeks, there was much carpentry and furniture repair needed. Dr. Don Baker, a long time board member of Summit (and co-author of this chapter), faithfully came to the Summit Hotel every day to find the pieces and put things back together again. Dr. Baker and Dr. Noebel knew every rusty pipe and electrical circuit in the hotel (and ultimately in the VanHorne cottages across the street). As well, many lunches found Dr. Baker at a table in the dining room sitting with students or staff as he shared the great things the God of the Bible had done in his life and in the history of Summit. Mary, Dr. Baker's wife, was a powerful prayer warrior, standing in the gap for Summit Ministries.

The Jim Bowers family played strategic roles in these early years of Summit. From financial support; to the lecture hall; to helping in the kitchen; and even extending to the custodial services; Jim, Carole, Curtis, Clark, and daughter Kellie all pitched in. At one point in the 1990s, the Bowers family taught nineteen hours of the two-week curriculum. Some of their topics included communism, socialism, marriage and the family, and postmodernism. Dr. Bowers' daughter-in-law, Amanda, was Dr. Noebel's cheerful and helpful personal secretary for several years. Jim Bowers' sister, Margaret Sanders, oversaw the cleaning and domestics staff. Doug Sanders, Margaret's husband, lectured on sciences and archeology, and he also turned the Summit Bookhouse into a profitable store.

Betty Gasper was indispensable in the formative years of Summit. Betty and Alice Noebel compiled the *Summit Cookery* cookbook after testing and tasting each recipe. *"Neither have I gone back from the commandment of His lips; I have esteemed the words of His mouth more than my necessary food"* (Job 23:12).

To bring the financial aspects of Summit into conformity with *501 c 3* non-profit standards, Robert McBurney came to Summit. McBurney had been an economics professor at Baylor University. Professor McBurney set up the financial books and simplified the ways that supplies were purchased and statements paid. He also was given lecture time with the students and had the opportunity to explain the Christian worldview on economics.

Working with McBurney in the business office was Mary Hines. When Prof. McBurney decided to go back to teaching in Texas, Mary assumed his position as chief financial officer, where she continues to faithfully serve today. Some of the information in this chapter came through Mary's willing help. Working in the office with Mary is Trudy Friesma. Trudy has been Dr. Noebel's faithful executive assistant for many years and both of Trudy's children have been Summit students and employees.

In the mid 1990s, Todd and Renee Cothran joined the permanent staff. Renee's abounding joy and musical abilities enabled her to play piano and lead the singing at many of the Summit worship times. Renee was also one of Dr. Noebel's secretaries until she began raising a family. Renee, Amanda Bowers, Kellie Bowers McGuire, and Lauren MacAlvany Bowers formed a legendary Summit quartet that could have won awards. Todd was staff director for a few years and then took over the production of Summit's videos. New videos were produced dealing with Humanism, Marxism, New Age, and other topics. As older Summit videos become outdated, Todd replaces them with the current technology and knowledge of our times.

David Akridge (a.k.a. Tiger Woods, to the more precocious students) added patience and polite stability to the permanent staff for many years. David improved and directed the Excellence program, drove busloads of Summit students to visit Focus on the Family and the Air Force Academy, and was Assistant Dean of Men for three years. Fellow staff member Rachel Davis displayed the kind of servant character David was looking for in a wife, and they married in 2004.

It was also in the mid 1990s that Doc welcomed the Honken family to Summit. Rich and Sherri Honken, along with their eight children—Jen, Shellie, Heather, Sara, Ben, Peter, Rob, and Luke—worked together as a family for many years at the Summit providing help in nursing, maintenance, construction, cooking, housekeeping, and a host of other projects. Shellie Honken's testimony on evangelism night was always a favorite with the students. Jen Honken is currently Dr. Noebel's secretary.

Food at the Summit has always been a point of justifiable pride. Vivacious Bonnie McGuire took over the duty of head chef in the 90s. Bonnie did the cooking and Alice Noebel did the grocery shopping. Many of the summer staff learned how to cook delicious meals, make salads (enough for 250 people) and bake rolls and deserts under Bonnie's tutelage. Two of Mrs. McGuire's best apprentices were her daughters, Brooke and Meagan.

Over the more than forty year history of Summit Ministries, the Lord Jesus not only provided the best teachers in each area of the Christian worldview, but also provided a constant supply of patrons and volunteer workers. Men and women with just the right gifts and talents would arrive at Summit at just the right time to fill a particular need. It would be impossible to name all these wonderful people, but it is certain our loving Lord will credit their eternal accounts for their often sacrificial investments in all aspects of the Summit. *"And whatsoever ye do, do it heartily, as to the Lord, and not unto men"* (Colossians 3:23).

As Summit grew, so did the demand for its teaching. A grant was given to the ministry to teach Christian school teachers how to teach worldviews. This paved the way for the adult worldview conferences, now held annually at the Navigator headquarters of Glen Eyrie castle. Sandi Banks has been the developer and organizer of these special weeks. Sandi works very hard throughout the year ministering to graduates of the Adult Worldview program and recruiting new students. *"Thou therefore, my son, be strong in the grace that is in Christ Jesus. And the things that thou hast heard of me among many witnesses, the same commit thou to faithful men, who shall be able to teach others also"* (2 Timothy 2:1, 2).

As teachers came to these Adult Worldview sessions and began asking for curriculum materials, teachers and writers rose to the forefront. Kevin Bywater became the developer of the basic Summit Worldview curriculum for high school, and is a lecturer during the summer camps as well. Working with Kevin on curriculum was Micah Wierenga, who also leads the summer praise and worship times. Chuck Edwards authored a study of worldviews designed especially for church Sunday Schools, along with a teacher's manual to complement the student workbook. Chuck joined the full time staff in the late 1990s. As the curriculum needs developed and grew, John Hay, an expert in writing curriculum for the primary grades, joined the team. Dr. Noebel urged Mr. Hay to bring his expertise to Summit and complete a worldview curriculum for the primary grades. These materials have recently been completed and published.

With all the curricular materials being produced, including Dr. Noebel's *Understanding the Times*, more space was needed to house and ship these educational materials. A small ranch was donated to the ministry with several sturdy cinder-block horse barns. With some creative thinking and a bit of rearranging, the ranch stables became the Summit Bookhouse shipping and warehouse facility. Josh Wierenga did much in the beginning with Doug Sanders to get the Bookhouse working smoothly. Then a young lady named Rachel Shanahan showed just the right talents and temperament to govern the busy, but rather remote, Summit Ranch Bookhouse. Of course her parents, Bill and Paula, along with her sister, Loral, step in and volunteer to help when things get hectic.

With the increasing size of the permanent staff, more housing was needed. As properties adjacent to the Summit Hotel came up for sale, they were (and are) purchased as our faithful God provides the resources. As most properties surrounding the hotel are single family dwellings, and since there are times when 180 young people can make a bit of noise, it has been advantageous to purchase these dwellings. The Summit Hotel is located in a residential neighborhood, not an area with commercial zoning, and there have been times when the neighbors have threatened to shut the ministry down due to some high volume Summit students. There always seems to be a neighbor with a hot-line to the police department. In 1999 four of the summer staff men formed a quartet and practiced singing the song *Goodnight Sweetheart*. One night the four believed themselves practiced enough to serenade the campers at their 11:00 pm lights out. With students leaning out of windows and hanging from the balconies to be serenaded, the quartet sang their hearts out in the center courtyard, lovingly called "the well." The whistles and applause were so overwhelmingly loud that within a few minutes the police were at the door of the hotel. The neighbors had complained we were disturbing the peace.

Dr. Jobe Martin sang the bass line in that quartet. The Martin family was involved at Summit from the mid 80s through 2001. Dr. Martin's lectures included the evolution/creation controversy, the New Age movement, relationships, leadership, and morning devotionals. For a few years, he was Director of Summer Staff, Dean of Students, and a member of the Board of Directors. His daughters, Taryn and Mirren, were part of the kitchen and classroom staff and recited chapters of Scripture at the beginning of Dr. Martin's lectures to challenge the students to memorize God's Word, for it is His Word that is *living and active and sharper than any two-edged sword* (Hebrews 4:12). There were many Summit students who memorized chapters of Scripture after seeing that it was possible. Mrs. Jenna Dee Martin was always in prayer for the Summit staff and students and hung many framed Scriptures on the walls of the Summit Hotel. *"Because I will publish the name of the Lord: ascribe ye greatness unto our God. He is the Rock, His work is perfect: for all His ways are judgment: a God of truth and without iniquity, just and right is He"* (Deuteronomy 32:3, 4).

Other than Dr. Noebel, the most dynamic speaker from the late 1990s until the present has been an evangelist named Mark Cahill. Mark played basketball with Charles Barkley on the Auburn Dream Team. His youthful vigor (and face) belie his true age. Mark is a major factor at Summit Ministries in motivating the students to get busy practicing their faith and spreading the Gospel. Mark always uses God's word to back up his lectures. He reminds them that when witnessing, it is important to use the Ten Commandments so people can first see their sin and thus see their need for a Savior—the Lord Jesus Christ. When students shrink from sharing the Gospel due to fear of rejection, Mark encourages them with two Scriptures. 1 Peter 4:14: *"If ye be reproached for the name of Christ, happy are ye; for the spirit of glory and God resteth upon you: on their part He is evil spoken of, but on your part He is glorified."* Luke 6:22, 23: *"Blessed are ye, when men shall*

*hate you, and when they shall separate you from their com-*
*pany, and shall reproach you, and cast out your name as*
*evil, for the Son of Man's sake. Rejoice ye in that day, and*
*leap for joy: for, behold, your reward is great in heaven: for in*
*the like manner did their fathers unto the prophets."*

After Mark shared the above Bible verses to one of the
1999 Summit classes, three students felt compelled to go
onto the streets of the old hippy town of Manitou Springs to
share the Gospel. One of the students found an old follower
of Timothy Leary sitting on the curb and he began reading
the plan of salvation to this "Manitou's Finest." Suddenly
the old hippy jumped up, grabbed the student's Bible out
of his hands, and began ripping the pages out. The surprised student decided to claim 1 Peter 4:14 and Luke 6:22,
23. He turned to his two friends and exclaimed, "I'm being
rejected for the name of Jesus! Give me a high five!" His
friends gave him a high five and said, "Let's leap for joy!" So
the three young men started leaping for joy in front of the
old hippy. The old fellow probably thought he was having
some sort of pathological flashback. The summer staff took
up a collection and bought the young man a new Bible.

Much of the popularity of Summit Ministries comes
from the faculty employed by Dr. Noebel. During the 1990s
some of Christianity's most well-known teachers became
a part of the Summit faculty team. The fruit of some of
these speakers will be seen in the remaining pages of this
memorial book. Teachers such as Dr. Michael Bauman, Dr.
Frank Beckwith, Dr. Ron Nash, Dr. Jeff Meyers, Dr. Robert
Linden, Dr. Del Tackett, and political cartoonist Mr. Chuck
Asay continue to rearrange their busy schedules to teach
each session of Summit students. Other well-known apolo-
gists join the lecture team a few times a summer. These
include Dr. J.P. Moreland, Dr. Norman Geisler, Dr. Charles
Thaxton, Dr. Chris Osborne, Dr. and Mrs. Dave Nutting, Dr.
Charles White, Greg Koukl, Don MacAlvany (whose wife,
Molly, serves on the Summit board), and Phyllis Schlafly.

And what would Summit ministries be without its
devoted Board of Directors and Trustees? The board has
provided consistent ministry leadership and special encour-

agement to David and Alice Noebel and the Summit family. The Summit board meetings always begin with prayer and a biblical devotional by the board chaplain (for most of the history of Summit the chaplain of the board was Allen Nebergall). The directors have never flinched from dealing with the thorns and thistles that crop up from time to time. Our Lord brings board members with different gifts. Some are always looking ahead and setting goals and plans. Others look back and see ways to improve and expand the ministry. During one particularly trying time, Dr. James Bowers chaired the board and guided Summit along its God-ordained path. Board member Julie Hays was always full of constructive ideas. Another long time member with a generous heart toward Summit was Mr. Kris Arbury. Mr. Stu Mast (for many years the CEO of the busy airport at Tampa, Florida) donated his gifts of leadership as chairman of the board. Under Mr. Mast's leadership in the 1990s, Summit realized its most rapid growth.

David and Alice Noebel, in the grace and power of the Lord Jesus Christ, began a legacy in an old hotel on the side of a Colorado mountain in 1962. As a result of their vision and faithfulness, thousands of young people have been equipped to defend their Christian worldview in the battlefields of the classrooms and workplaces across the United States of America and around the world. *"Faithful is He that calleth you, who also will do it"* (1 Thessalonians 5:24). May the generations to come be so impacted by this legacy that they go out into the classrooms and marketplaces of the world for the glory and praise of the Almighty God of the Bible.

# Never Read a Bible Verse
## The Most Important Thing I Can Teach You

Gregory Koukl

If there was one bit of wisdom, one rule of thumb, one single skill I could impart, one useful tip I could leave that would serve you well the rest of your life, what would it be? What is the single most important practical skill I've ever learned as a Christian? Here it is: *Never read a Bible verse.* That's right, never read a Bible *verse.* Instead, always read a paragraph—at least—if you want to unlock the meaning of a passage.

Think of it this way. When you stumble into the middle of a conversation and hear a phrase or a sentence that piques your curiosity, what's your next question? You ask, "What are you talking about?" You instinctively know you need the context to make sense of the conversation and benefit from it.

The same is true when we stumble into the middle of a Bible passage. We can't know what God is talking about by looking at an isolated sentence or phrase. We must consider the bigger picture.

This works because of a basic rule of all communication: Meaning always flows from the top down, from the larger units to the smaller units, not the other way around. The key to the meaning of any verse comes from the paragraph, not just from the individual words.[1]

## My Radio "Trick"

When I'm on the radio, I use one simple rule to help me answer Bible questions I'm asked about, even when I'm unfamiliar with the passage. I call it my radio "trick," and it's an amazingly effective technique you can use, too—*I read the entire paragraph, not just the verse.* I take stock of the relevant material above and below the reference I'm focusing on. Since the context frames the verse and gives it specific meaning, I let it tell me what's going on. Sometimes the most obscure passages come into focus with this simple technique.

The numbers in front of the sentences in your Bible give the illusion that the verses stand alone in their meaning. Verse numbers were not in the originals, though. They were added hundreds of years later. As a result, chapter and verse breaks sometimes pop up in unfortunate places, separating relevant material that should be grouped together.

Here's how you employ the simple rule, Never read a Bible verse.[2] First, ignore the verse numbers and try to get the big picture by looking at the larger unit. Then begin to narrow your focus. It's not very hard or time consuming. It takes only a few minutes of careful reading.

It works like this. Begin with the broad context of the book. What type of literature is it—history, poetry, proverb? Different genres require different approaches. Next,

---

[1] Notice I didn't say "Never *quote* a Bible verse." Rather, beware of simply reading the verse expecting to get the accurate meaning in isolation from the full passage.

[2] I highly recommend Fee and Stuart's popular *How to Read the Bible for All Its Worth* (Zondervan) as a guide to proper Bible study habits, or Walt Russell's *Playing with Fire: How the Bible Ignites Change in Your Soul* (NavPress). See also D.A. Carson's *Exegetical Fallacies* (Baker), and James Sire's *Scripture Twisting* (InterVarsity Press). For a thorough treatment I recommend *Introduction to Biblical Interpretation* by Klein, Blomberg, and Hubbard (Thomas Nelson).

stand back from the verse and look for breaks in the text that identify major units of thought. Then ask, "What in this paragraph or group of paragraphs gives any clue to the meaning of the verse in question?" Look especially at the flow of thought in the passage. What ideas are in play and how are they being developed?

There is a reason this little exercise is so important. Words have different meanings in different contexts (that's what makes puns work). When we consider a verse in isolation, one meaning may occur to us. But how do we know it's the right one? Help won't come from the dictionary. Dictionaries only complicate the issue, giving us more choices, not fewer. Help must come from somewhere else, bit it's not very far away. It comes from the surrounding paragraph.

With the larger context in view, focus on the meaning of the verse itself. When you think you have a handle on the author's intent based on your analysis—your careful observation, research, and study—sum up the passage in your own words. Then employ what I call the "paraphrase principle." It's an incredibly simple way to find out if your interpretation is in the running.

Here's how it works. *Just replace the text in question with your paraphrase and see if the passage still makes sense in light of the larger context.* Does it dovetail naturally with the bigger picture?

This technique will immediately weed out interpretations that are obviously erroneous. Remember, an interpretation is your ability to say essentially the same thing as the author, but in your own words.

Here is an example of how the paraphrase principle can effectively clear up a common misunderstanding.

## A "Spirit of Fear"

In 2 Timothy 1:7 we read, "For God has not given us the spirit of fear; but of power, and of love, and of a sound mind" (KJV). Some have taken Paul to mean that whenever a believer feels fearful, it is the result of a demonic spirit that needs to be resisted, bound, or even cast out.

The word *spirit*, though, is equivocal. It is open to more than one interpretation because it has more than one meaning. It could refer to an immaterial, spiritual person— a demon, an angel, the Holy Spirit, a human soul, etc. (e.g., Luke 4:33, Acts 16:16), which is the sense taken in the interpretation above. However, *spirit* could also mean a disposition, frame of mind, mood, or defining characteristic. In 1 Corinthians 4:21, Paul talks about dealing with the errant Corinthians either "with a rod or with love and a spirit of gentleness" (see also Galatians 6:1, Romans 8:15). [3]

What sense of the word *spirit* does Paul have in mind when writing to Timothy? The paraphrase principle comes to our rescue. Here's our paraphrase of the first option: "For God hath not given us *the demonic spirit of fear; but a demonic spirit [or an angelic spirit?] of power, and of love, and of a sound mind.*" This seems odd. Does the Bible teach that the qualities of power, love, and a sound mind are the result of spiritual beings that have power over us, or are they virtuous dispositions we develop and possess?

Let's try the alternate meaning: "For God has not given us *a fearful disposition; but a disposition of power, and of love, and of a sound mind.*" This makes much more sense, especially when you consider the larger context (remember, "Never read a Bible verse"), which includes Paul's admonition that Timothy rekindle his spiritual gift (v. 6), not being ashamed of the "testimony of our Lord" (v. 8). Timothy was not possessed of a demonic spirit of fear; he was timid. This is why the NASB renders the verse, "For God has not given us a spirit of timidity, but of power and love and discipline."[4]

[3]All Scripture references are from the *New American Standard Bible* unless otherwise noted.
[4] The archaic renderings in the *King James Bible* create unnecessary confusion for modern readers. I recommend the KJV for any reader who is 350 years old or older. All others would do better with a more recent translation.

# Jesus, the Uncreated Creator

Let me give you another example. In John 1:1 the apostle states plainly that "the Word was God." Two verses later John provides backup support for his claim. He writes, "All things came into being by Him, and apart from Him nothing came into being that has come into being." In verse three John says the same thing in two different ways for emphasis and clarity: Everything that ever came into being owes its existence to the Word who caused it all to happen. If the Word caused all created things to come into existence, then He must have existed *before* all created things came into existence. Therefore, the Word could not have been created. The Word—Jesus—is the uncreated Creator; Jesus is God.

Those who deny the deity of Christ offer this rebuttal, however. "Wait a minute. You missed something in the text because you didn't read the verse carefully. Notice the phrase 'apart from Him.' The apostle excludes Jesus from the count. If you said, 'Apart from Billy, the whole family is going to Disneyland,' you wouldn't mean that Billy wasn't part of the family, just that he wasn't included in the count. Every member of the family is going to Disneyland *with the exception of* Billy. In the same way, every created thing was created by Jesus *with the exception of* Jesus Himself. Jehovah created Jesus first, then Jesus created everything else. Jesus is not God."

Note that this rebuttal turns on the ability to replace "apart from Him" with the phrase "with the exception of Jesus." On this interpretation the phrases are synonymous. Let's make the replacement by applying the paraphrase principle and see what happens. The verse then looks like this: "*With the exception of Jesus*, nothing came into being that has come into being."

If this seems confusing, I'm not surprised. On this reading Jesus is a created being, clear enough, but now there's another problem. It turns out that Jesus is the *only* created thing that exists. Obviously, the phrase "apart from Jesus" cannot mean "with the exception of Jesus." These phrases are not synonymous in this passage.

"Apart from Him" means something entirely different. It means "apart from His agency." It's the same as saying, "Apart from me you'll never get to Disneyland. I've got the car." On this interpretation our paraphrase looks like this: "Apart from *Jesus' agency* nothing came into being that has come into being." This makes perfect sense in the context. Jesus is the Creator of all created things. Jesus is God, just as John 1:1 clearly states.

## Having a "Peace" about It

Let's try another. Colossians 3:15 is a text that is constantly misunderstood by well-meaning Christians. Paul writes, "And let the peace of Christ rule in your hearts." Some have accurately pointed out that the Greek word for "rule" means to act as arbiter or judge. They see this verse as a tool for knowing God's will for our lives.

The conventional thinking goes something like this. An internal sense of peace acts like a judge helping us make decisions according to God's will. When confronted with a decision, pray. If you feel a "peace" in your heart, take it as a "green light;" God is giving you the go-ahead. If you don't feel peace, don't proceed. On this interpretation, a paraphrase might be: "And let feelings of peacefulness in your heart be the judge about God's individual will for your life."

This is a classic example of how knowledge of the Greek can be dangerous if context is not taken into consideration. The word *peace* actually has two different meanings. It could mean a sense of inner harmony and emotional equanimity. Paul seems to have this definition in mind in Philippians 4:7: "And the peace of God, which surpasses all comprehension, shall guard your hearts and your minds in Christ Jesus." This is the subjective sense of peace.

The word *peace* also has an objective sense: lack of conflict between two parties formerly at war with each other. This definition is what Paul intends in Romans 5:1: "Therefore having been justified by faith, we have peace with God through our Lord Jesus Christ." (Note the distinction between the peace *of* God and peace *with* God here.)

Here's our question: What sense of peace did Paul have in mind when writing to the Colossians? The Greek gives us no indication because the same word is used in all these cases. Once again, context solves the problem. The specific meaning can only be known from the surrounding material.

In verse 11, Paul says that in the Body of Christ there are no divisions between Greek and Jew, slave and free, etc. On this basis he appeals for unity in the church characterized by forgiveness, humility, and gentleness. He then adds that harmony (peace) should be the rule that guides our relationships.

Paul has the objective sense of peace in mind here—lack of conflict between Christians—not a subjective feeling of peace in an individual Christian's heart. This becomes obvious when we join the paraphrases with the context:

Put on a heart of compassion, kindness, humility, gentleness, and patience; bearing with one another, and forgiving each other, whoever has a complaint against anyone; just as the Lord forgave you, so also should you. And beyond all these things put on love, which is the perfect bond of unity. And *let feelings of peacefulness in your heart be the judge about God's will for your individual life*, to which indeed you were called in one body; and be thankful.

vs.

Put on a heart of compassion, kindness, humility, gentleness, and patience; bearing with one another, and forgiving each other, whoever has a complaint against anyone; just as the Lord forgave you, so also should you. And beyond all these things put on love, which is the perfect bond of unity. And *let harmony, not conflict, be the rule that guides you* [plural], to which indeed you were called in one body; and be thankful.

The first is completely foreign to the context; the second fits right in with everything that comes before and after. In the context of Colossians 3, there is no hint of using internal feelings as a divine stamp of approval on our decisions. Personal decision-making is not the message of the paragraph. Harmony in the Body is.

## Context Is King

Both of these examples illustrate a deeper truth about properly understanding the Bible, or any other communication for that matter: Context is king. The paraphrase principle works so well because it plays on the fact that the meaning of any particular word or phrase is always governed by the role it plays in the context of larger units like sentences and paragraphs.

Think of it this way: Wouldn't it be convenient to have a biblical tour guide on call to clear up confusion in the text any time you open your Bible, someone who could tell you the explicit meaning of a verse in many cases, or at least help you to know what the verse doesn't mean and thus narrow your options?

Wouldn't it be helpful to have a tutor who could point out critical clues to the meaning, identify conditions that limit the application of the verse, or indicate the audience the verse may be limited to? If that sounds appealing, then pay attention to what the context can tell you, because it does each of these things. Let's look at them one by one.

## "If I Be Lifted Up"

Context often clearly and unambiguously gives us the exact meaning of a passage. John 12:32 is a case where a phrase can have two widely divergent meanings, yet right in the text the author tells us exactly which one he has in mind.[5]

---

5 This happens with some frequency in the Scriptures. Compare Matthew 13:24-30 with 13:36-43 where Jesus gives an explicit interpretation of His own parable.

"And I, if I be lifted...will draw all men to Myself," is a statement of Jesus that worship leaders love to cite. They then go on to explain that in worship we "lift up" the Lord when we exalt Him and declare His glory. If we focus on Jesus and ascribe glory to Him, the power of Christ is released to transform the hearts of those listening and they are drawn to Him.

This is the meaning the worship leader has in mind, but it isn't what Jesus was talking about. John tells us in the very next verse precisely what Jesus meant: "But He was saying this to indicate *the kind of death* by which He was to die."

When we apply our paraphrase test, the results look like this: "'And I, *if I be exalted before the people*, will draw all men to Myself.' But He was saying this to indicate the kind of death by which He was to die." Jesus wasn't executed by praise, but by a cross. In this instance, being "lifted up" clearly means to be crucified, not exalted.

Understanding this phrase in context sheds light on another familiar passage, John 3:14-15: "And as Moses lifted up [raised in the air] the serpent in the wilderness, even so must the Son of Man be lifted up [raised in the air] that whoever believes may in Him have eternal life."

Our corrected paraphrase looks like this: "And as Moses lifted up the serpent in the wilderness, even so must the Son of Man be *crucified* that whoever believes may in Him have eternal life."

This makes perfect sense. Jesus had to be crucified before salvation could be offered, an appropriate lead-in to the verse that comes next, the most famous salvation verse in the Bible, John 3:16.

## Beware the Ellipses...

If you looked closely, you would have noticed that the worship leader mentioned above did not quote the verse correctly. He left something out. The full text actually reads, "And I, if I be lifted up *from the earth*, will draw all men to Myself."

John 12:32 is nearly always misquoted, albeit unwittingly. Inaccurate quoting, though, leads to inaccurate interpretations. Beware of ellipses—the three dots (...) that signal something has been left out of a quote—because the omission may be vital to a verse's meaning.

A prime example of the "error of the ellipses" comes from John 5:17, 19-20 which one author quotes this way:[6]

> My Father has been working until now, and I have been working....Most assuredly, I say to you, the Son can do nothing of Himself; but what He sees the Father do; for whatever He does, the Son also does in like manner. For the Father loves the Son, and shows Him all things that He Himself does.

The author's point was that Jesus received guidance directly from the Father. Since Jesus is our model, each of us should likewise learn to "hear the voice of God" in order to know and do His will, just as Jesus did.

The omission of verse 18, a portion of 19, and verses 21-23 is unfortunate. Each is vital to our understanding and seriously qualifies the meaning of the passage, as this more complete citation of John 5:17-23 shows:

> (17) But He answered them, "My Father is working until now, and I Myself am working."
>
> (18) For this cause therefore the Jews were seeking all the more to kill Him, because He not only was breaking the Sabbath, but also was calling God His own Father, *making Himself equal with God.*
>
> (19) Jesus *therefore* answered and was saying to them, "Truly, truly, I say to you, the Son can do nothing of Himself, unless it is something He sees the Father doing; for whatever the Father does, these things the Son also does in like manner. (20) For the Father loves the Son, and shows Him all things that He Himself is doing; and greater works than these

---

[6] Henry Blackaby and Claude King, *Experiencing God* (Nashville, TN: Broadman & Holman, 1994), 65.

will He show Him, that you may marvel. (21) For just
as the Father raises the dead and gives them life,
even so the Son also gives life to whom He wishes.
(22) For not even the Father judges anyone, but
He has given all judgment to the Son, (23) in order
that all may honor the Son, even as they honor the
Father. He who does not honor the Son does not
honor the Father who sent Him." [emphasis added]

Note first of all verse 18, the verse that had been completely omitted. The Jews, understanding Jesus' comments to be a clear claim to deity, seek to kill Him. The word *therefore* in verse 19 indicates that what follows is Jesus' specific response to the Jews' concern about His singular claim.

Note also the three phrases in parallel construction: "For the Father loves the Son and shows Him all things...," "For just as the Father raises the dead...," and "For not even the Father judges anyone...."

These verses are a complete unit. If the Father showing Jesus "all things that He Himself is doing" is an example for us to model, then we are also to give life to whom we wish, judge the world on the Father's behalf, and demand that all people honor us as they honor the Father.

Obviously, that is not Jesus' teaching here. Once again, context is king. In context, these verses have to do with the deity of Christ. Jesus is unique as the incarnate Son of God and therefore has unique obligations, unique abilities, and a unique relationship with the Father.

Verses 26-27 clear up any question on this score: "For just as the Father has life in Himself, even so He gave to the Son also to have life in Himself; and He gave Him authority to execute judgment, *because He is the Son of Man.*" "Son of Man" is a Messianic title from Daniel 7:13 that Jesus used frequently.

As Messiah and as the incarnate Son of God, Jesus has a singular role. This is why Jesus never directs His disciples to follow His example in John 5. No subsequent writers—Peter, John, Paul, Luke—ever make that connection. Jesus is unique in this regard.

We are not to imitate those things pertaining to Jesus' divinity or His Messianic office. This passage is not given so we would emulate Christ, but so we would adore Him. We know this because we followed the rule of context.

## The Eliminator

Sometimes context eliminates possible options by clearly indicating what a verse does *not* mean. In John 20:29, Jesus says to the no-longer-doubting Thomas, "Because you have seen Me, have you believed? Blessed are they who did not see, and yet believed."

These words are often taken as a criticism of those seeking evidence for faith. On this view, Jesus commended "blind" faith as more virtuous. But this interpretation is not possible in light of what John writes next:

Many other signs, therefore, Jesus also performed in the presence of the disciples, which are not written in this book; *but these [signs] have been written that you may believe* that Jesus is the Christ, the Son of God, and that believing you may have life in His name.

If Thomas wasn't to rely on evidence, then why did John say he included the evidence of miraculous signs expressly for the purpose of aiding belief?

No, Jesus was objecting to something else. Thomas's problem wasn't that he wanted evidence. Most likely his error was that he didn't believe the evidence already adequate to establish the fact of the resurrection: the testimony of his fellow disciples ("We have seen the Lord!" v. 25). Thomas demanded an extreme standard of proof: "Unless I shall see in His hands the imprint of the nails, and put my finger into the place of the nails, and put my hand into His side, I will not believe."

Whatever the meaning behind Jesus' words, it's clear He did not mean that a leap of faith is better than a reasoned response of trust.

## Truth Shall Set You Free?

Contrary to popular belief, Jesus never said that truth sets us free. His words in John 8:32, "You shall know the truth, and the truth shall make you free," are frequently read as a simple truism: Truth sets free. Learn the truth and freedom follows.

Context, our faithful guide, reveals a condition that limits the application of Jesus' remarks about the impact of truth:

> Jesus therefore was saying to those Jews who had believed Him, "If you abide in My word, then you are truly disciples of Mine; and you shall know the truth, and the truth shall make you free." (John 8:31-32)

Context shows that Jesus' remarks are conditional: If we do one thing, then another thing follows. If the result is freedom, what are the conditions? In short, faithful discipleship. We are set free when we abide in (obey, live in accordance with) God's Word while following Jesus. If someone doesn't fulfill the conditions, he won't experience the result.

Many other passages taken naively as unqualified promises actually have conditions attached to them. Claiming them out of context is a fruitless enterprise.

## "My Sheep Hear My Voice"

Once in a while context will give us a critical clue that helps us decipher a text. Miss the clue and you'll be lost, because the clue changes everything.

For example, much has been made of Jesus' words in John 10 that His sheep "know" and "hear" His "voice."[7] Many have taken these words as a promise that every believer can learn to "tune in" to the "still, small voice"[8] of God and develop a conversational relationship with Him.

---

[7] John 10:4-5, 16, 27.
[8] Another phrase taken out of its context in 1 Kings 19.

Jesus has nothing like this in mind, though. I know because of a key clarification, often overlooked, a clue that John himself gives early in the chapter. In verse six, John specifically states that when Jesus speaks of His sheep knowing His voice He is using a figure of speech.

The word *voice*, then, can't actually mean some kind of inner voice because a thing is never a metaphor of itself. A figure of speech is a picture of *something else*. Jesus must be referring, in a figure, to something else that the phrase "hear my voice" represents. But what?

The context tells the story. Jesus is warring with belligerent Pharisees who refuse to believe in Him in spite of miraculous works that bear Him witness (v. 25). By contrast, Jesus says, "my sheep hear My voice, and I know them, and they follow Me," and then adds, "and I give eternal life to them" (v. 27-28). Note the sequence: His sheep hear His voice. They follow Him in response (unlike the Pharisees). He then gives them eternal life. Hearing Jesus' voice is a figure of speech for the inner working of the Holy Spirit that *leads* to salvation. It results *in* salvation; it's not the result *of* salvation. It's applied here to non-believers destined for the Kingdom, not believers already in the Kingdom.

This makes perfect sense in the broader context of the chapter. The Jews have no trouble *hearing* Jesus' words. They know what Jesus is *saying*. Their problem is that they don't *respond with belief*. Why don't the Jews "hear" Jesus by responding with belief? Jesus tells them plainly. They don't "hear" because God is not "speaking" to them. They are not among the sheep the Father gave the Son (v. 26).

The voice being referred to here is not the still, small voice of private conversations between God and individual Christians. It's the effective call of the Holy Spirit bringing non-Christians to salvation, the work of the Father that allows the non-believer to be drawn into Jesus' arms.[9]

[9] John 10 records the latest of a series of references Jesus makes to this concept: John 5:25, 37; 6:45; 8:43, 47. The same idea is expressed clearly by Jesus in Matthew 11:27.

**For Your Eyes Only**

Sometimes reading the Bible accurately in context can be disheartening. It's painful to discover that verses once cherished for the emotional comfort they give turn out to have a completely different meaning altogether. This often happens with Old Testament promises or encouragements originally meant for others that we mistakenly claim as our own without qualification.

A prime example comes from the prophet Jeremiah, through whom God spoke these words: "'For I know the plans that I have for you,' declares the Lord, 'plans for welfare and not for calamity to give you a future and a hope'" (Jeremiah 29:11).

The key question here is who is the "you" that God had in mind when He spoke these wonderful words of consolation. A careful examination of the context gives us the answer. The verse was limited to the specific audience identified in Jeremiah 29:1 and 4:

> Now these are the words of the letter which Jeremiah the prophet sent from Jerusalem *to the rest of the elders of the exile, the priests, the prophets, and all the people whom Nebuchadnezzar had taken into exile from Jerusalem to Babylon.*...Thus says the Lord of hosts, the God of Israel, *to all the exiles whom I have sent into exile from Jerusalem to Babylon...*

When we read the full paragraph instead of just one Bible verse, the larger picture begins to unfold.

> For thus says the Lord, "When seventy years have been completed for Babylon, I will visit you [the Jewish exiles] and fulfill My good word to you, to bring you back to this place, for I know the plans that I have for you [the exiles]," declares the Lord "plans for welfare and not for calamity to give you a future and a hope. Then you will call upon Me and come and pray to Me, and I will listen to you. And

you will seek Me and find Me, when you search for
Me with all your heart. And I will be found by you,"
declares the Lord, "and I will restore your fortunes
and will gather you from all the nations and from all
the places where I have driven you [Babylon, etc.],"
declares the Lord, "and I will bring you back to the
place [Jerusalem and Judea] from where I sent you
into exile." (Jeremiah 29:10-14)

Our faithful guide, context, tells us clearly what God
had in mind. After 70 years of discipline, the Jewish exiles
would be restored to their homeland in Judea and prosper
according to the Lord's plans. This was a promise for the
Jews in exile, not for storm-tossed Christians uncertain
about their future. We may learn broader principles from
passages like these, like the principle that God keeps His
promises—a valuable lesson for believers of all eras—but
the particular promise in this passage is not for us.[10]

In times of distress or uncertainty, we would do better
to focus on promises specifically directed to followers of
Christ, verses like "Come to Me, all who are weary and
heavy-laden, and I will give you rest" (Matthew 11:28), or
"Lo, I am with you always, even to the end of the age" (Matthew 28:20).

The practice of citing a verse without addressing the role
it plays in a passage is called "prooftexting."[11] It's a dangerous habit; simply claiming a verse doesn't make it ours.

Whether claiming promises during difficult times or
citing verses to substantiate my own biblical views, I want
to be confident the texts I use as proof of my point actually
mean what I think they mean. That's why I'm always on the
alert when reading popular books written on biblical issues.
Are the authors simply quoting verses to buttress their
points (prooftexting), or are they interpreting the Scripture
carefully by looking at the details of the context?

---

[10] To sharpen the point, the prophet Daniel confirms this meaning. He refers to
the Jeremiah text in Daniel 9:1-2 and clearly understands it as applying to exiled
Judah. He follows with his famous prayer of confession, repentance, and request
for restoration of the exiles to the Promised Land.

## Biblical Fast Food?

The concept of "Never read a Bible verse" raises legitimate questions concerning the daily devotionals that are so popular today, handbooks of short messages built around single verses, sometimes only a phrase.

For many, these vignettes have become a primary source of daily nourishment. They're inspirational and short, able to be wedged into the busiest schedule. But they come with a serious drawback.

By focusing only on pieces of a passage, readers may actually miss the point of the passage. If we're just reading snatches of text, what's our guarantee that the inspirational feelings we experience aren't just false hopes or mere emotion? The difference is critical. It's the distinction between believe and make-believe.

We can't know what God is talking about or teaching us by looking at an isolated sentence or phrase. And if we take the Scripture in a way God did not mean it—if what we're getting *from* the verse is not really the teaching *of* the verse—then the words lose their authority. As Christians, our commitment should be to the truth of the passage, not to the feeling a certain reading of that passage gives us. If we ignore that priority, then whatever feeling we may have had will have been based on fantasy—make-believe.

Fortunately, the liability can be overcome by remembering our basic rule: Never read a Bible verse. Instead, read a paragraph, at least. Always check the context. Observe the flow of thought. Then focus on the verse itself.

Remember, meaning always flows from the top down, from the larger units to the smaller. A reflection on a Bible passage from a devotional or a sermon may be edifying, encouraging, and uplifting. But if it's not the message of the text—God's message—it lacks power even when the quote comes right out of the Bible.[12]

[11] See Gregory Koukl's "The Perils of Prooftexting," at www.str.org.
[12] A notable exception is *Our Daily Bread* (Radio Bible Class Ministries, rbc.org). Their devotions consistently work with a paragraph or more—sometimes an entire chapter—and do not wrench a text out of context to make a devotional point.

Misconstruing a passage can actually neutralize the Word of God. It can rob the Scripture of its authority and influence. God's Word only has power when it is used as God intended. The entire reason we go to the Bible in the first place—to get God's truth and apply it to our lives—is thwarted when we ignore the context.

If you habitually take the fast food approach when it comes to the Bible, try this experiment. For the next three months, put away your one-verse devotionals and make the time to sit down with the Lord to a real meal. Don't be satisfied with tidbits; commit yourself to reading whole chapters.

I suspect that if you'll do this you will quickly begin to feel the difference as you "renew your mind" each day. You'll be confident that the sense of comfort and safety you experience will be grounded in truth and not presumption, fact and not fantasy. You may even find you'll never go back to biblical fast food again.

## The Role of the Holy Spirit

Some think that the Holy Spirit is a substitute for careful Bible study. But it's not wise to simply ask the Holy Spirit to give you a personalized interpretation of a text. He has not committed Himself to do that for you. The Holy Spirit does not give us secret messages hidden between the lines. Instead, the Spirit illuminates—sheds light on—the Word, helping us to see what is *already there* in words the Holy Spirit Himself inspired through the initial writers (see 1 Corinthians 2:10-16). God will help us, but He won't do the work for us. This is why Paul tells Timothy, "Be diligent to present yourself approved to God as a workman who does not need to be ashamed, handling accurately the word of truth" (2 Timothy 2:15).

If you think God is telling you something through Scripture that is not connected to the meaning of the words in their context, it can't be God because He chose to communicate through language, not around it. God will not twist, distort, or redefine His own Word for your private consumption.

The Holy Spirit does not give new information beyond what is already evident in the inspired words. The curriculum, so to speak, is standardized for all Christians. Every person has equal access to the meaning. *There are no private messages in Scripture.* Peter is clear on this point:

> But know this first of all, that no prophecy of Scripture is a matter of one's own interpretation, for no prophecy was ever made by an act of human will, but men moved by the Holy Spirit spoke from God. But false prophets also arose among the people, just as there will also be false teachers among you, who will secretly introduce destructive heresies, even denying the Master who bought them, bringing swift destruction upon themselves. (2 Peter 1:20-2:1)

Because there is a Divine author behind prophesy, the Apostle argues, there is a particular truth—a determined meaning—that God intends to convey. Individual, personalized interpretations that obscure and even distort this meaning bring danger (note the reference to false prophets and false teachers).

The same reasoning applies to all of Scripture, not just to the words of the prophets, because the same rationale applies—the same Divine author stands behind the entire Bible. The meaning God originally intended when He gave the Scripture through the inspired writers is the same meaning for anyone reading the verse today.

Don't look for private messages in the Bible. They're not there. Simply put, "a text cannot mean what it never meant."[13] The Holy Spirit did not mean one thing when Paul wrote to the church at Ephesus, for example, and then something entirely different when a Spirit-filled Christian reads it 2,000 years later. The applications may vary, but the meaning remains the same. Ironically, evangelicals pride themselves on being biblical literalists, yet feel com-

---

[13] Gordon Fee and Douglas Stuart, *How to Read the Bible for All Its Worth* (Grand Rapids, MI: Zondervan, 1982), 27.

fortable abandoning the plain, literal sense of the passage whenever "the Spirit leads." You should always take the text at face value instead of looking for personal messages in words that were originally intended by the Spirit to mean something else.

## Take It "Literally"

"Do you take the Bible literally?" is a question frequently asked about biblical interpretation. I answer that I try to read the Bible with the precision the writer intended. I take it at its plain meaning unless I have some good reason to do otherwise. When you think about it, this is the basic rule we apply to everything we read: novels, newspapers, periodicals, and poems.

Remember our basic rule: Never read a Bible verse. Always check the context, observe the flow of thought, then focus on the verse.

If you will do this one thing—if you will read carefully in the context applying the paraphrase principle—you will begin to understand the Bible as God intended and Scripture will open up for you like never before. Without the bigger picture, though, you'll be lost.

Only when you are properly informed by God's Word the way it was written—in its context—can you be transformed by it. Every piece becomes powerful when it is working together with the whole as the Holy Spirit intended.

It's the most important practical spiritual lesson I've ever learned...and the single most important thing I could ever teach you.

*One-time rights only granted by Gregory Koukl, 417 E. 212th St., Carson, CA 90745, SSAN: 350-42-3075.

# What Went Wrong
## How Islam Lost Its Lead

Charles Edward White

Please imagine that you are a farmer living in Britain in the year 1000 A.D. You have a field that is twenty-six paces long and forty-eight paces wide, and you need to sow it with wheat. You know you need one handful of wheat to properly seed an area of your field that is one pace long and one pace wide. How many handsful of wheat do you need to save from your harvest in September to have enough wheat to plant next March? Oh, and remember, since it is the year 1000, you only have Roman numerals to help you do the math. Since there is no way to easily multiply XXVI by XLVIII, the only way to solve this problem is to draw a rect-angle twenty-six units long and forty-eight units wide. Then you count all the squares and find out that the answer is MCCXLVIII.

Or let's say you are a seamstress with a piece of cloth that is eighty-eight inches long. You need to cut your cloth into four pieces. The biggest piece must be ten inches longer than the smallest piece, and the two larger pieces must have a difference of two inches and the two shorter pieces must also have a two-inch difference. How long should you make each piece?

A seamstress living in Britain in 1000 A.D. would have no easy way to solve that problem. Even making a diagram like the farmer's would not help her much. But to a Muslim living in Damascus, neither of these questions would be problem. Using the Arabic numerals, the farmer would multiply 26 x 48 and get 1,248. Using algebra (which in Arabic means "the restoration"), the seamstress would call the smallest piece X, the largest piece X+10, and the two middle pieces X+10-2 and X+2. Then she would know that X+X+2+X+10-2+X+10=88. She would simplify 4X=68 and then know that the pieces would be seventeen, nineteen, twenty-five, and twenty-seven inches long.

Having Arabic numerals and knowing algebra gave Muslims in 1000 A.D. a tremendous advantage in solving the problems of daily life. Besides this practical superiority, Muslims also enjoyed a level of theoretical knowledge not even dreamed of in the West. In addition to their lead in mathematics, they also possessed the pre-eminence in chemistry, medicine, optics, and philosophy.[1] They made better maps of the earth and more accurate charts of the skies. In wealth, intellect, sophistication, and resources, the cities of Islam far outshone the cities of Christendom.[2]

Despite this incredible head-start, by 1600 the West had forged ahead in technology and science, and by 2000 led the Muslim world in every positive cultural and economic indicator. It has been almost a thousand years since a Muslim made an important advance in science, and only by the importation of Western technology have the masses in the Islamic world been lifted from poverty. Muslim nations fell under the influence of the Western colonialists, and have only tasted independence since Western nations decided it was good for them.

Westerners often have a simple explanation for Islam's precipitous decline. They say it is the absence of freedom. Charles Murray states it in a sentence, saying, "Islam could not accommodate itself to the degree of autonomy required

[1] Charles Murray, *Human Accomplishment* (New York: HarperCollins, 2003), 399.
[2] Norman F. Cantor, *The Meaning of the Middle Ages* (Boston: Allyn and Bacon, 1973), 141.

to sustain [cultural progress]."[3] Bernard Lewis, after spending one-hundred-fifty-eight pages explicating the problem, agrees with Murray, and offers a similarly brief explanation: "... it is precisely the lack of freedom—freedom of the mind from constraint and indoctrination, to question and inquire and speak; freedom of the economy from corrupt and pervasive mismanagement; freedom of woman from male oppression; freedom of citizens from tyranny—that underlies so many of the troubles of the Muslim world."[4]

As persuasive as this explanation appears to be, it is unsatisfactory on at least two counts. First, what accounts for this lack of freedom? What in Islam mitigates against individual autonomy and personal freedom? Second, why did Islam lose its lead after the eleventh century? Why were Islam's first four centuries so productive, and its next nine so barren? Any accounting for Islam's calamitous fall must consider factors that changed after 1100.

Obviously historical phenomena as vast as the rise or decline of a civilization cannot be explained by a single cause. A cultural transformation is the result of the thoughts and actions of millions of people, as well as non-human factors such as climate, disease, and natural disasters. However, different occurrences rely to varying degrees on the actions of a single individual. Some cultural events, like the discovery of calculus, seem to be "out there," waiting in the future to occur. That Leibniz and Newton developed the methods of calculus at about the same time argues that this event was bound to happen. Like Everest, these cultural events mark the high point of a whole mountain range of happenings. Other cultural events are more isolated. They are not the culmination of a series of trends, but represent a sharp departure from the way things were headed. They are like Kilimanjaro, which, without a peer, bursts from the plains of Africa. It seems that both the rise and fall of Islam represent not the tectonic movement of historical plates, but the eruptions of a single individual.

---

[3] Murray, 399.
[4] Bernard Lewis, *What Went Wrong?* (New York: Oxford University Press, 2002), 159.

The emergence of Islam in the eighth century and its rapid spread across the Middle East is too large an event to be explained entirely by the life of a single man, but obviously without the life of Mohammed it would never have occurred. Likewise the decline of Islam from its position of cultural superiority does not have merely a single cause, but it was precipitated by the life of Abu Hamid Muhammad ibn Muhammad ibn Ta'us Ahmed al-Tusi al-Shafi'I al-Ghazali.[5]

Al-Ghazali is considered by many Muslims to be the greatest human being to live after Mohammed. He has been called "The Proof of Islam," "The Ornament of the Faith," and "The Renewer of Religion." It is said, "If there were a prophet after Mohammed, Al-Ghazali would have been the man." Born in Persia in 1058, Al-Ghazali came from a religious family. His father was a dervish who practiced a life of self-denial and experienced religious ecstasy. As a boy, Al-Ghazali rejected his father's beliefs and made it his ambition to be rich and famous. His extreme intelligence made him impatient in school. He disliked his teachers and began to doubt whether they really knew anything at all. Despite his early rejection of his father's mysticism, his experience in school led him to question whether learning was a road to satisfaction in life. Finally disillusioned with academic life, he quit school, and like his father before him, sought enlightenment through mystical practices. In this quest he was disappointed. He did not attain the bliss he expected, so he returned to the ordinary life of humanity. He was disappointed in himself, and felt he had sold out. His intellectual gifts offered him a place in the academic world. Having failed in the attempt to attain spiritual enlightenment, he turned to the pleasures which wealth and notoriety could afford.

At the age of thirty-four his learning was recognized, as he was appointed to the position which later academics would have called "the chair of the theology department at

[5] The most accessible information on Al-Ghazali is found at www.ghazali.org, from which most of the following information is taken. Two articles have been the most useful: Kojiro Nakamura, "Al-Ghazail, Abu Hammid" and M. Saeed Sheikh, "Al-Ghazali" in *A History of Muslim Philosophy*, part 4, chapter 30.

Nizamiya University" in Baghdad. Being the leading teacher of the most important subject in the most prestigious institution in the most powerful country in the world should have brought him unqualified joy, but he found no peace because his intellect was unsatisfied by Muslim theology. As he taught larger and larger classes, he became less and less satisfied with the answers he was giving his students. His position as the expert on religious matters brought him to the attention of the vizier of the Sultan, who began to seek his advice on religious and even political affairs. Like Henry Kissinger, his learning made him one of the most powerful people in the world.

Even though he had achieved his boyhood goal of being rich and famous, his doubts refused to leave him. His reason insisted that the ideas he taught in class could not be true, but his teaching opened the door to every earthly satisfaction. He knew he had everything his heart desired— everything, that is, except integrity. This lack of integrity gnawed at him, and made him afraid. He was afraid that what he taught was true, and if it were true, then he knew that to teach it without believing it was a great sin. In the classroom, his mouth spoke Islamic orthodoxy, but his mind rebelled at that orthodoxy, and his heart feared that it might be true. That orthodoxy told him that to profess without belief was the road to Hell.

Even worse than his skepticism about the content of the faith he taught was his disbelief in the way one obtained it. He rejected not just specific tenets, but the whole method of rational inquiry. He was faced with double doubt: his reason led him to disbelieve the doctrines of Islam, but he also doubted that reason itself was reliable. He was convinced that the Sufis were right when they insisted that the way to God lay not through the intellect, but through the heart. Yet all his worldly prestige, all the acclaim he received from others, and all the wealth he treasured came from the rational defense of the faith of Islam. How could he, the main teacher of theology in the most prestigious institution in the most powerful country in the world tell his students that studying about God would not enable them to know anything meaningful about God? He feared the only way for him to be right with God was to give up everything he had worked so hard to obtain.

Day after day he wrestled with his conscience about what he was teaching in class. Soon the conflict spread from his mind and began to affect his body. He lost his appetite, and when he did force himself to eat, his stomach often refused to function. Finally he was so conflicted he even lost his ability to speak. Not being able to speak made it easier for him to resign his teaching position. He established a trust fund to provide for his family, gave away his other possessions, and set out on a pilgrimage to find God. He wandered all over the Muslim world, visiting Mecca, Jerusalem, and other holy sites. He submitted himself to various religious exercises and practiced rigorous ascetic discipline. Finally, at the end of eleven years he returned to his home village and announced that he had experienced the ineffable.

He reported that during his time of solitary wandering there had been revealed to him "things innumerable and unfathomable." He resumed teaching, but now the message he tried to communicate was that the most important truths in life were incommunicable. He used rationality to argue that rationality was flawed. Thus his message was essentially negative. It was reflected in the title of his most important work: *Tahafut al-Falasifah, The Destruction of the Philosophers.*

The thesis of *The Destruction of the Philosophers* is that reason does not work in the world of nature or in the world of the spirit. Solutions to problems in physics and metaphysics cannot be proved or disproved, so reasoning about them is a waste of time. Al-Ghazali uses reason to prove that reason is untrustworthy. He argues this way. First, one cannot use one's senses to learn the truth about the material world. For instance, if one holds a coin out at arm's length, it is possible to cover a star in the sky by carefully positioning the coin in the line of sight. Thus it appears to the eye that the nearby coin is larger than the distant star. Obviously this sensation is not true, so one cannot always trust one's senses about the physical world. In addition, by definition, the metaphysical world is what exists beyond the reach of our senses, so one cannot use any of the five senses to learn metaphysical truths. Thus the senses are unreliable for determining physical or metaphysical truth. When one sees that the nearby coin covers the distant star, one uses reason to correct the erroneous conclusion. Thus reason is more reliable than sense perception. While reason may be a corrective for the misinformation of sense perception, reason itself can be fooled. Al-Ghazali makes this point in twenty ways, but three are the easiest to understand.

First, one cannot trust reason, because the philosophers use reason to argue that the world must have always existed. Since by reason we know that if a moment of creation is to exist, then it must be different from every other moment when creation did not occur, and since every moment of time is the same to God, then no moment of creation can exist. Because no moment of creation exists, the world must be uncreated and eternal. But since the Qu'ran states that God created the world, reason must be wrong.

A second reason that reason is wrong comes from the philosopher's conclusion that God cannot know anything specific about the world. Reason tells us that the world changes, and so whoever keeps abreast of the facts of the changing world must have changing knowledge. Since God is unchanging, his knowledge cannot change, so reason leads to the conclusion that God does not know anything specific about the world. But since the Qu'ran states that God knows everything, reason's conclusions cannot be trusted.

The third evidence of the failure of reason is that reasoning depends on the idea of cause and effect. People reason from cause to effect or think back from effect to cause. The belief in cause and effect is essential for rationality. Without the idea, "if p, then q" no one can draw any conclusions. Al-Ghazali, however, pointed out that people see events in succession and jump to the conclusion that the first event causes the second. This reasoning is false, because the two events may have no necessary connection. In pointing out the *post hoc ergo prompter hoc* fallacy in cause-and-effect thinking, Al-Ghazali anticipated Dave Hume by almost seven hundred years. Both were led to the same inescapable conclusion, that there is no reason to trust reason.

Thus Al-Ghazali eliminated the two most obvious sources of certain truth. He used reason to show that sense perception was not a reliable guide, and then he turned reason upon itself to show that it too was faulty. His conclusion was that the mystical knowledge of the Qu'ran taught by the Sufis was the only straight path.

In addition to concluding that reason is worthless in science and theology, Al-Ghazali believed that it is also valueless in ethics. The good person will spontaneously know what is good, so any choice one has to think about is a bad choice. Ethical reasoning, then, is an oxymoron, because all reasoning about ethical choices is itself an immoral action.

Because of this criticism, philosophy declined in the Islamic world. First the Sunnis abandoned it and then the Shi'ites neglected to pursue it. *The Destruction of the Philosophers* became the second-most influential book in the Islamic world, following only the Qu'ran in its impact. Almost a century later, Averroes wrote his *Tahaful al-tahafut, Destruction of the Destruction*, but his effort was ineffectual. Muslims followed Al-Ghazali and turned away from rationality. Since perception and reason were both useless, and since God revealed the only certain truth to Mohammed in the Qu'ran, that sacred book was the only necessary object of study. Because other cultures did not have the infallible revelation from God, Islam has nothing to learn from them.

After the time of Al-Ghazali, Islam turned its back on the world, feeling it had nothing to learn from the rest of humanity. This rejection of infidel knowledge is epitomized by Arab efforts at translation. Before the time of Al-Ghazali the Muslim conquerors had made the learning of the ancient world their own by translating the treasures of Greek classical thought into Arabic. With the coming of the barbarians and the fall of Rome, the study of Greek vanished from the West and the copying of Greek manuscripts almost ceased. Greek literature was preserved only by its friends in the East who translated it into Persian. Between about 800 and 1050, Muslim scholars once again translated these Greek texts from Persian into Arabic. In fact, the Renaissance began in the West only after they rediscovered the literature of the ancient world in Arabic translation. Thanks to the openness and curiosity of the Muslims before Al-Ghazali, the Western world recovered its Greek heritage.

After the time of Al-Ghazali however, efforts to translate the discoveries of the other nations into Arabic dropped off drastically. In fact, in the nine hundred years since Al-Ghazali's death only about ten thousand books have been translated into Arabic. That means that Muslims have had access to only about eleven new books a year from the outside world. Spain translates as many books in a single year as the Muslim Arabs have translated in the last millennium. In the early seventies, the Greeks, with twelve million speakers, translated five times the number of books produced in the same period for the eight hundred million speakers of Arabic. Even in the 1980s, the Arabs translated less than one book a year into Arabic for each million speakers of the language, whereas for every million Hungarians, people translated five hundred nineteen books![6]

Hence it is no wonder Islamic civilization fell off the table while Western civilization skyrocketed. Refusing to learn from the observations of natural science or to use reason to manipulate the data gathered from those observations kept their own thinkers from making important scientific discoveries. Thinking that the only reliable information in the world came from the Qu'ran shut the door on borrowing the discoveries of other nations. Without native discovery and lacking shared information, Islam found itself mired in the eleventh century. Al-Ghazali's life and thought caused a decline in Islam almost as spectacular as its rise under Mohammed.

---

[6] United Nations Development Programme Arab Fund for Economic and Social Development, *Arab Human Development Report 2003* (New York: United Nations Publications, 2003), 67-8.

Christians living in a postmodern world have much to learn from Al-Ghazali's effect on Islam. When people are decrying "modernity," "foundationalism," and "linear thinking," we would do well to remember what happened to Islam when it abandoned its trust in rationality and opened itself to unreason. During the same centuries that Islam was shutting down its interest in the natural world and the speculations of its philosophy, Christians were beginning to think rigorously about the universe and humanity's place in it. When thinkers like Roger Bacon and Francis Bacon began to reason about data from experimental observations, and were convinced that those data fit a pattern because they were created by a reasonable God, science emerged. When philosophers like Thomas Aquinas began to systematize biblical truths and reconcile them with the reasoning of Aristotle, systematic theology resulted. The resulting worldview, called theism, was supported both by nature and by grace, by science as well as scripture, and by faith in tandem with reason.

Therefore we Christians need to remember that when our God appeared in our world he called himself *logos*, reason (John 1:1), and that we dare not abandon him.

# What's Wrong With Moral Relativism?[1]

Francis J. Beckwith

In his important and influential work, *The Closing of the American Mind*, late philosopher Allan Bloom makes the observation that "there is one thing a professor can be absolutely certain of: almost every student entering the university believes, or says he believes, that truth is relative...The students, of course, cannot defend their opinion. It is something with which they have been indoctrinated."[2] Bloom is talking about moral relativism as well as epistemological relativism. The latter is the view that there is no such thing as objective truth, that knowledge is relative to one's self, culture, and/or point of view. In this chapter, we will focus primarily on moral relativism, a view that is not limited to indoctrinated college freshmen, but is dominant in North American culture.

Moral relativism is the view that when it comes to questions of morality, there is no absolute or objective right

---

[1] This chapter is adapted from "Why I Am Not a Relativist," which appeared in *Why I Am a Christian*, eds. Norman L. Geisler and Paul Hoffman (Grand Rapids, MI: Baker Book House, 2001).
[2] Allan Bloom, *The Closing of the American Mind* (New York: Simon and Schuster, 1987), 25.

and wrong—moral rules are merely personal preferences and/or the result of one's cultural, sexual, or ethnic orientation. Many people see relativism as necessary for promoting tolerance, non-judgmentalism, and inclusiveness, for they think if one believes one's moral position is correct and other positions are incorrect, one is close-minded and intolerant. I will argue in this chapter that not only do the arguments for relativism fail, but that relativism itself cannot live up to its own reputation, for it is promoted by its proponents as the only correct view on morality. This is why relativists typically do not tolerate non-relativist views, judge those views as mistaken, and maintain that relativism is exclusively right.

A critical evaluation of relativism is important to the case for the Christian faith because Chrsitianity teaches that there are objective moral norms that apply to all persons in all places and in all times.[3] Relativism says that there are no such norms. So, if relativism is incorrect, Christianity cannot be dismissed on the grounds that it affirms objective moral norms.

Since September 11, 2001, relativism has lost a lot of its rhetorical edge. Given the horrific events of that grim morning, most Americans have no problem with embracing the judgment that there are just some activities that are simply wrong no matter what a particular culture, religion, individual, public figure, or Baldwin brother may think. Nevertheless, many still resort to embracing relativism on a variety of issues (especially those that touch on personal and sexual morality), maintaining that reasoning, especially moral reasoning (if they believe there is such a thing), has no place in these disputes.

I will first explain what it means to make a moral claim. I will then move on to critique moral relativism by assessing two of the most-often cited arguments offered for it—the argument from cultural and individual differences, and the

---

[3] There are many works that defend the notion that the Bible and the Christian tradition teach objective moral norms. See, for example, Pope Benedict XVI, *Truth and Tolerance* (San Francisco: Ignatius, 2004); and C. S. Lewis, *Mere Christianity* (New York: MacMillan, 1943).

argument from tolerance. This will take up the bulk of this chapter. I will conclude with a brief section in which I show, by employing several examples, how it is possible to provide reasons for a particular moral point of view.

## Moral Relativism and Moral Discourse[4]

Moral relativism has stunted our ability to grasp the nature of moral claims. People in our culture often confuse *preference-claims* with *moral-claims* or reduce the latter to the former. To understand what I mean by this, consider two statements:[5]

(1) I like vanilla ice cream
(2) Killing people without justification is wrong.

The first statement is a preference-claim, since it is a description of a person's subjective taste. It is not a *norma-tive* claim. It is not a claim about what one ought or ought not to do. It is not saying, "Since I like vanilla ice cream, the government ought to coerce you to eat it as well" or "Every-one in the world ought to like vanilla ice cream too." A claim of subjective preference tells us nothing about what one *ought to* think or do. For example, if someone were to say, "I like to torture children for fun," this would tell us noth-ing about whether it is wrong or right to torture children for fun.

The second claim, however, is quite different. It has little if anything to do with what one likes or dislikes. In fact, one may *prefer* to kill another person without justification and still know that it is morally wrong to do so. This statement is a *moral-claim*. It is not a descriptive claim, for it does not tell us what, why, or how things are, or how a major-ity of people in fact behave and think. Nor is it a prefer-

---

[4] The ideas and argument of this section have been significantly shaped by a portion of the book by Hadley Arkes, *First Things: An Inquiry Into the First Principles of Moral and Justice* (Princeton NJ: Princeton University Press, 1986), 20-22.
[5] Arkes' work (ibid) was instrumental in helping me to better understand the dif-ferences between the two statements.

ence-claim, for it does not tell us what anyone's subjective preference may be or how one prefers to behave and think. Rather, it is a claim about what people *ought to do*, which may be contrary to how people in fact behave and how they prefer to behave.

Unfortunately, the espousal of moral relativism has made it difficult for many people in our culture to distinguish between preference-claims and moral-claims. Rather than pondering and struggling with arguments for and against a particular moral perspective, people sometimes reduce the disagreement to a question of "personal preference" or "subjective opinion." For example, many who defend the abortion-choice[6] position sometimes tell pro-lifers: "If you don't like abortion, then don't have one." This instruction reduces the abortion debate to a preference-claim. That is, the objective moral rightness or wrongness of abortion (i.e., whether or not it involves the unjustified killing of a being who is fully human) is declared, without argument, not relevant. But this is clearly a mistake, for those who oppose abortion do so because they believe that the unborn during most if not all of a woman's pregnancy is a full-fledged member of the human community and it is *prima facie* wrong, both objectively and universally, to kill such a being. For this reason, when the pro-lifer hears the abortion-choice advocate tell her that if she doesn't like abortion she doesn't have to have one, it sounds to her as if the abortion-choicer is saying, "Don't like murder, then don't kill any innocent persons." Understandably, the pro-lifer, committed to objective moral norms, finds such rhetoric perplexing as well as unpersuasive. Of course, many sophisticated abortion-choice advocates are opponents of moral relativism as well.[7] But it just seems that in the

---

[6] As far as I know, it was the President of the Libertarians for Life, Doris Gordon, who first coined the term "abortion-choice." See, for example, her introductory essay in *International Journal of Sociology and Social Policy* 19.3/4 (1999).

[7] See, for example, Louis P. Pojman, *Ethics: Discovering Right and Wrong*, 3rd ed. (Belmont, CA: Wadsworth, 1998). Pojman, a supporter of abortion rights, is a critic of moral relativism as well as a defender of moral objectivism. For his defense of the abortion-choice position, see Louis P. Pojman, "Abortion: A Defense of the Personhood Argument," in *The Abortion Controversy 25 Years After* Roe v. Wade:

popular debate, abortion-choicers tend to reduce the issue of abortion to a matter of preference and thus seem to have been more affected by moral relativism than have their opponents. (But they are *not completely* affected, for they do appeal to "fundamental rights" typically grounded in objective morality).[8] It is true that the pro-lifer's arguments may be flawed, but the abortion-choice advocate does not critique those flawed arguments when he mistakenly turns a serious moral disagreement into a debate over preferences.

## Arguments for Moral Relativism

There are two arguments that are often used to defend moral relativism. The first is the argument from cultural and individual differences, and the second is the argument from tolerance.

### Argument from Cultural and Individual Differences

In this argument, the relativist concludes that there are no objective moral norms because cultures and individuals disagree on moral issues. In order to defend this premise, the relativist typically cites a number of examples, such as cross-cultural and intra-cultural differences over the morality of sexual practices, abortion, war, and capital punishment. In the words of Hadley Arkes, an opponent of moral relativism: "In one society, a widow is burned on the funeral pyre of her husband; in another, she is burned on the beach in Miami. In one society, people complain to the chef about the roast beef; in another, they send back the roast beef and eat the chef."[9] There are at least four problems with this argument.

---

*A Reader*, 2nd ed., eds. Louis P. Pojman and Francis J. Beckwith (Belmont, CA: Wadsworth, 1998) Another well-known defender of abortion-choice, David Boonin, seems to be no friend of moral relativism. See David Boonin, *A Defense of Abortion* (New York: Cambridge University Press, 2003), 13-14.
[8] For an assessment of the apparent incoherence of this position, see Hadley Arkes, *Natural Rights and the Right to Choose* (New York: Cambridge University Press, 2002).
[9] Arkes, *First Things*, 149.

## Relativism does not follow from disagreement

The fact that people disagree about something does not mean that there is no truth. For example, if you and I were to disagree on the question of whether or not the earth is round, our disagreement would certainly not be proof that the earth has *no* shape. The fact that a skin-head (a type of young neo-Nazi) and I may disagree on the question of whether we should treat people equally and with fairness is certainly not sufficient reason to conclude that equality and fairness are not objective moral values. Even if individuals and cultures hold no values in common, it does not follow from this that nobody is right or wrong about the correct values. That is, there could be a mistaken individual or culture, such as Adolf Hitler and Nazi Germany.

If the mere fact of disagreement were sufficient to conclude that objective norms do not exist, then we would have to believe that there is no objectively correct position on such issues as slavery, genocide, and child molestation, for the slave owner, genocidal maniac, and pedophile have an opinion that differs from the one held by those of us who condemn their actions. In the end, moral disagreement proves nothing.

## Disagreement counts against relativism

Suppose, however, that the relativist, despite the logical failure of his case, sticks to his guns and maintains that disagreement over objective norms proves the correctness of relativism. But this will not work. For the relativist has set down a principle—disagreement means there is no truth—that unravels his own case. After all, some of us believe that relativism is a mistaken view. We, in other words, *disagree* with the relativist over the nature of morality. We believe that objective moral norms exist whereas the relativist does not. But, according to the relativist's own principle—disagreement means there is no truth—he ought to abandon his opinion that relativism is the correct position. And to make matters worse for the relativist, his principle is a proposition for which there is not universal agreement, and thus on its own grounds must be rejected. As Arkes points out, "My disagreement establishes that the proposition [i.e., disagreement means there is no truth] does not enjoy a universal assent, and by the very terms of the proposition, that should be quite sufficient to determine *its own invalidity.*"10

## Disagreement is overrated

Although it is true that people and cultures disagree on moral issues, it does not follow from this that they do not share the same values or that there are not moral norms that are binding on all nations in all times and in all places. Take, for example, the Salem witch trials. In colonial Massachusetts certain individuals were put to death as punishment for practicing witchcraft. We do not execute witches today, but not because our moral norms have changed. Rather, the reason why we don't execute witches is because we do not believe, as the 17th-century residents of Massachusetts did, that the practice of witchcraft has a fatal affect upon the community. But suppose that we had good evidence that the practice of witchcraft did effect people in the same way that second-hand cigarette smoke affects the non-smoker. We would alter the practice of our values to take into consideration this factual change. We might set up non-witch sections in restaurants and ban the casting of spells on interstate airplane flights. The upshot of all this is that the good of the community is a value we share with the 17th century residents of Salem, but we simply believe that they were factually wrong about the effect of witches upon that good.

Consider again the issue of abortion. The conventional wisdom is that the moral and legal debate over abortion is a dispute between two factions that hold incommensurable value systems. But the conventional wisdom is mistaken, for these factions hold many principles in common.

First, each side believes that all human persons possess certain inalienable rights regardless of whether their governments protect these rights. That is why both sides appeal to what each believes is a fundamental right. The pro-life advocate appeals to "life," whereas the abortion-

10 Ibid., 132.

choice advocate appeals to "liberty" (or "choice"). Both believe that a constitutional regime, in order to be just, must uphold fundamental rights.

Second, each side believes that its position best exemplifies its opponent's fundamental value. The abortion-choice advocate does not deny that "life" is a value, but argues that his position's appeal to human liberty is a necessary ingredient by which an individual can pursue the fullest and most complete life possible.

On the other hand, the pro-life advocate does not eschew "liberty." She believes that all human liberty is at least limited by another human person's right to life. For example, one has a right to freely pursue any goal one believes is consistent with one's happiness, such as attending a Los Angeles Lakers basketball game. One has, however, no right to freely pursue this goal at the expense of another's life or liberty, such as running over pedestrians with one's car so that one can get to the game on time. And of course, the pro-life advocate argues that the unborn are persons with a full right to life. And because the act of abortion typically results in the death of the unborn, abortion, with few exceptions, is not morally justified, and for that reason ought to be made illegal.

The abortion-choice advocate does not deny that human persons have a right to life. He just believes that this right to life is not extended to fetuses because they are not full members of the human community. Others, such as Judith Jarvis Thomson and Eileen McDonagh,[11] argue that even if the unborn entity is a full-fledged member of the human community, he or she has no right to use the body of another against that person's will, because such a usage of another's body demands of that person great risk and sacrifice beyond any ordinary moral obligation. Hence, because a pregnant woman is not morally obligated to put herself at great risk and to make a significant sacrifice for another, she is morally justified in removing her unborn

11 Judith Jarvis Thomson, "A Defense of Abortion," in *Philosophy & Public Affairs* 1 (1971): 57-66; and Eileen McDonagh, *Breaking the Abortion Deadlock: From Choice to Consent* (New York: Oxford University Press, 1996).

offspring even if such a removal results in his or her death. The pro-life advocate does not deny that people have the liberty to make choices that they believe are in their best interests. She just believes that this liberty does not entail the right to choose abortion because such a choice conflicts with the life, liberty, and interests of another human being (the fetus), who is defenseless, weak, and vulnerable, and has a natural claim upon its parents' care, both pre- and post-natally. Thus, when all is said and done, the debate over abortion is not really about conflicting moral systems. After all, imagine if a pro-life politician were to say the following in a campaign speech: "My party's platform affirms a woman's right to terminate her pregnancy if and only if it does not result in the death of her unborn child." Disagreement over such a plank would not be over the morality of killing human persons; it would be over the metaphysical question of whether the unborn human is included in that category.[12]

## Absurd consequences follow from moral relativism

First, if there are no objective moral norms that apply to all persons in all times and in all places, then certain moral judgments, such as the following, cannot be universally true: Mother Teresa was morally better than Adolf Hitler; rape is always wrong; and it is wrong to torture babies for fun. But to deny that these judgments are not universally true seems absurd. For there seem to be some moral judgments that are absolutely correct regardless of what cultures or individuals may think.

Second, if the relativist claims that morality is relative to the individual, what happens when individual moralities conflict? For example, suppose that Jeffrey Dahmer's morality permits him to cannibalize his neighbor, but his neighbor disagrees. What would the relativist suggest be done in this case, since, according to this form of relativism, nobody's morality is in principle superior to any other?

[12] Sophisticated abortion-choice advocates argue that fetuses are not human persons. And for this reason, a fetus does not have a right to life if her life hinders the liberty of a being who is a person (i.e., the pregnant woman).

In addition, if the moral life is no more than a reflection of people's individual tastes, preferences, and orientations, then we cannot tell young people that it is morally wrong to lie, steal, cheat, smoke, abuse drugs, kill their newborns, and drop out of school, even though these behaviors may be consistent with the students' own personal tastes, preferences and/or orientations.

Third, even if the relativist were to make the more modest claim that morality is not relative to the individual but to the individual's culture, that one is only obligated to follow the dictates of one's society, other problems follow.

(a) The cultural relativist's position is self-refuting. What does it mean for a position to be self-refuting? J.P. Moreland explains:

> When a statement fails to satisfy itself (i.e., to conform to its own criteria of validity or acceptability), it is self-refuting....Consider some examples. "I cannot say a word in English" is self-refuting when uttered in English. "I do not exist" is self-refuting, for one must exist to utter it. The claim "there are no truths" is self-refuting. If it is false, then it is false. But if it is true, then it is false as well, for in that case there would be no truths, including the statement itself.[13]

How is cultural relativism self-refuting? The supporter of cultural relativism maintains that there are no objective and universal moral norms, and for that reason everyone ought follow the moral norms of his or her own culture. But the cultural relativist is making an absolute, universal claim—that everyone is morally obligated to follow the moral norms of his or her own culture. So, if this moral norm is absolute and universal, then cultural relativism is false. But if this moral norm is neither absolute nor universal, then cultural relativism is still false, for I would not have any obligation to follow my culture's moral norms.

13 J.P. Moreland, *Scaling the Secular City* (Grand Rapids: Baker Book House, 1987), 92.

(b) Because each of us belongs to a number of different "societies" or "cultures," which one of them should be followed when they conflict? For example, suppose a woman named "Carla" is a resident of a liberal upscale neighborhood in Hollywood, California, attends a Christian church, and is a partner in a prestigious law firm. In her neighborhood, having an adulterous affair is considered "enlightened" and those who do not pursue such unions are considered repressed prudes. At her church, however, adultery is condemned as sinful, while at her law firm adultery is neither encouraged nor discouraged. Suppose further that Carla chooses to commit adultery in the firm's back office with a fellow churchgoer, Winston, who resides in a conservative neighborhood in which adultery is condemned. The office, it turns out, is adjacent to the church as well as precisely halfway between Carla's neighborhood and Winston's neighborhood. It is not clear which society is morally relevant.[14]

(c) There can be no moral progress or moral reformers. If morality is reducible to culture, then there can be no real moral progress. For the only way one can say that a culture is *getting better*, or progressing, is if there are objective moral norms that are not dependent on culture to which a society may draw closer. But if what is morally good is merely what one's culture says is morally good, then we can only say that cultural norms change, not that the society is progressing or getting better. Yet, it seems, for example, that the abolition of slavery and the establishment of civil rights of African Americans in the United States were instances of moral progress. In addition, there can be no true moral reformers if cultural relativism is true. Moreland writes:

> If [cultural] relativism is true, then it is impossible in principle to have a true moral reformer who changes a society's code and does not merely bring out what was already implicit in that code. For moral reformers, by definition, *change* a society's code by arguing

---

[14] Moreland offers a similar illustration in Ibid.

that it is somehow morally inadequate. But if [cultural] relativism is true, an act is right if and only if it is in society's code; so the reformer is by definition immoral (since he adopts a set of values outside the society's code and attempts to change that code in keeping with these values). It is odd, to say the least, for someone to hold that every moral reformer who ever lived—Moses, Jesus, Gandhi, Martin Luther King—was immoral by definition. Any moral view which implies that is surely false.[15]

Thus, in order to remain consistent, the cultural relativist must deny that there can any real moral progress or any real moral reformers. Such judgments presuppose the existence of real objective and absolute moral norms.

*Argument from Tolerance*

Many people see relativism as necessary for promoting tolerance, non-judgmentalism, and inclusiveness, for they think if you believe your moral position is correct and the position of others is incorrect, you are close-minded and intolerant. They usually base this premise on the well-known differences of opinion on morality between cultures and individuals. So, the moral relativist embraces the view that one should not judge other cultures and individuals, for to do so would be intolerant. There are at least four problems with this argument, all of which maintain that tolerance (rightly understood) and relativism are actually *incompatible* with each other.

Tolerance supports objective morality, not relativism

Ironically, the call to tolerance by relativists presupposes the existence of at least one nonrelative, universal, and objective norm: tolerance. Bioethicist Tom Beauchamp explains:

If we interpret normative relativism as requiring tol-

[15] Ibid., 243.

erance of other views, the whole theory is imperiled by inconsistency. The proposition that we ought to tolerate the views of others, or that it is right not to interfere with others, is precluded by the very strictures of the theory. Such a proposition bears all the marks of a non-relative account of moral rightness, one based on, but not reducible to, the cross-cultural findings of anthropologists. . . .But if this moral principle [of tolerance] is recognized as valid, it can of course be employed as an instrument for criticizing such cultural practices as the denial of human rights to minorities and such beliefs as that of racial superiority. A moral commitment to tolerance of other practices and beliefs thus leads inexorably to the abandonment of normative relativism.[16]

Thus, if everyone ought to be tolerant, then tolerance is an objective moral norm. And therefore, moral relativism is false. Also, tolerance presupposes that there is something good about being tolerant, such as being able to learn from others with whom one disagrees or to impart knowledge and wisdom to that person. But that presupposes objective moral values, namely, that knowledge and wisdom are good things. Moreover, tolerance presupposes that someone may be correct about his or her moral perspective. That is to say, it seems that part of the motivation for advocating tolerance is to encourage people to be open to the possibility that one may be able to gain truth and insight (including moral truth and insight) from another who may possess it. If that is the case, then there are objective moral truths that I can learn.

In addition, tolerance presupposes a moral judgment of another's viewpoint. That it to say, I can only be tolerant of those ideas that I think are mistaken. I am not tolerant of ideas with which I agree; I embrace them. And I am not tolerant of topics for which I have no interest (e.g., European professional soccer); I merely have benign neglect for them

[16] Tom L. Beauchamp, *Philosophical Ethics: An Introduction to Moral Philosophy* (New York: McGraw-Hill, 1982), 42.

(that is, I don't care one way or another). Consider the following example. Suppose I tell a friend that I believe that homosexuality is immoral. And suppose my friend requests that I be tolerant toward homosexuals in my community. If I accept this advice, and choose to be civil, respectful, and gracious to gay men and women with whom I have contact, while at the same time judging their sexual practices as immoral, it seems that I would be truly tolerant. But suppose that someone says that my judging of homosexuality as immoral still makes me "intolerant." At that point, given my understanding of "tolerance," I have no idea what I am supposed to do. For if I change my view of homosexuality, and say either that it is not immoral or that I have no opinion (i.e., I have benign neglect), then I cannot be tolerant, for I can only be tolerant of that which I believe is wrong or mistaken. On the other hand, if judging another's position as wrong or mistaken makes one intolerant, then the person who judges my negative assessment of homosexuality is, by that person's own definition, intolerant. But that is absurd. For if "tolerance" means that one ought not to judge a view as morally wrong, then it seems to be consistent with either embracing the view or having benign neglect for it. If that is the case, then "tolerance" has lost its meaning and is simply a cover for trying to shame and coerce others not to publicly (and/or perhaps privately) disagree with one's controversial and disputed position on human sexuality. This, ironically, is an example of intolerance (as traditionally understood). So, it seems to me, that the appeal to tolerance, once we have a clear understanding of its meaning, is *inconsistent* with relativism.

## Relativism is itself a closed-minded and intolerant position

After all, the relativist dogmatically asserts that there is no moral truth. To illustrate this, consider a dialogue (based loosely on a real-life exchange) between a high-school teacher and her student, Elizabeth.[17] The teacher instructs her class, "Welcome, students. This is the first

---

[17] This dialogue is presented in similar form in Francis Beckwith and Gregory Koukl, *Relativism: Feet Firmly Planted in Mid-Air* (Grand Rapids: Baker, 1998), 74.

day of class, and so I want to lay down some ground rules. First, since no one has the truth about morality, you should be open-minded to the opinions of your fellow students." The teacher recognizes the raised hand of Elizabeth, who asks, "If nobody has the truth, isn't that a good reason for me not to listen to my fellow students? After all, if nobody has the truth, why should I waste my time listening to other people and their opinions? What's the point? Only if somebody has the truth does it make sense to be open-minded. Don't you agree?"

"No, I don't. Are you claiming to know the truth? Isn't that a bit arrogant and dogmatic?"

"Not at all. Rather I think it's dogmatic, as well as arrogant, to assert that no single person on earth knows the truth. After all, have you met every person in the world and quizzed them exhaustively? If not, how can you make such a claim? Also, I believe it is actually the opposite of arrogance to say that I will alter my opinions to fit the truth whenever and wherever I find it. And if I happen to think that I have good reason to believe I do know the truth and would like to share it with you, why wouldn't you listen to me? Why would you automatically discredit my opinion before it is even uttered? I thought we were supposed to listen to everyone's opinion."

"This should prove to be an interesting semester."

Another student blurts out, "Ain't that the truth," provoking the class to laughter.

## Relativism is judgmental, exclusivist, and partisan

This may seem like an odd thing to say, since the relativist would like you to think his viewpoint is non-judgmental, inclusivist, and neutral when it comes to moral beliefs. But consider the following.

First, the relativist says that if you believe in objective moral truth, you are *wrong*. Hence, relativism is judgmental. Second, it follows from this that relativism is *excluding* your beliefs from the realm of legitimate options. Thus, relativism is exclusivist. And third, because relativism is exclusive, all non-relativists are automatically not members of the "correct thinking" party. So, relativism is partisan.

Tolerance only makes sense within the framework of a moral order, for it is within such a framework that one can morally justify tolerating some things while not tolerating others. Tolerance without a moral framework, or absolute tolerance, leads to a dogmatic relativism, and thus to an intolerance of any viewpoint that does not embrace relativism. It is no wonder that in such a climate of "tolerance" any person who maintains that there is an objective moral order to which society ought to subscribe is greeted with ferocious hatred.

## The "tolerance" of moral relativism either condones barbarism or is self-refuting

As I pointed out above, some moral relativists embrace tolerance because they believe that such a posture is appropriate given the diversity of moral and cultural traditions in the world today. Humanist author Xiaorong Li points out the fallacy in this reasoning:

> But the existence of moral diversity does no more to justify that we ought to respect different moral values than the existence of disease, hunger, torture, slavery do to justify that we ought to value them. Empirical claims thus are not suitable as the basis for developing moral principles such as "Never judge other cultures" or "We ought to tolerate different values."
>
> What if the respected or tolerated culture disrespects and advocates violence against individuals who dissent? When a girl fights to escape female genital circumcision or foot-binding or arranged marriage, when a widow does not want to be burned to death to honor her dead husband, the relativist is obligated to "respect" the cultural or traditional customs from which the individuals are trying to escape. In so doing, the relativist is not merely disrespecting the individual but effectively endorsing the moral ground for torture, rape and murder. *On moral*

*issues, ethical relativists can not possibly remain neutral—they are committed either to the individual or to the dominant force within a culture.*

Relativists have made explicit one central value—equal respect and tolerance of other ways of life, which they insist to be absolute and universal. *Ethical relativism is thus repudiated by itself.*[18]

## Reasoning About Moral Matters

Morality is clearly more than mere reasoning, just as architecture is more than mere mathematics. One can immediately grasp as well as appreciate the moral virtue of Mother Teresa or the monumental elegance of the Eiffel Tower without having studied Thomas Reid's moral philosophy or mastered geometry and calculus. Nevertheless, just as one cannot build the Eiffel Tower without mastering certain mathematical disciplines, one cannot attribute the label "just" or "right" to one's point of view without offering justification for its rightness.

The logic of moral reasoning has been part and parcel of our discourse for as long as human beings have occupied the Earth. It has stirred souls, shamed sinners, moved nations, energized social movements, and provided us a potent grammar in numerous areas of private and public life. Consider just three examples, though numerous others could be conscripted for our purposes.

In the book of II Samuel (chapter 11) in the Jewish Tanuch (the Christian Old Testament), one finds the story of King David's encounter with Nathan after the King had taken himself a wife, Bathsheba, a woman whom he had first encountered one evening while he strolled on the palace roof. He noticed, from a distance, Bathsheba bathing. Overwhelmed by her beauty, he sent his messengers to fetch her, and he quickly came to know her (in the Biblical sense). That union resulted in a pregnancy. But there was a problem, for Bathsheba, as David knew, was married to

[18] Xiaorang Li, "Postmodernism and Universal Human Rights: Why Theory and Reality Don't Mix," *Free Inquiry* 18.4 (Fall 1998): 28.

Uriah the Hittite. So, the King assigned Uriah, a member of the army, to the front lines where the fighting is the most ferocious, and instructed Joab, the leader of the Israelite army, to leave Uriah there unprotected so that he would surely be killed. David married Bathsheba soon after Uriah died on the battlefield.

But David did not live happily ever after, for first among the punishments that followed was Nathan's rebuke, which Nathan introduced with an elegant form of moral reasoning that forced the King to confront the gravity of his offense:

> When [Nathan] came to [David], he said, "There were two men in a certain town, one rich and the other poor. The rich man had a very large number of sheep and cattle, but the poor man had nothing except one little ewe lamb he had bought. He raised it, and it grew up with him and his children. It shared his food, drank from his cup and even slept in his arms. It was like a daughter to him.
>
> "Now a traveler came to the rich man, but the rich man refrained from taking one of his own sheep or cattle to prepare a meal for the traveler who had come to him. Instead, he took the ewe lamb that belonged to the poor man and prepared it for the one who had come to him."
>
> David burned with anger against the man and said to Nathan, "As surely as the LORD lives, the man who did this deserves to die! He must pay for the lamb four times over, because he did such a thing and had no pity."
>
> Then Nathan said to David, "You are the man!" (II Samuel 12:1b-7a).

David fully grasped the moral principles by which we judge that the rich man's behavior was wicked and that it should result in severe punishment against him. But those very same moral principles, and the punishments that follow from violating them, apply to David as well. One need not accept the divine inspiration and/or historicity

of this biblical account in order to appreciate the wisdom
of Nathan's judgment, the aptness of his analogy, and
the clarity that one acquires when grasping a scintillating
instance of moral reasoning.

In his failed 1858 bid for a U.S. Senate seat from Illi-
nois, Abraham Lincoln engaged in a series of public debates
with his Democratic opponent, Stephen A. Douglas. Among
the many topics on which they disputed was the question
of whether U.S. terrorities should be allowed by the federal government to permit slavery if they so chose. Douglas maintained that although he believed that slavery was
wrong (i.e., he personally opposed it), he was not willing
to require that the federal government eliminate slavery,
for to do so would be to violate the principle of popular
sovereignty, i.e., that local majorities should be permitted to vote on such issues free of any and all federal constraints.[19] But, as Lincoln aptly pointed out, "when Judge
Douglas says he 'don't care whether slavery is voted up or
down,'...he cannot thus argue logically if he sees anything
wrong in it;...He cannot say that he would as soon see a
wrong voted up as voted down. When Judge Douglas says
that whoever, or whatever community, wants slaves, they
have a right to have them, he is perfectly logical if there is
nothing wrong in the institution; but if you admit that it is
wrong, he cannot logically say that anybody has a right to
do a wrong."[20] Lincoln, a practical man with uncommon
wisdom, grasped an important conceptual truth not often
apprehended by those, such as Douglas, who inadvertantly
stumble into the arena of moral reasoning and think they
are somewhere else. To claim that something is a wrong is
to claim that it is impermissible, but it would inexorably
follow from that truth that one cannot claim that one has a
*right* to perform the wrong, for that would mean the impermissible is permissible.[21] Or, as Arkes puts it: "[O]nce we
come to the recognition that any act stands in the class of a

---

[19] Arkes, *First Things*, 24.
[20] *The Collected Works of Abraham Lincoln*, ed. Roy Basler (New Brunswick, NJ:
Rutgers University Press, 1953), 3: 256-57, as quoted in Arkes, *First Things*, 24.
[21] Arkes, *First Things*, 24-25.

wrong...the logic of that recognition forbids us from treating that act any longer as a matter merely of personal taste or private choice."[22]

In notes he had prepared for himself, Lincoln provided another example of principled moral reasoning in assessing the sorts of arguments that his contemporaries put forth to defend the enslavement of black people by white people:

> You say A. is white and B. is black. It is *color*, then: the lighter having the right to enslave the darker? Take care. By this rule, you are to be slave to the first man you meet, with a fairer skin than your own.
>
> You do not mean *color* exactly?—You mean the whites are *intellectually* the superiors of the blacks, and therefore, have the right to enslave them? Take care again. By this rule, you are to be slave to the first man you meet, with an intellect superior to your own.
>
> But, say you, it is a question of interest; and, if you can make it your *interest*, you have the right to enslave another. Very well. And if he can make it his interest, he has the right to enslave you.[23]

Lincoln was making the point that if one were to apply the arguments for slavery to the prospective and current slave-owners, whites, then one has put in place premises that may be employed by the government to undermine the rights of all human beings under its authority.[24] For the premises of the pro-slavery arguments contain propositions that appeal to degreed properties that carry no moral weight—color, intellect, and interest—when it comes to the question of human equality. Lincoln's assessment of these arguments is an impressive example of moral reasoning.

---

[22] Ibid., 25.
[23] *The Collected Works of Abraham Lincoln*, 2:222, as quoted in Arkes, *First Things*, 43-44 (emphasis in original).
[24] Arkes, *First Things*, 43.

## Conclusion

Moral relativism is a philosophical failure. The two main arguments for moral relativism—the argument from disagreement and the argument from tolerance—are seriously flawed in numerous ways. Given the failure of moral relativism, it seems reasonable to believe in objective morality. Moreover, there is a logic of moral reasoning that has been employed by numerous people throughout the ages for the purpose of providing for their fellow citizens moral clarity and/or moral justification. There is no reason why we cannot do the same today.

## Suggested Readings

Hadley Arkes. *First Things: An Inquiry Into the First Principles of Moral and Justice.* Princeton, NJ: Princeton University Press, 1986.

Francis J. Beckwith and Gregory P. Koukl. *Relativism: Feet Firmly Planted in Mid-Air.* Grand Rapids, MI: Baker Book House, 1998.

Allan Bloom. *The Closing of the American Mind.* New York: Simon & Schuster, 1987.

Peter Kreeft. *A Refutation of Relativism: Interviews with An Absolutist.* San Francisco, CA: Ignatius, 1999.

Pope Benedict XVI. *Truth and Tolerance.* San Francisco, CA: Ignatius, 2004.

# A Critique of the Worldview of Scientific Naturalism

J.P. Moreland

## Part 1: Naturalism and Evolution

In 1941, Harvard sociologist Pitirim A. Sorokin wrote a book entitled *The Crisis of Our Age.* In it Sorokin claimed that cultures come in two major types: sensate and ideational. A sensate culture is one in which people only believe in the reality of the physical universe capable of being experienced with the five senses. A sensate culture is secular, this-worldly, and empirical. By contrast, an ideational culture embraces the sensory world, but goes on to accept the notion that an extra-empirical immaterial reality can be known as well, a reality consisting of God, the soul, immaterial beings, values, purposes, and various abstract objects like numbers and propositions. Sorokin claimed that a sensate culture will eventually disintegrate because it does not have the intellectual resources necessary to sustain a public and private life conducive of corporate and individual human flourishing.

Sorokin's claim should come as no surprise to students of the Bible. Proverbs tells us that we become the ideas we cherish in our inner being and Paul reminds us that we transform our lives through a renewed intellectual life. Scripture is quite clear that our "world view"—the way we think about things and the beliefs we actually come to have—will determine the shape of our cultural and individual lives. Because this is so, the war of worldviews raging in our modern context is a struggle with absolutely far-reaching and crucial implications.

In my opinion, given the death of communism, there are three main worldviews currently contending for prominence in the marketplace of ideas, especially the universities: postmodernism, Christian theism, and scientific naturalism. Very roughly, postmodernism is the idea that there is no such thing as objective truth —there are only a multiplicity of equally valid, relative perspectives. So understood, postmodernism is a self-defeating form of conceptual relativism. I shall not examine it further because, at least for now, it is not as influential as scientific naturalism. Instead, I intend to examine scientific naturalism and, more specifically, to provide an analysis and critique of some of its major aspects.

## What is Scientific Naturalism?

Just what is scientific naturalism (hereafter, naturalism)? Succinctly put, it is the view that the spatio-temporal universe of physical objects, properties, events, and processes that are well established by scientific forms of investigation is all there is, was, or ever will be.

There are three major components of naturalism. First, naturalism begins with an epistemology, a view about the nature and limits of knowledge, known as scientism. Scientism comes in two forms: strong and weak. Strong scientism is the view that the only things we can know are what can be tested scientifically. Scientific knowledge exhausts what can be known and if some belief is not part of a well established scientific theory, it is not an item of knowledge. Weak scientism allows some minimal, low-grade degree of rational justification for claims in fields outside of science, like ethics. But scientific knowledge is taken to be so vastly superior to other forms of reasonable belief that, if a good scientific theory implies something that contradicts a belief in some other discipline, the other field will simply have to adjust itself according to science.

Second, naturalism contains a theory—a causal story—about how everything has come-to-be. The central components of this story are the atomic theory of matter and evolution. The details of this story are not of concern here. But two broad features are of critical importance. First, the explanation of macro-changes in things (a macro-change is a change in some feature of a normal sized object that can be detected by simple observation, such as the change in a leaf's color) in terms of micro-changes (changes in small, unobservable entities at the atomic or sub-atomic level). Chemical changes are explained in terms of re-arrangements of atoms only; phenotype changes are due to changes in genotypes. Causation is from bottom-up, micro to macro—for instance, we explain why heating water causes it to boil in terms of the excitation of water molecules. Second, all events that happen are due to the occurrence of earlier events plus the laws of nature, regardless of whether the laws of nature are taken to be deterministic or probablistic.

Third, naturalism has a view about what is real: physical entities are all that exist. The mind is really the brain, free actions are merely happenings caused in the right way by inputs to the organism along with its internal "hardware" states, and there is no teleology or purpose in the world. History is just one event following another. The world is simply one big cluster of physical mechanisms effecting other physical mechanisms.

As we will see shortly, the order among these three components of naturalism is quite important. The naturalist view of knowledge is what justifies the naturalist causal story. For example, we have purged the world of real teleology and accepted the evolutionary story largely because the latter can be tested scientifically and the former cannot. Or so we are lead to believe. And the naturalist causal story is used to justify the naturalist view of what is real. We know we are merely creatures of matter because we are solely the product of evolution, and evolution is a story of physical processes operating on physical things to produce more adaptive physical things.

So far, I have been using the term *evolution* without defining it, but in reality, it can be used to mean three different things: the fact that organisms change over time (micro-evolution), the thesis of common descent, and the blind watchmaker thesis. The thesis of common descent can be interpreted in two ways: the mere claim that 1) life appeared on earth in a general pattern of simple to complex in a certain order or 2) the pattern just mentioned was one in which latter forms of life somehow (naturalistically or by Divine action) *came from* earlier ones. The blind watchmaker thesis is that the processes and mechanisms of evolution are solely naturalistic with no specific intervention of a deity. So understood, a theistic evolutionist could accept the blind watchmaker thesis so long as he limited God's activity to that of a first cause or of a being who sustains the world in existence while it unfolds according to natural law and "chance."

It is the third notion of evolution that is crucial to the naturalist. And it is precisely this sense of evolution that has far less evidence in support of it than is often realized. Whether or not you agree with this statement, one thing seems clear. The certainty claimed for evolution and the ferocity with which it is held go far beyond what is justified by scientific evidence and empirical testing. No one could read Phillip Johnson's *Darwin on Trial* (InterVarsity, 1991), Michael Denton's *Evolution: A Theory in Crisis* (Adler & Adler, 1986), Jonathan Well's *Icons of Evolution* (Washington, DC: Regnery, 2000), or *The Creation Hypothesis* (InterVarsity, 1994; edited by the present author) without realizing that a serious, sophisticated case can be made against the blind watchmaker thesis even if one judged that, in the end, the case is not as persuasive as the evolutionary account. The problem is that most intellectuals today act as if there is simply no issue here and that if you do not believe in evolution, then you must believe in a flat earth.

Why is this? Why do so many people, including some well-intentioned Christians, heap so much scorn on creationists (either young earth or progressive) who reject the evolutionary story, and act as though no informed, modern person can believe otherwise? I believe the answer lies in two directions, neither of which is empirical or purely scientific.

## Two Reasons For the Modern Certainty About Evolution

Let us recall that our question is not about the empirical evidence for evolution. I think this evidence is quite meager. But in any case, even if we grant for the sake of argument that there is a decent bit of positive evidence for it, the degree of certainty claimed on its behalf, along with the widespread attitude towards creationists, is quite beyond what is warranted by the evidence alone. What is going on here? What are the reasons behind the seemingly unshakable modern belief in evolution?

First, the monolithic intellectual authority of science, coupled with the belief that creation science is religion, not science, means that evolution is the only view of origins that can claim the backing of reason. In our sensate culture, science and science alone has unqualified intellectual acceptance. When a scientist makes a pronouncement on the evening news about what causes obesity, crime, or anything else, he is taken as speaking *ex cathedra*. When was the last time you saw a philosopher, theologian, or humanities professor consulted as an intellectual leader in the culture? All supposedly extra-scientific beliefs must move to the back of the bus and are relegated to the level of private, subjective opinion.

Now, if two scientific theories are competing for allegiance, then most intellectuals, at least in principle, would be open to the evidence relevant to the issue at hand. But what happens if one rival theory is a scientific one and the other is not considered a scientific theory at all? If we abandon the scientific theory in favor of the non-scientific one, then given the intellectual hegemony of science, this is tantamount to abandoning reason itself. If we draw a line of demarcation between science and non-science—a set of necessary and sufficient conditions that form a definition of science—and show that creationism is religion masquerading as science, then the creation/evolution debate turns into a controversy that pits reason against pure subjective belief and opinion. In the infamous creation science trial in Little Rock, Arkansas, in December of 1981, creation science was ejected from public schools, not because of the weak evidence for it, but because it was judged religion and not science. Today in the state of California you cannot discuss creationist theories in science class for the same reason.

Space forbids me to present reasons why almost all philosophers of science, atheist and Christian alike, agree that creation science is at least a science and not a religious view, regardless of what is to be said about the empirical evidence for or against it. I have presented these arguments in *The Creation Hypothesis* and in *Christianity and the Nature of Science* (Baker, 1989). Suffice it to say that philosophical naturalists are currently in control of who sets the rules for what counts as science. The bottom line is this: philosophical naturalism is used to argue both that evolution is science and creation science is religion, and that reason is to be identified with science. Thus, the empirical evidence for or against evolution is not the core issue when it comes to explaining why so many give the theory unqualified allegiance.

There is a second reason for the current over-belief in evolution: it functions as a myth for secularists. By myth I do not mean something false (though I do believe evolution is false), but rather a story of who we are and how we got here that serves as a guide for life. Evolutionist Richard Dawkins said that evolution made the world safe for atheists because it supposedly did away with the design argument for God's existence. In graduate school, I once had a professor say that evolution was a view he embraced religiously because it implied for him that he could do anything he wanted. Why? Given that there is no God and that evolution is how we got here, there is no set purpose for life given to us, no objective right and wrong, no punishment after death, so one can live for himself in this life anyway he wants. Serial killer Jeffrey Dahmer made the same statement on national television. Dahmer said that naturalistic evolution implied that we all came from slime and will return to slime. So why should he resist deeply felt tendencies to kill, given that we have no objective purpose or value and there is no punishment after death?

I am not arguing here that secularists cannot find grounds for objective purpose and value in their naturalistic world view (though I do believe that to be the case). I am simply pointing out that evolution functions as an egoistic myth for many intellectuals who have absolutized freedom, understood as the right to do anything I want. Philosophical naturalists *want* evolution to be true because it provides justification for their lifestyle choices.

For these two reasons—first, the identification of evolution as the only option on origins that claims the support of reason and, second, the function of evolution as a convenient myth for a secular lifestyle—the widespread overcommitment to evolution is not primarily a matter of evidence. That is why people *react* to creationism with hatred, disgust, and loathing, instead of responding to creationist arguments with calm, but open minded counter arguments. This situation is tragic, because it has produced a cultural log jam in which philosophical naturalism is sustained as our source of cultural authority, protected from serious intellectual criticism and scrutiny. And as Phillip Johnson has recently argued in *Reason in the Balance* (InterVarsity, 1995), philosophical naturalism has had a devastating impact on modern society.

For Christians, there is a lesson to be learned from all this and an application to be followed. The lesson is this: The debate about creation and evolution is not primarily about how to interpret certain passages in Genesis (though it is that). Rather, it is primarily about the adequacy of philosophical naturalism as a worldview and the hegemony of science as a cognitive authority which relegates religion to private opinion and presuppositional faith. The application is this: Believers owe it to themselves and the church to read works that present a well-reasoned alternative to evolution and to keep an eye on the broader implications of employing theistic evolution as a viable compromise. Theistic evolution may well be inadequate to stop our cultural slide toward a thoroughly sensate culture, which, if Sorokin is correct, is to head toward disaster.

## Part 2: The Ethical Inadequacy of Naturalism

You don't have to be a rocket scientist to recognize that our society is in a state of moral chaos. The simple fact that Jerry Springer and his talk show competitors are such popular theaters of moral expression is enough to send shivers down the spine of anyone with an ounce of moral sensibility. This moral chaos should come as no surprise to Christians, who know well that there is a deep connection between the world view of a culture and its moral beliefs and behaviors. The shift from a Judeo-Christian worldview to a naturalistic one is what lies behind much of the moral chaos we now face.

In April, 1986, Steven Muller, the president of Johns Hopkins University, got it right when he warned that our crisis in moral values is due largely to the loss of a Judeo-Christian worldview and the substitution of secularism, the major component of which is scientism. During the Los Angeles riots following the Rodney King beating, an African-American bystander said on a TV interview how surprised she was that people were acting like animals. What was unclear was why this should surprise anyone, given that we were and are taught all week long in public schools that this is exactly what we are—animals.

Muller was right to center the source of our moral crisis in the emergence of scientific naturalism as the dominant worldview among cultural elites. In what follows, I will add a bit of meat to the bones of Muller's statement by discussing three areas of moral life where the intellectual resources of naturalism are weighed in the balance and found wanting.

## The Existence and Exemplification of Value

Consider the statement "The ball is hard." If this statement is true, it has implications for the way the world is. There is some specific ball that exists and there is a real property, hardness, that it possesses or exemplifies. Now consider the following value statements: "Mercy is a virtue." "Friendship is good." "Human beings have worth." Each of these statements is true and through common sense ascribes non-natural, intrinsically normative value properties to mercy, friendship, and human beings. By a non-natural property I mean an attribute that is not a scientific, physical characteristic of physics or chemistry, (e.g., being a C fiber, having negative charge, or being magnetic). By intrinsically normative I mean a property that is 1) valuable in and of itself, and 2) something we ought to desire. Now it is easy to explain how these properties could exist and "show up," as it were, in the spatio-temporal universe on a Christian view of things. For Christians, the most fundamental entity in being is not matter or energy or any other physical thing studied by science. It is God, and among His attributes are those of moral and ontological excellence: wisdom, kindness, goodness, and the like. God also created the world to be a place where these values are exemplified and play a role in the course of things.

How is a naturalist to treat statements like these? The problem is that the properties expressed in them are just not scientifically testable, physical properties, nor are they at home in a naturalist view of how we know things, how things came to be, and what is real. Intrinsically normative, non-natural properties are not known by the methods of science. I cannot find out that mercy is a virtue by some laboratory experiment. Nor are they the kinds of properties that could come to be present by strict physical laws. And it is obvious that no property that science studies is normative. So what's a naturalist to do?

There are three main courses of action available. First, a naturalist can try to paraphrase sentences like "Mercy is a virtue" as mere expressions of emotion ("Hooray! Mercy!") or as mere commands ("Prefer mercy!"). But these paraphrases don't work because although "Mercy is a virtue" is true, mere expressions of emotion or pure imperatives are neither true nor false, and they leave unanswered why it is we should express emotions in this way or obey this command.

Second, a naturalist can paraphrase "Mercy is a virtue" in a reductionist way where the normative property "virtue" is replaced by a scientific, natural property, e.g., "I like mercy" or "Merciful acts tend to promote survival." The first sentence is a statement of psychology, the second one of evolution. Unfortunately, these paraphrases don't work either. Why? They leave out the normative component of "Mercy is a virtue." It does not follow from the fact that someone likes mercy that mercy is something we ought to value. Nor does it follow that mercy is intrinsically valuable from the fact (if it is a fact) that merciful acts promote survival, unless, of course, we are already assuming that survival is an intrinsically good, normative state of affairs. But such an assumption would merely relocate normative value for the naturalist; it would not naturalize it.

These days, most naturalists have seen the folly of these two moves and, for those who try to preserve objective, non-natural value, an evolution-of-the-gaps move is made: somehow, mysteriously, at some point in the history of evolutionary development, values simply emerged. Now, apart from the fact that this is just a name for the problem to be solved and not a solution, it should be clear that this move is an *otiose ad hoc* abandonment of naturalism. Why? Because the existence and emergence of value is not something that is compatable with a naturalist worldview, given its three components. It is interesting to note that naturalist J.L. Mackie agreed and argued that the emergence of moral properties would constitute a refutation of naturalism and evidence for theism: "Moral properties constitute so odd a cluster of properties and relations that they are most unlikely to have arisen in the ordinary course of events without an all-powerful god to create them."[1] Mackie's nat-

---

1 J.L. Mackie, *The Miracle of Theism* (Oxford: Clarendon Press, 1982), 115. Cf. J.P. Moreland, *Does God Exist?* (Buffalo, NY: Prometheus, 1993), chapters 8-10.

uralistic "solution" is to opt for subjectivism about values, a solution, I suppose, that the L.A. rioters following the King beating could have nicely appropriated, had they taken the time to read Mackie.[2]

*Naturalism, Proper Function, and the Good Life*

The Declaration of Independence tells us that all men are endowed by their Creator with certain inalienable rights, among them the right to pursue happiness. Now, happiness or the good life has come to mean a life of pleasure and the possession of consumer goods. But historically, happiness or the good life meant a life of eudaimonia—a state of ideal human flourishing and proper human functioning constituted by a life of character and virtue lived the way human beings were meant to live. It is easy to see how this notion of the good life makes sense in a Christian worldview. For a human being to live the good life is for him or her to function in the way proper to ideal human living. And one functions properly as one functions the way one was meant to function by one's Designer. Since the Designer is Himself a virtuous person of character, and since He made us to imitate Him, the good life of proper functioning is a life of virtue and character. In this way, we see how Christian theism clarifies and justifies a rich conception of the good live of virtue and character as a life in which humans function as they were meant to by God.

Christian theism also provides a satisfying answer to the question of why we should care about the good life: Why should I be moral? If I am trying to decide what my life plan will be—what I will care about, live for, spend my time seeking—and if I want my life plan to be rationally justified and sensible, then why is it reasonable for morality and the life of virtue to be a key part of my life plan? Why isn't it more reasonable to live a life of pure egoism in which my own self interests, defined any way I wish, are all that should matter

2 J.L. Mackie, *Ethics: Inventing Right and Wrong* (New York: Penguin Books, 1977). Cf. Louis Pojman, *Ethics: Discovering Right and Wrong* (Belmont, CA: Wadsworth, 1990).

to me, rationally speaking. Why should I not just pretend
to care for morality when it is in my self interests to do so,
all the while not really adopting the moral point of view
at all? Christian theism says we should be moral because
the moral life of virtue is real, we know some truths about
it, and to live in disregard of the moral life is to live out of
touch with a real and important part of reality made by
God. Moreover, God made us to function best when we live
the life of virtue. To live in disregard of morality and virtue
is to live like a fish out of water, i.e., to live contrary to our
proper functioning.

Obviously, naturalists cannot help themselves to this
depiction of the nature of and grounds for the good life.
While not all naturalists agree about the nature of morality
and the good life—how could they when it is hard enough to
have any clear room for objective value in a naturalist view
of things—many tough-minded naturalists opt for a view of
morality which Daniel Callahan calls "minimalist ethics"—
one may act in any way one chooses so far as one does not
do harm to others.[3] Unfortunately, such an ethic draws
too sharp a distinction between public and private morality—it reduces humans to isolated moral atoms who create
their own moral universe, and it deprives us of meaningful and true ways to discourse about the good life of virtue
in its individual and communal forms. Other naturalists
follow Alasdair MacIntyre, taking virtues and the good life
of human excellence to be mere expressions of value rela-
tivized to one's culture and tradition (not Nazi culture, presumably) or to one's private beliefs and choices (not Jeffrey
Dahmer's, presumably).

Both of these naturalist strategies—minimalist ethics
and the relativization of virtue—are simply inadequate
to capture the nature of morality and the good life or to
explain why they have such hegemonic authority. This
inadequacy can be seen in three areas. First, these naturalist strategies take the good life to be whatever an individual or culture chooses to create and value as long as no

3 See Callahan's statement and critique of this position in "Minimalist Ethics,"
*The Hastings Center Report* 11 (Oct. 1981): 19-25.

harm is done to others. But as Harvard philosopher John Rawls admits, this view implies that a person who chooses to spend his entire life counting blades of grass is living the good life of virtue as equally as Billy Graham or Mother Teresa as long as both freely choose their activities and can pursue them in a satisfying way.[4]

Second, naturalists have no way of expressing what it means to function properly in a normative way. Because they do not believe we were created by God, there is no higher way we were meant to function, no form of life that is proper to our nature as creatures in God's image. This can be seen in Georgetown Philosopher Tom Beauchamp's attempt to protect a relativistic view of the good from certain obvious problems. Beauchamp discusses the view within our purview, viz., that the good is whatever satisfies the relativistic preferences freely chosen by individuals.[5] Beauchamp recognizes that if everyone happened to prefer certain horrible desire satisfactions (e.g., regularly fondling children), then this would have to count as the good on this definition. Beauchamp responds by saying that the good should be redefined as whatever satisfies the relativistic preferences freely chosen by individuals *if they are choosing rationally*, i.e., if they are functioning properly in their choices.

Unfortunately, rationality for Beauchamp does not mean "choosing the way we ought to choose, the way we were designed to choose" since this would be circular—the good would be defined in terms of choosing what we ought, but choosing what we ought would be defined as choosing what is really good. The only solution here is to say either that rational behavior is simply what is statistically regular among adults who grow up in a typical way in society or it is behavior that promotes the survival of the species. It should be obvious that this will not work. It is easy to conceive of possible worlds where adults prefer to fondle children or where such behavior could have survival value.

[4] John Rawls, *A Theory of Justice* (Cambridge: Harvard University Press, 1971), 424-33.
[5] Tom Beauchamp, *Philosophical Ethics* (New York: McGraw-Hill, 1982), 84-86.

But in these possible worlds, fondling children would still not constitute the life of virtue. Without a normative notion of proper functioning, the naturalist is stuck with problems like this.

Finally, many naturalists agree with atheist Kai Nielsen, who acknowledges that there is no answer to the question of why we should be moral. For Nielsen, the choice between adopting the moral point of view vs. living a life of pure selfishness in total disregard for morality and virtue is a arbitrary, non-rational choice.[6] But any view that reduces the difference in worth between the overall lifestyle of an greedy, hateful racist and the life of St. Benedict to being nothing more than an arbitrary choice (like the one between being a fast-food lover vs. learning to play the tuba) is deeply flawed. It is no wonder that moral chaos has resulted from the hegemony of naturalism among our cultural elites.

## The Special, Equal Value of All Human Beings

It is a cherished belief of most people that human beings simply as such have equal value and rights and that they have significantly greater value that animals. However, this claim is difficult if not impossible to justify given a naturalist worldview. For many naturalists, the best, perhaps only way, to justify the belief that all humans have equal and unique value simply as such is in light of the metaphysical grounding of the Judeo-Christian doctrine of the image of God.[7] Such a view depicts humans as substances with a human nature. For at least two reasons, that framework must be abandoned by naturalists. For one thing, the progress of science has regularly shifted entities (e.g., heat) from the category of substance to the category of quality, relation, or quantity. Thus, most likely there is no such thing as a human nature, and should be limited within the categories of biology, chemistry, and physics and with a view of

[6] See J.P. Moreland, Kai Nielsen, *Does God Exist?* (Buffalo, NY: Prometheus, 1993), 97-135.
[7] Helga Kuhse, Peter Singer, *Should the Baby Live?* (Oxford: Oxford University Press, 1985), 118-39.

humans as mere ordered aggregates of parts.

Second, Darwin's theory of evolution has made belief in human nature, though logically possible, nevertheless quite implausible. As E. Mayr has said:

> The concepts of unchanging essences and of complete discontinuities between every eidos (type) and all others make genuine evolutionary thinking impossible. I agree with those who claim that the essentialist philosophies of Aristotle and Plato are incompatible with evolutionary thinking.[8]

This belief has, in turn, led thinkers like David Hull to make the following observation:

> The implications of moving species from the metaphysical category that can appropriately be characterized in terms of "natures" to a category for which such characterizations are inappropriate are extensive and fundamental. If species evolve in anything like the way that Darwin thought they did, then they cannot possibly have the sort of natures that traditional philosophers claimed they did. If species in general lack natures, then so does *Homo sapiens* as a biological species. If *Homo sapiens* lacks a nature, then no reference to biology can be made to support one's claims about "human nature." Perhaps all people are "persons," share the same "personhood," etc., but such claims must be explicated and defended *with no reference to biology*. Because so many moral, ethical, and political theories depend on some notion or other of human nature, Darwin's theory brought into question all these theories. The implications are not entailments. One can always dissociate "*Homo sapiens*" from "human being," but

[8] E. Mayr, *Populations, Species, and Evolution* (Cambridge: Harvard University Press, 1970), 4.
[9] David Hull, *The Metaphysics of Evolution* (Albany, NY: State University of New York, 1989), 74-75, emphasis added.

the result is a much less plausible position.[9]

Finally, this observation has led a number of thinkers to claim that the traditional sanctity of life view of human beings is guilty of speciesism (an unjustified bias towards one's own biological classification) and to settle on person-hood and not simply on being human as constituting our locus of value. Thus, value resides in personhood, not humanness. What is a person? A person is anything that satisfies the right list of criteria, e.g., has a self concept, can form meaningful relations with God or others, can use language, can formulate goals and plans, etc. There are two key implications of this view. First, there can be human non-persons (e.g., defective newborns, people in comas) and personal non-humans (e.g., orangutans) and the latter have more value than the former. Second, since the features that constitute personhood can be possessed to a greater or lesser degree, then some individuals can be more of a person and thus claim more rights and value than other individuals. In my view, the first is false. Humanity is too closely tied to personhood to be separated—being a person is to being a human as being a color is to being red. There can be non-human persons (angels), but there cannot be human non-persons just as there can be colored non-red things (blue things), but no red non-colored things.[10] The second proposition is one that naturalists have worked hard—and in my view, unsuccessfully—to avoid.[11] In any case, it should be clear that the high intrinsic and equal value of all human beings is easy to justify given Christian theism, but is hard to square with naturalism.

In summary, ideas matter. A culture cannot adopt any worldview it chooses without having to face serious implications of that choice. Once the ethical implications of taking the naturalistic path are laid bare, it becomes clear just exactly where a major source of our current moral chaos

[10] Cf. J.P. Moreland,"Humanness, Personhood, and the Right to Die," *Faith and Philosophy* 12 (January 1995): 95-112; J.P. Moreland, Stan Wallace, "Aquinas vs. Descartes and Locke on the Human Person and End-of-Life Ethics," *International Philosophical Quarterly* 35 (September 1995): 319-30.

[11] For a response to the main naturalist attempt to avoid proposition two, see J.P. Moreland, John Mitchell, "Is the Human Person a Substance or Property-Thing?" *Ethics & Medicine* 11 (1995).

lies: the worldview of naturalism.

# Part 3: The Nature and Value of Religious Experience

If you poll a typical Christian congregation, you will discover that the majority of church members have had very deep encounters with God. Most have had at least a few occasions of dramatic answer to prayer, some have seen physical healings of various sorts, and many have had moments when God was intensely real to them. Moreover, these phenomena happen not only to individual believers, but also when Christians gather together in community. Speaking more generally, it is safe to say that millions upon millions of people worldwide have had some sort of religious experience at one time or another. What should we make of these facts? Do they provide evidence for the existence of God? For the truth of Christianity? How is a naturalist supposed to take these facts?

Typically, naturalists make two claims about religious experience that serve to rebut its evidential value. First, a naturalist will say that adherents of various world religions have different and, in fact, contradictory religious experiences. Therefore, these different experiences cancel each other out, so to speak, and provide no evidence for the truth of a specific religion or even for the reality of a Supreme Being. Second, a naturalist will give a reductive analysis of religious experience (e.g., religious experience is nothing but psychological projection that expresses the need for a father figure, religious experience is nothing but a culturally relative form of group behavior expressing a certain conception of transcendence, and so forth). In this way the naturalist can treat religious experience as merely a natural psychological or sociological phenomenon.

I want to defend the evidential value of religious experience for both the existence of God and the truth of Christianity by looking at skepticism in general, analyzing different types of religious experiences, and offering two arguments for the existence of the Christian God based on religious experience.

## Dealing with Skepticism in General

Since the naturalist claims stated above are an expression of skepticism about religious experience, it will be useful to begin our exploration by taking a brief look at skepticism in general. A skeptic raises doubts about claims to have knowledge or justified belief in various areas of our intellectual life. A skeptic will point out that in the past our senses, our memory, our moral insights, our religious perceptions, and so forth have been mistaken. In light of this, surely it is possible, he will say, that our current experiences or beliefs are faulty. How then do we know that our senses, memory, or moral and religious beliefs are not misleading us right now? By raising these doubts, the skeptic is trying to get us to believe two things. First, that we cannot have particular examples of knowledge unless we can answer the broad question of how we know things in general. For example, I cannot know that there is a computer before me unless I can say how it is that I know in general that my senses are reliable. Second, the skeptic wants to place a burden of proof on the person who claims to know something. Particular knowledge claims are guilty until proven innocent.

Now neither of these two approaches to knowledge is correct. If I have to know how I know things generally before I can know something in a specific case, then I will be involved in a vicious cycle of infinite regress. Why? Before I can know that p, I will have to know how I know that p, but before I can know how I know that p, I will have to know how I know how I know that p...and so on and so forth. The fact is we start the enterprise of knowing with specific items of knowledge and go on to formulate criteria for knowledge based on the specific cases. I know there is a computer before me right now. I know a rug is on the floor. I go on and formulate general criteria for knowledge (if something appears to be in front of me, then I should believe that it is in front of me unless there is reason to doubt such a claim, e.g., I am on drugs or the lighting is bad.) If God appears to be present to someone, then one should believe that He is, in fact, present unless there is reason to doubt my faculties at this moment (e.g., this experience contradicts what some certified form of revelation says about God).

What about the burden of proof issue? Why should we let the skeptic tell us that a burden of proof is on the one who claims to know? After all, we all do, in fact, know many things before we ever consider the skeptic's questions. We should place the burden of proof on the skeptic—our beliefs are innocent unless there is reason to think they are guilty. By way of application to religious experience, we only need to rebut the skeptic (show why he has not demonstrated that his skepticism is correct) rather than needing to refute him (show that he is in fact wrong before we can claim to know something). We can approach religious experience without some heavy burden of proof against us before we are allowed to proceed.

*Types of Religious Experience*

There are at least three main types of religious experiences.[12] First, there are *sensory* experiences in which the person claims to have actual sounds or visions present to him. Second, there are *numinous* experiences in which the object is experienced as overwhelmingly powerful, willful, and active. Numinous experiences are accompanied by a sense of dread, awe, astonishment. Finally, there are *mystical* experiences in which the person is caught up in a different form of awareness that produces a deep joy, exultation, ecstasy, and a sense of union with God.

Two important observations should be made about these different types of religious experiences. For one thing, sensory experiences are by far the more culturally relative and conditioned of the three. In fact, numinous and mystical experiences have elements that transcend culture and are more uniform worldwide. This is not surprising when we recognize that the God of the Bible is not a sense-per-

---

[12] For a brief treatment of these, see William Wainwright, *Philosophy of Religion* (Belmont, CA: Wadsworth, 1988), chapter 5.

ceptible object, but rather the type of being reported in most numinous or mystical experiences. Further, sense perception is the most relative part of more ordinary forms of mental life. For example, two people can be thinking of the very same object of thought, say London, but because of differences in background, one may be using a mental image of a foggy scene to help focus his mind on London, while the other may be using the image of Big Ben. The two are not thinking *about* these images, they are thinking *with* them *about* London. In this case, the images are relative to one's background, but the object of thought is not.

Second, in numinous and mystical experience, people worldwide report three different things: an experience of a personal God, an experience of an impersonal It, and an experience of nothing. How would a Christian analyze this? One thing to say is this: When a mystic experiences an impersonal It, he may be experiencing God's impersonal, metaphysical nature (e.g., His infinity, His self existence, His immutability). When a mystic experiences nothingness, he may be experiencing his own empty ego. When a mystic experiences a personal deity, he may be experiencing God Himself.

But should a Christian hold that people in other religions experience the true God? That depends. A believer will not say that such people experience the true God *because of* their religion, but rather *in spite of* their religion, if in fact God is being experienced at all. Further, the Bible teaches that God is evident to all and that all people have some sort of awareness of God Himself. Remember, a genuine experience of God (who, after all, exists) is not the same thing as having a salvific experience of God. So there is no reason to think that people in parts of the world outside the Christian faith never experience God at all, though there are good reasons to say that such experiences are not means of salvation.

Still, any experience of God can be filled with errors and may not even be an experience of God at all. To see this, consider the act of seeing a hat on a table. There are four aspects to such an act. For starters, there is the conscious sensation of the hat inside the mind of the perceiver. If you are having a sensation of a hat, no one else can see your private, mental sensation. Second, there is the phenomenological object, i.e. that part of the hat directly present to you. Two people seeing the same hat will have two different phenomenological objects, two different parts of the hat present to each, e.g, one sees the top of the hat from above, the other a side of the hat. Third, there is the apparent object, the entire hat of which the phenomenological object (the top, the side) is but a part. One does not have the entire apparent object directly present in acts of seeing, e.g., the back side is hidden from view. Finally, there are interpretations given to the act of seeing the hat, e.g., "I am seeing my uncle's hat" or "I am seeing a stolen hat." Now each component of seeing is a source of error. My sensations can be defective because I am color blind. The phenomenological object may not be the way it appears to me because the lighting in the room is wrong. It may be red but appear orange to me due to lighting. I may hold mistaken beliefs about the whole object based on my angle of seeing. If there are no buttons on the surface of the hat I am seeing, I may infer that there are no buttons on the hat at all, but there may be some on the back surface. Finally, I can interpret the experience wrongly: this may not be my uncle's hat at all.

Now an experience of God can go wrong in all these ways and more. Sin may have made my faculty of experiencing God so defective that my experiential awareness of God may be hallucinatory and He might not be present at all. I will not draw out further parallels since they should be obvious. Moreover, the devil can cause problems in experiencing God and God Himself can simply hide His presence for reasons He does not share. All of this means that religious experience can go wrong and we should not build an entire case for God or an entire theology on religious experience. Still, it would be equally wrong to conclude that no one can have a veridical experience of God.

How, then, should religious experience factor in to a case for God's existence and the truth of Christianity? I suggest the following. We start with knowledge of God from creation based on arguments for God in natural theology.[13] For example, we know that the universe began to exist, that there are too many types of design in the universe to be explained without an intelligent designer, that objective value exists and a personal God is the best explanation for this fact, and so on. I will not develop a case for God's existence here, but if such a case is successful, it means that we have a strong basis for believing in monotheism prior to our consideration of religious experience.

Second, we have an objective revelation of God in the Bible that offers us tests for judging the authenticity of religious experience. But why accept the Bible instead of, say, the Qu'ran? My answer would appeal to things like the uniqueness of the Bible, along with indications of its supernatural origin from historical evidence, miracle, and prophecy. Given this background, religious experience forms additional confirming proof that God exists and Christianity is true. Religious experience by itself carries some weight, but it is even more powerful if used to complement the whole of Christianity. This means that we can form arguments for Christianity based on religious experience and these arguments can serve as additional indicators of the truth of the Christian faith.

## Two Different Arguments from Religious Experience

There are two different ways of using religious experience to help justify belief in the Christian God: the *causal argument* and *religious perception*.[14] Let us begin by looking at the causal argument. Very often, we either cannot or have not seen some thing, but we nevertheless are justified in believing in its reality because postulating the existence of the thing in question can explain a range of data that needs explaining. For example, no one has seen an electron.

[13] For a similar approach to the problem of evil, see Douglas Geivett, *Evil and the Evidence for God* (Philadelphia: Temple University Press, 1993).

[14] See J.P. Moreland, *Scaling the Secular City* (Grand Rapids: Baker, 1986), 231-42; Cf. J.P. Moreland, Kai Nielsen, *Does God Exist?* (Buffalo, NY: Prometheus, 1993), 233-36.

But there is a range of observational effects associated with electrical phenomena that requires explanation. If we postulate electrons as the things that are causing these effects, then we have an explanation of the facts. Similarly, in religious experience, there is a range of effects that no one can deny—a new power to lead holy lives, specific answers to prayer, an new ability to sacrifice for others, etc. William James' work *The Varieties of Religious Experience* contains the classic statement of this argument: "When we commune with it [God], work is actually done upon finite personality....God is real since he produces real effects."[15]

Philosopher Patrick Sherry has advanced a communal form of this argument. Sherry argues that if one examines the church through history—specifically those parts of the church where authentic spiritual practices were flourishing—and compares the church with any other community (e.g., Marxist, Buddhist), then the church is vastly superior in the regular production of moral saints and heroes with a higher quality of spiritual power and devotion to God and others, often in the face of martyrdom and other forms of opposition.[16] Sherry's argument does not claim that the church has not had periods of hypocrisy or that there are no moral heroes outside the Christian church. But he insists, rightly in my view, that there is a superior number, quality, and depth of such heroes produced by authentic Christian practice. These real effects, says Sherry, have a real cause: the Holy Spirit.

The strength of the causal argument depends on how well the postulation of God explains the data compared to naturalistic explanations. Suffice it to say here that naturalists will have a difficult time explaining the actual religious power and lives that fill church history and the specific answers to prayer that many of us have seen. Imagine what world history would be like if the church were taken out of it compared to what would be the case for world his-

---

[15] William James, *The Varieties of Religious Experience* (New York: Modern Library, 1902), 506-7.
[16] Patrick Sherry, *Spirit, Saints, and Immortality* (Albany, NY: State University of New York Press, 1984), 31-63.

tory if some other community were excluded.

The second approach to religious experience goes something like this: In normal sensory experiences of tables, chairs, etc., if something seems to be present before us, then even though we could be hallucinating, we are justified in believing that something is, in fact, in front of us as it seems to be unless we have reason to think otherwise. Now, religious forms of awareness are closely analogous to normal sensory perception. Therefore, if a being who is good, personal, holy, etc. seems to be present to someone, then we ought to believe that such a being is, in fact, present unless we have reason to think otherwise. This approach is not really an argument at all. Rather, it is a report that we sometimes directly experience God Himself and others may do so as well if they follow the correct procedures that are relevant to being aware of God (e.g., repentance, humility of heart, seeking God).

To understand the force of this approach, compare the difference between having a pain vs. having an experience of an apple. A pain does not present itself as an experience of something outside us, say of something on a table. Rather, it is experienced as something totally within our own self. But the apple experience is different. Part of the experience itself is the awareness that the object experienced is outside of us, say, on a table. This is not an interpretation of the experience, it is an aspect of the experience every much as real as the color or shape of the perceived object. Similarly, in experiences of God, the externality of the object (God) is not an interpretation of the experience. It is a part of the experience itself, just as much as the awareness of holiness, personhood, etc. Here the believer invites the naturalist to do certain things, e.g., seek God in the name of Jesus and on the basis of His gospel, humble one's heart, and God Himself will be experienced directly as real in the same way that we can invite someone to do certain things (e.g., turn the light on, look in a certain direction) and see an apple.

To be sure, we cannot predict the nature or even the occurrence of an awareness of God with the same degree of accuracy as we can a prediction of an experience of an apple if certain things are done. But this is not surprising for two reasons. First, our faculties of awareness become more distorted the closer we get to perceiving things deeply related to our sinful lifestyle choices, e.g., moral values and God Himself. This explains the greater diversity of moral or religious awarenesses compared to sense perceptions of apples or tables. Second, God is a person, and an uncontrollable, infinite one at that! And persons (finite or infinite) can hide themselves, fail to show themselves, and in general, refuse to cooperate with our efforts to know them due to reasons they may not share with us. Thus, we can do certain things conducive to being aware of a person, but there is no guarantee the person will cooperate. By contrast, physical objects like tables are inert, passive things and our experiences of them are not dependent on their cooperation. That's why we can predict experiences of tables with greater precision than an experience of another person or God. Note that if tables or apples were like quantum entities—they disappeared randomly and showed up at unpredictable locations moments later—then we would not be able to accurately predict our experiences of "normal" objects either.

On the basis of these various facets of religious experience, I recommend that we challenge a sincere naturalist who is a seeker of truth to perform a devotional experiment. First, we talk to the naturalist about the existence of God in light of arguments that are part of natural theology. Then we get the naturalist to consider the human condition in its alienation from God, one another, and ourselves; our sense of guilt and shame; and our desire to have objectively meaningful lives and life after death. We then invite the naturalist to consider the evidence for the authority of Scripture based on its uniqueness among world literature, the historical evidence for its miracle claims and accuracy in general, and its cases of fulfilled prophecy. Then we invite the naturalist to consider the two approaches to religious experience just discussed. Finally, we invite him to engage in a devotional experiment: accept the gospel as best you can, try to live as though Christianity were true with all the sincerity of heart you can muster, and see what happens. After all, that is how many enter the Kingdom of God.

The naturalist skeptic needs to be careful, however. This strategy has worked for twenty centuries and the naturalist camp has lost a number of adherents in this way, myself included. The Bible says that if you seek God with all your heart, you will find Him. And while religious experience does not stand on its own as we have seen, at some point the naturalist must stop arguing and seek, if he has the courage to do so. What he will find, of course, is that God has never been far away because in Him we live and move and have our very being.

## Part 4: Naturalism, Christianity, and the Human Person

Cultural myths die hard. For example, the belief that movie stars are qualified to speak as moral authorities persists in spite of the flood of evidence to the contrary virtually every time a famous actor tries to do so. After all, the name "Tinseltown" as a title for Hollywood has more than a little ring of truth to it. Another cultural myth that manages to stick around is the idea that most thinking people are naturalists. As naturalist philosopher David Papineau opines, "...nearly everybody nowadays wants to be a 'naturalist'..."[17] But no matter how loudly this opinion is shouted, it is plainly false. The overwhelming number of people around the world, including educated people in developed nations, are theists of some sort or another. And in Papineau's own discipline, philosophy, it is a safe bet to say that if one were to add up all the members of the Society of Christian Philosophers and toss in Catholic and Protestant philosophers worldwide, the total would most likely surpass the number of naturalists in the discipline. But even if this is wrong, it is clearly true that not everyone in philosophy wants to be a naturalist.

It is important to make this point about numbers because naturalists often try to give the impression that

17 David Papineau, *Philosophical Naturalism* (Oxford: Basil Blackwell, 1993), 1.

the really smart people all end up on their side, so there must be some secret knowledge or insight they possess to which average folks don't have access or else they would be naturalists too. Nothing could be further from the truth. In the final analysis, of course, the issue is not numbers, but arguments and evidence. Therefore, in this final installment of my four-part series on naturalism, I want to wrap-up my critique of naturalism by showing what is wrong with the most consistent naturalist view of human beings: physicalism.

In Part 1 of this series, I described naturalism in this way: the spatio-temporal universe of physical objects, properties, events, and processes that are well established by scientific forms of investigation is all there is, was, or ever will be. There are three major components of naturalism. First, naturalism begins with an epistemology, a view about the nature and limits of knowledge, known as scientism. Second, naturalism contains a theory, a causal story, about how everything has come-to-be. The central components of this story are the atomic theory of matter and evolution. Third, naturalism has a view about what is real: physical entities are all there are. In Part 1 we also saw that the naturalist's creation myth—evolution—is religiously embraced with a fervency well beyond what the evidence justifies because evolution 1) is thought to be the only scientific, and therefore, rational alternative to origins available, and 2) serves as a convenient myth for a secular lifestyle.

In Part 2, I argued that naturalism is inadequate because it fails to provide room for the existence of objective, normative values—virtues, proper human functioning, and moral rules. I also claimed that naturalism fails to give metaphysical grounding for equal human rights.

In Part 3, I showed that the nature and evidential value of religious experience provides grounds for believing in God and the truth of Christianity over and against naturalism. In what follows, I shall argue for the same conclusion in

---

18 For more on this, see Gary Habermas, J.P. Moreland, *Immortality: The Other Side of Death* (Nashville: Thomas Nelson, 1992), chapters 1-3; J.P. Moreland, *Scaling the Secular City* (Grand Rapids: Baker, 1986), chapter 3.

light of the nature of human persons.[18]

*Naturalism, Christianity, and the Human Soul*

Physicalism is the view that human beings, including all their parts, features, abilities, and internal states, are nothing but physical objects. To be sure, humans are very complicated, even computer-like physical objects, but for all of that, physicalists still insist that humans are mere arrangements of physical stuff. Though some would demur, most naturalists have taken their position to require strict physicalism precisely because the latter seems to be implied by the constraints placed on their anthropology by the three aspects of naturalism mentioned above. William Lyons' statement is representative of most naturalists on this point: "[Physicalism] seem[s] to be in tune with the scientific materialism of the twentieth century because it [is] a harmonic of the general theme that all there is in the universe is matter and energy and motion and that humans are a product of the evolution of species just as much as buffaloes and beavers are. Evolution is a seamless garment with no holes wherein souls might be inserted from above."[19] For the naturalist, there should be a coherence among third person scientific ways of knowing, a physical, evolutionary account of how our sensory and cognitive processes came to be, and an analysis of what those processes are. Any entities that exist should bear a relevant similarity to those that characterize our best physical theories, their coming-to-be should be intelligible in light of the naturalist causal story, and they should be knowable by scientific means.

Historically and biblically, Christianity has held to a dualist notion of the human being. A human being is a unity of two distinct entities—body and soul.[20] The soul, while not by nature immortal, is nevertheless capable of entering an intermediate disembodied state upon death

---

[19] William Lyons, "Introduction," in *Modern Philosophy of Mind*, ed. by William Lyons, (London: Everyman, 1995), lv. In context, Lyons' remark is specifically about the identity thesis, but he clearly intends it to cover physicalism in general.
[20] For my purposes, I will use *soul*, *mind*, and *spirit* interchangeably. I actually take the mind and the spirit to be different faculties of the soul, but the differences among these entities are not relevant for our current discussion.

and, eventually, being reunited with a resurrected body. The name for this view is substance dualism. On this view, the self or I is a substantial, unified reality that informs and causally interacts with its body and that contains various mental states within it—sensations, thoughts, beliefs, desires, and acts of will. A *sensation* is a state of awareness or sentience, a mode of consciousness, (e.g., a conscious awareness of sound, color, or pain). A *thought* is a mental content that can be expressed in an entire sentence and that only exists while it is being thought. Some thoughts logically imply other thoughts. For example "All dogs are mammals" entails "This dog is a mammal." Some thoughts don't entail, but merely provide evidence for, other thoughts. For example, certain thoughts about evidence in a court case provide evidence for the thought that a person is guilty. A *belief* is a person's view, accepted to varying degrees of strength, of how things really are. At any given time, one can have many beliefs that are not currently being contemplated. A *desire* is a certain inclination to do, have, or experience certain things. Desires are either conscious or such that they can be made conscious through certain activities, for example, through therapy. An *act of will* is a volition, an exercise of power, an endeavoring to do a certain thing.

Now if something is merely physical, then in principle it can be given a complete description in physical terms, say, in the categories of physics, chemistry, biology, and neurophysiology. Substance dualists want to insist, however, that neither the self nor its internal states can be described physically. Briefly put, the dualist claims that no material thing, e.g., the moon or a carbon atom, presupposes or requires reference to consciousness for it to exist or be characterized. You will search in vain through a physics or chemistry textbook to find consciousness included in any description of matter. A completely physical description of the world would not include any terms that make reference to or characterize the existence and nature of the self or any of its states of consciousness. Yet the self and its internal states do require consciousness to characterize them adequately. So the self and its internal states are not physical.

To understand more fully why dualism is to be preferred to physicalism, we need to look briefly at what is called the nature of identity. Bishop Joseph Butler (1692-1752) once remarked that everything is itself and not something else. This simple truth has profound implications. Suppose you want to know whether J.P. Moreland is Eileen Spiek's youngest son. If J.P. Moreland is identical to Eileen Spiek's youngest son, then in reality, there is only one thing we are talking about: J.P. Moreland who *is* Eileen Spiek's youngest son. Furthermore, J.P. Moreland is identical to himself; he is not different from himself. Now if J.P. Moreland is *not* identical to Eileen Spiek's youngest son, then in reality we are talking about two things, not one.

This illustration can be generalized into a truth about the nature of identity: For any x and y, if x and y are identical (they are really the same thing, there is only one thing you are talking about, not two), then any truth that applies to x will apply to y and vice versa. This suggests a test for identity: if you could find one thing true of x not true of y, or vice versa, then x cannot be identical to (be the same thing as) y. Keep in mind that the relation of identity is different from any other relation, for example, causation or constant connection. It may be that brain events cause mental events or vice versa (e.g. having certain electrical activity in the brain may cause me to experience a pain, having an intention to raise my arm may cause bodily events). It may be that for every mental activity a neurophysiologist can find a physical activity in the brain with which it is correlated. But just because A causes B (fire causes smoke), or just because A and B are constantly correlated with each other, that does not mean that A is identical to B. Something is trilateral if and only if it is triangular. But trilaterality (the property of having three sides) is not identical to triangularity (the property of having three angles), even though they are constantly conjoined.

In order to establish physicalism, it is not enough that mental states and brain states are causally related or constantly conjoined with each other in an embodied person.

Physicalism needs identity to make its case, and if something is true, or possibly true of a mental substance, property, or event that is not true, or possibly true of a physical substance, property, or event, physicalism is false. With this in mind, here are four arguments for a dualist construal of human persons.

First, there is the simple fact that consciousness itself is not something that can be described in physical categories. For example, the felt, experienced texture of our sensory states of awareness—the hurtfullness of pain, the experienced tone of an awareness of sound, the vivacity of an awareness of red—cannot be captured by physics, chemistry, or neurophysiology. A pain is not a hardware state of the brain nor is it a tendency to grimace and shout "Ouch!" A pain is a certain felt state of consciousness to which I have first-person, private access. No one can be aware of my pain in this way, but others can be aware of the brain state correlated with my pain in the same ways I have available to me. If a red object seems orange to me for some reason or another, then the statement "the object is orange" is false (since it is red), but the statement "the object seems orange to me" is true. The former statement is about a physical object, say a red ball, and could be—and in this case, is—false; the latter statement is about a private state of my own consciousness—the state in which something seems or appears orange to me, and it is hard to see how I could be wrong about such a claim. If the object appears orange to me then I know this for certain, even if my claim about the ball itself could be mistaken. A scientist deaf from birth who knew everything there was to know about the physical aspects of hearing would, if she suddenly regained her ability to hear, learn completely new facts totally left out of her prior exhaustive knowledge of the physical aspects of hearing, viz., what it is like to hear. If one hallucinates a pink elephant, then there is an awareness of pink in one's mind, but there is no awareness of pink in the brain as would become evident if a detailed brain scan were done at that moment. All such a scan would reveal would be chemical and electrical activity, but no awareness of pink would be detected.

Second, our conscious states have intentionality, but no physical state has intentionality, so our conscious states are not physical. Intentionality refers to the "ofness" or "aboutness" of our mental states. I have a thought *of* the President, a hope *for* rain, a fear *about* a coming visit to the dentist. No physical state is of or about another physical state. One state of the brain may cause another one to follow, but no brain state is about anything. A thought is only one type of mental state that has intentionality. Sensations, beliefs and desires have this feature as well. But while we are on the topic of thoughts as an illustration of intentionality, it will be useful to say a few more things about thoughts that show they are not physical. To repeat, thoughts are of things, but nothing physical is of anything. Second, a thought—for example, that triangles have 180 degrees—does not have size, shape, spatial location, chemical composition, or electrical properties. But the state of my brain correlated with a thought does have these features. Third, some thoughts logically entail other thoughts. For example, the thought "grass is green" logically entails the thought that "it is false that grass is not green." There is no possible world that even God could create where grass would be both green and not green at the same time in the same sense. But no physical thing entails another physical thing. Moreover, the laws of nature (e.g., the law of gravity) are not necessary as are the logical laws of thought. It is easy to conceive of possible worlds where the laws of nature are quite different from their character in our world. But there is no possible world in which the laws of logic do not pertain. Finally, certain thoughts are normative with respect to other thoughts, that is, if I hold to certain thoughts, then I ought to hold to other thoughts. If I believe that P is taller than Q and Q is taller than R, then I ought to hold that P is taller than R. But no physical state is normative with respect to another. Physical states just are; they have no normative character whatsoever.

Third, a physical object like a desk or car does not stay literally the same object if it looses its old parts and gains new ones. If, for example, you take a car and replace all of its parts with new ones, then the car is literally a different car. By contrast, a human being remains literally the same human person even if he has an entire replacement of parts and mental states like memories or personality traits. If God wished, he could give a person an entirely new body, set of memories, and personality traits and that person could still be literally the same individual. In fact, it is possible for a human person to exist with no memories or personality traits at all, say the first few seconds after God created Adam. Moreover, it is surely possible that a human person could exist even if no physical object whatever existed. These considerations point to the conclusion that a human person is more that his body, memories, and personality traits. A human person is a substantial, unified ego, an enduring I who has a body, memories, and personality. Substance dualism makes sense of this fact.

Finally, what is sometimes called libertarian freedom is real and sufficient to refute physicalism because physicalism implies determinism.[21] But, libertarians claim, the freedom necessary for responsible action is not compatible with determinism. Real freedom requires a type of control over one's action—and, more importantly, over one's will—such that, given a choice to do A (raise one's hand and vote) or B (leave the room or simply refrain from raising one's hand), nothing determines which choice is made. Rather, the agent himself simply exercises his own causal powers and wills (or has the power to refrain from willing) to do one or the other. When an agent wills A, he could have also willed B or at least refrained from willing A without anything else being different inside or outside of his being. He is the absolute originator of his own actions. When an agent acts freely, he

---

[21] Even if physicalism is taken to imply indeterminism, this is not sufficient to allow for libertarian freedom. This is because physicalism, in both its deterministic and indeterministic forms, implies event causation: All events are (deterministically or probabilistically) caused by prior events and no room is allowed for a first-moving, substantial agent who initiates action. The discussion of event causation is a bit technical, so I will continue to talk about freedom and determinism instead of freedom and event causation. For more, see William Rowe, *Thomas Reid on Freedom and Morality* (Ithaca, NY: Cornell Univ. Press, 1991).

is a first or unmoved mover; no event causes him to act. His desires, beliefs, etc. may influence his choice, but free acts are not caused by prior states in the agent. Such freedom is real—moral responsibility requires it and we are aware of exercising such freedom when we act—and it presupposes a substantial, immaterial self to be possible.

## Naturalism, Christianity, and the Origin of the Human Soul

We have seen that there are good reasons to accept substance dualism and reject physicalism. It should come as no surprise to Christians that if we are made in God's image, there should be something about us that reflects our Creator and, therefore, that would be very difficult to treat in strictly naturalistic terms. Given the truth of substance dualism, how are we to explain the origin of mental selves and their states? These broader worldview implications of the mind/body debate are what have driven many thinkers to embrace physicalism in spite of its obvious weaknesses. As UC Berkeley philosopher John Searle has noted:

> How is it that so many philosophers and cognitive scientists can say so many things that, to me at least, seem obviously false?....I believe one of the unstated assumptions behind the current batch of views is that they represent the only scientifically acceptable alternatives to the anti scientism that went with traditional dualism, the belief in the immortality of the soul, spiritualism, and so on. Acceptance of the current views is motivated not so much by an independent conviction of their truth as by a terror of what are apparently the only alternatives. That is, the choice we are tacitly presented with is between a `scientific' approach, as represented by one or another of the current versions of `materialism,' and an `unscientific' approach, as represented by Cartesianism or some other traditional

22 John Searle, *The Rediscovery of the Mind* (Cambridge: MIT Press, 1992), 3-4.

religious conception of the mind.[22]
Naturalist philosopher Paul Churchland asserts:

The important point about the standard evolutionary story is that the human species and all of its features are the wholly physical outcome of a purely physical process.... If this is the correct account of our origins, then there seems neither need, nor room, to fit any nonphysical substances or properties into our theoretical account of ourselves. We are creatures of matter. And we should learn to live with that fact.[23]

For the naturalist, there is in principle no scientific explanation as to how evolution, a strictly physical process operating on physical materials, could give rise to something utterly non-physical. How can unconscious, purposeless, mindless particles give rise to unified immaterial selves with internal mental states by simply re-arranging according to strict physical laws? The naturalist simply has no answer to this question. By contrast, the Christian theist has an excellent answer as to how mind could arise in the course of events that constitute the history of the universe. For the Christian, personhood and, in fact, a Specific Person, is more fundamental to reality than matter. So it is no problem to conceive of a personal God creating finite personal selves by an act of His will. But no amount of study of matter will make it at all conceivable that physical stuff, all by itself, could give rise to mind. Howard Robinson was right when he said, "The idea that science captures everything, except the centre of everyone's universe, his own consciousness, makes a laughing-stock of its [naturalism's] claim to present a plausible world view."[24] John Calvin once remarked that when we contemplate our own souls and their faculties, our minds are directed immediately to the Creator who gave us such endowments. Calvin was right. The nature of the human person is the final nail

---

[23] Paul Churchland, *Matter and Consciousness* (Cambridge: MIT Press, 1984), 21.
[24] Howard Robinson, *Matter and Sense* (Cambridge: Cambridge University Press, 1982), 2. See also Searle, 10.

in the naturalist's coffin.

# Attitudes of the Christian Leader
Who is Really Sovereign?

Robert B. Linden

The topic of attitudes can be misunderstood by some Christians. It immediately brings to mind all that is written from the humanistic and other non-Christian points of view about having a positive mental attitude. Because of that, those who think that way will tend to reject the topic out-of-hand. However, just because the world talks about some subject doesn't mean that Christians shouldn't. When I was part of the New Age movement before becoming a Christian, I was told I was responsible for what happened in my life because I was either on my way to becoming a god or already was one. But just because they said I was responsible does not mean that, as a Christian, I can't talk about responsibility because God talks about it and did so long before the New Agers. Likewise, there are non-Christian groups that have adopted the rainbow as their symbol but that doesn't mean we can't display one. After all, God gave us the rainbow first. Witches, I am told, fast and pray. Because they do this, does this mean that I can't? Of course not. Attitudes are much like the foregoing. Just because the world talks about attitudes doesn't mean that we shouldn't.

Let me assure you that having a proper attitude was originally God's idea. Romans 12:2 says, "Do not conform any longer to the pattern of this world but be transformed by the renewing of your mind." Ephesians 4:22-24 says, "You were taught with regard to your former way of life, to put off your old self, which is being corrupted by its deceitful desires; to be made new in the attitude of your minds; and to put on the new self, created to be like God in true righteousness and holiness." The phrase "attitude of your minds" comes from the Greek term which means "spirit of the mind." Both phrases refer to one's mental disposition, bent, leaning, the inward man. For example, Romans 8:28 says, "And we know that all things work together for good to those who love God, to those who are called according to His purpose." So you see, while the world can talk about attitudes that one generates within oneself and with the object being oneself, we as Christians can have a right, proper, even a positive attitude, based on Who God is, what He intends for us, and the fact that He is sovereign.

But what does God's being sovereign mean? A.W. Pink, in his book, *The Sovereignty of God*, writes, "The sovereignty of God! What do we mean by this expression? We mean the supremacy of God, the kingship of God, the Godhood of God. To say that God is sovereign is to declare that God is God. To say that God is sovereign is to declare that He is the Most High, doing according to His will in the army of heaven, and among the inhabitants of the earth, so that none can stay His hand or say unto Him, What doest Thou? (Daniel 4:35). To say that God is sovereign is to declare that He is the Almighty, the Possessor of all power in heaven and earth, so that none can defeat His counsels, thwart His purposes, or resist His will (Psalm 115:3). To say that God is sovereign is to declare that He is 'The Governor among the nations' (Psalm 22:28), setting up kingdoms, over throwing empires, and determining the course of dynasties as pleaseth Him best. To say that God is sovereign is to declare that He is the 'Only Potentate, the King of kings, and the Lord of lords.' (I Timothy 6:15). Such is the God of the Bible."[1]

---

[1] A.W. Pink, *The Sovereignty of God* (Grand Rapids, MI: Baker Books, 1984), 20

Likewise, Jerry Bridges, in his book, *Trusting God Even When Life Hurts*, states, "In the arena of adversity, the Scriptures teach us three essential truths about God— truths we must believe if we are to trust Him in adversity. They are:

> God is completely sovereign;
> God is infinite in wisdom;
> God is perfect in love."[2]

He goes on to say, "The sovereignty of God is asserted, either expressly or implicitly, on almost every page of the Bible."[3] He quotes many passages from the Bible to back up this assertion, including Lamentations 3:37,38; Proverbs 16:9, 19:21, and 21:30; Ecclesiastes 7:13; Jeremiah 29:11; Romans 11:33,34; Ephesians 1:11; and James 4:15.

Here is the sum of the points I have made thus far. For leaders to be Christian leaders—and not just leaders who also happen to be Christians—they must accept at their very core that God is in charge; that He and He alone is sovereign. That must be their preeminent attitude. That, however, does not absolve them of responsibility.

## The Question Is: What Is Leadership?

Dr. Warren Bennis, known as the dean of leadership research, says that one of the broader definitions of leadership is, "The manner in which individuals choose to exercise and carry out their responsibilities." This means that everyone, at some level, is a leader. He also says that, "The true north of leadership is character." For Christians, this means that we must develop the character qualities of Christ so that we can better reflect His image (Romans 8:29). By contrast, Steve Kerr, in a talk given at a Chicago leadership conference, states that, "Only the mediocre are always at their best." If you feel you are always at your best,

---

[2] Jerry Bridges, *Trusting God Even When Life Hurts* (Colorado Springs, CO: NavPress Publishing Group, 1990), 18
[3] Ibid.

you might want to examine yourself. It could be, according to Steve, that you are only performing at a mediocre level. Doctors Charles Manz and Henry Sims, in an article entitled "SuperLeadership: The Myth of Heroic Leadership," say that, "The most appropriate leader is one who can lead others to lead themselves." The implication of that statement is that such leading "others to lead themselves" continues *ad infinitum*. However, their statement sounds like an application of II Timothy 2:2, which says, "And the things you have heard me say in the presence of many witnesses entrust to reliable men who will also be qualified to teach others." Another statement by Manz and Sims says, "Our position is that true leadership comes mainly from within a person, not from outside." From the Christian perspective the inner source of leadership is the Holy Spirit. II Timothy 1:7 states, "For God has not given us a spirit of fear, but of power and of love and of a sound mind."

As I present my first example showing the importance of the attitudes we adopt, be aware that I will use a lot of examples from all walks of life, all ages, and both sexes. I don't have any idea, except in one case, whether or not the people I use as examples are Christians. I use them to show the impact attitudes have on our lives. But think for a moment. What if all of the examples I use are non-Christians except for the one person I know to be Christian? If what they have accomplished has been accomplished in the arm of the flesh, just think of what we, as Christians, can do in the power of the Holy Spirit! But there is a catch. For Christians to truly operate in the power of the Holy Spirit, they must believe that God is sovereign. To be sure, God is sovereign whether or not we believe Him to be so. His sovereignty does not hinge on our beliefs. However, for any of us to be able to more fully operate in His power, we must acknowledge to ourselves—that is, our attitude must be—that God is completely sovereign.

How many of you have listened to Zig Ziglar or read his materials? For those of you who don't know, Zig has a strong Christian testimony. Zig tells the story of David Lofchick, who was born with cerebral palsy. Over a period of time, his parents took David to a total of thirty-nine doctors, all of whom correctly diagnosed his medical condition, saying that he would never walk, talk, count to ten, or ride a bicycle and that he should be put into an institution. His parents did not like the diagnosis, prognosis, or prescription and sought out Dr. Perlstein, then a leading researcher in cerebral palsy, living in Chicago. After a thorough analysis of David, he indicated that, indeed, David had a severe case of cerebral palsy saying that half of his brain was not attached to half of his body. However, he also gave a different prognosis and prescription from the other thirty-nine doctors. He said, "I am not a problem-oriented doctor. I am a solution-oriented doctor." (That shows a significant difference in attitude. All forty doctors saw the same information. Thirty-nine came to negative conclusions and a negative prescription. Only one, Dr. Perlstein, came to positive conclusions and a positive proactive prescription.)

He suggested that they not take David to therapy because he was concerned that David would have a strong inclination to imitate other children who had cerebral palsy instead of only having examples of people without the disease to follow. He recommended they bring a therapist and a body builder to their home. After a significant amount of time, David was able to perform his first four-point push-up—something he wasn't supposed to be able to do. Later he learned how to ride a bicycle and then to ice skate. He got good enough at ice skating to be chosen for a neighborhood ice hockey team. At the age of thirteen he performed his Bar Mitzvah in English and Hebrew. He was also able to do 1,000 push-ups at one time and complete a six-mile run. As an adult he became a leading real estate salesman of condominiums in Winnipeg, Canada. None of these things would have been accomplished had his parents just accepted the diagnosis, prognosis, and prescription of the first thirty-nine doctors.

So what are the components of an attitude? An attitude is made up of thoughts, feelings, actions, or their potential. There must be some thought or belief about an event, person, or thing. But there also must be some emotional content about that event, person, or thing for there to be an attitude. An attitude is either positive or negative, and the strength of that attitude is dependent on the emotional content. The more formal definition of an attitude is, "A predisposition to act toward some person, thing or event in a positive or negative way."[4] Zig Ziglar's daughter, as a young girl, defined it as, "What can make you feel real good even when you feel real bad." She was illustrating the idea that one's attitude is a choice. Even when things are not going well in your life, in comparison to how you would want them to go, if you believe that God is sovereign, has a plan for you that according to Jeremiah 29:11 is for your prosperity, hope and future, then the proverbial glass is not just half full—it is overflowing (Psalm 23:5)! No one can force anyone else to have a certain attitude.

When our son Derek was very young, he came to me and said, "My sister makes me so mad!" I asked him what Kara had done. Quite vehemently he listed four things. I asked him, "Suppose your friend Clayton did the same things. Would you be mad at him?" He said, "No! He's my best friend!" I thanked him for the lesson he had just produced for himself. I explained, "You chose to get angry with your sister for doing the very things that, if Clayton had done them, you would choose not to become angry." I continued, "Anger (and every other emotion) is your choice. on't ever blame your sister for your anger. Now, she can do those things which can make your choice very easy, and we will hold her accountable for that behavior, but don't ever blame her for your anger. The extent to which you blame her for your emotions, you become her victim—she controls you. Do you want her to control you?" He was very clear that he did not want his sister to control him. Proverbs 15:13 says, "A happy heart makes the face cheerful." But what makes a happy heart? Eating properly, exercising, and getting enough sleep helps make a healthy heart, but not a happy one. The only way to have a happy heart is to choose to have a happy heart.

4 Websters Third International Dictionary (Springfield, MA: Merriam-Webster, 2002)

What if circumstances are significantly negative in one's life? Ephesians 5:20 says, "...always giving thanks to God the Father for everything, in the name of our Lord Jesus Christ." Our first response to adversity is to give thanks to God for what He intends to produce in us through the difficulty. A good set of companion verses is I Thessalonians 5:16-18 which says, "Be joyful always, pray continually, give thanks in all circumstances, for this is God's will for you in Christ Jesus."

There are two aspects of His will, one explicit and one implicit, contained in these verses. The explicit aspect is that these three actions—giving thanks, being joyful, and praying—are commands to us. These verses are written in the imperative. The implicit aspect is that whatever is going on in our lives is happening because He has either directly willed it or has at least allowed it. In the case of our sin, for instance, He will allow it and He can use it, but He does not will it in the sense of decreeing that it be done. The classic statement in this regard comes from Genesis 50:20 where Joseph says to his brothers, "As for you, you meant evil against me but God meant it for good...." His brothers were all responsible for their evil acts against Joseph, but God allowed it in carrying out His providential will to bring about good for others and ultimately glory to Himself.

The easiest of the three commands is to pray in all things. It is more difficult to thank God, especially in the midst of adversity. But most difficult, it would seem, would be to obey the command to be joyful in all things. How can one be joyful in all things—especially in adversity? In order to know how that is possible, we must understand what Christian joy is and Who is the focal point for this joy. John MacArthur's definition of Christian joy is, "The emotion springing from a deep-down confidence that God is in complete and perfect control of everything and will bring from it our good in time and our glory in eternity. It's an emotional response to what I know to be true about my God. There is no event or circumstance that can occur in the life of any Christian that should diminish that Christian's joy. If there is an event or circumstance, apart from sin, that does diminish your joy, you have sinned." He can say that it is sin not to have joy, even in adversity, because the actions stipulated in I Thessalonians 5:16-18 are commands. The result of such a view of joy is, as I have stated earlier, that the preeminent attitude one must have is that God is sovereign in all aspects of our lives. God is the focal point of our joy. If you do not have this attitude, you will not be able to carry out the command to be joyful.

Viktor Frankl is an excellent illustration of the impact of attitudes on one's life. Viktor was a Jewish psychiatrist living in Vienna who was rounded up by the Nazis and taken to Auschwitz, a German death camp. As he walked through the gate, he decided on three goals for himself: 1) I will survive; 2) As a physician, I will help those needing medical treatment; and 3) I will learn something from this experience. He accomplished all three goals and later wrote that one of the last capabilities we have is to choose our attitude in whatever situation we find ourselves. In a similar way Chuck Swindoll says that, "Life is 10% of what happens to us and 90% of how we choose to react to it."

Here are some things to remember about attitudes:

- I Corinthians 10:13 points out that nothing happens to us that is not commonly experienced by others. Here is a humorous way of putting this:

God
has you
right now in the
circumstances of His
own choosing—
so He can fix you!

God is fixin' to fix you.
But if you try to fix the fix
He's fixin' to fix you with,
He'll find another fix to fix you,
until you let the fix
He's fixed for you
—fix you!

- The Chinese word for crisis is a combination of two other Chinese words: danger and opportunity. If your attitude is that a current crisis is a danger to you, you are likely to avoid it, turn away from it, or stick your head in the sand in response to it. You are not likely to deal with or solve it. And you will be more closed to what God wants you to learn from the experience. However, if your attitude is that your crisis is an opportunity, you will be more likely to move toward it, to deal with it, and to solve it. And you will be more open to learning the lessons God wants you to learn.

- You don't need to be controlled by circumstances. Habakkuk 3:17,18 states that, "Though the fig leaf does not bud and there are no grapes on the vines, though the olive crop fails and the fields produce no food, though there are no sheep in the pen and no cattle in the stalls, yet I will rejoice in the LORD, I will be joyful in God my Savior." This individual is not in the midst of pleasant conditions. In spite of his circumstances, however, he chooses to rejoice in the LORD. James 1:2-4 says, "Consider it pure joy, my brothers, whenever you face trials of many kinds, because you know that the testing of your faith develops perseverance.  Perseverance must finish its work so that you may be mature and complete, not lacking anything." Again let me say that unless you hold the preeminent attitude that God is sovereign in all aspects of your life, you will not be able to carry out the demand of these verses. Just as there is a special word in Chinese for crisis, there is also a word for perseverance, which is made up of two other Chinese words: knife and heart. The picture is of a heart with a knife driven through it. Your life blood is flowing out, but you keep on keeping on anyway. What an excellent picture of perseverance.

- You decide to be positive or negative.

Below are some examples of people who succeeded in achieving things in their lives because of the attitudes they chose to have. Again, I don't know, except in one case, if any of these people are Christians, but consider for a moment: If they are able to do what they did in the arm of the flesh, think of what we as Christians who believe in the sovereignty of God can do in the power of the Holy Spirit.

1) Thomas Edison had to go through thousands of experiments to be able to get the incandescent light bulb like he wanted it to be. When asked by a reporter what it felt like to have failed so many times, Edison said he had not failed, but simply had found thousands of ways it wouldn't work. Had he believed he had failed, he might never have gotten past the first few experiments.

2) While playing a solo on stage, the famous violinist Paganini had a violin string break. However, he continued to play and then a second string broke. Again he contin-ued to play, when a third string broke. He finished his solo play-ing on only one string.

3) Many years ago I read of a blind man who rode his bicycle 150 miles by himself. I also met the first totally blind person to do downhill skiing.

4) Several years ago, a girl was in the goat roping con-test at the National Teen Rodeo Championship held in Pueblo, CO. She was deformed, blind, and hard of hearing, but she roped her goat.

5) George Blackman became a quadriplegic early in life. He learned how to type using his mouth and by the age of eight had written and published nine books.

6) Edith Ellexon was eighty-one years old when she completed her college degree. Excitedly, she planned and carried out an expedition to climb Mount Kilimanjaro, the twelfth tallest mountain in the world.

7) Erick Frisk is a blind artist.

8) Ray Charles, George Shearing, and Stevie Wonder are blind pianists.

9) Bob Hall was in a fifteen mile race in which there were 1504 entrants. Bob finished 300th, which is excellent given the fact that he has no legs.

10) Wendy Stoeker is a high diving champion who has no arms.

11) Jamie Russell was blind most of his life, but paints landscapes in detail.

12) Jerry Traylor ran sixty-nine marathons in fifty-two weeks. His last was run on crutches.

13) Dr. David Hartman was a blind physician specializing in surgery.

14) Mark Wilson came from a poor family with thirteen children. There were no funds for college, but he wanted to attend nonetheless. He decided to get involved with track and field to see if he could get a scholarship. The scouts came to look at his and his teammates' performances. Mark was able to do the high jump at 5'8". The scouts said he needed to be able to jump at least 6'6½". He worked at it and was able to clear 7'7½".

15) James Abbott was a pro baseball player. He was a pitcher with only one hand.

16) Mark Wellman taught mountain climbing as a profession. He became a paraplegic as a result of a mountain climbing accident. After recovering, he set a goal for himself to climb Mount El Capitan—a vertical 3500 foot granite cliff. He completed the climb in July, 1989, taking nine days and doing 7000 pull-ups.

17) In 2002, two Russian paraplegics climbed Mount McKinley (20,320 ft.), which is the tallest peak in North America. They took forty-two days to complete the trek.

18) Beethoven's music teacher said, "As a composer he is hopeless." His beautiful, well-composed music is still with us today.

19) Wernher von Braun was the father of American rocketry. He flunked ninth grade algebra.

20) Peter Strudwick runs an average of nine marathons a year, including the Pikes Peak Marathon, which requires him to run up and down a peak that is over 14,000 feet high. He has curvature of the spine, a tilted pelvic bone, and no feet, yet he is able to complete all these marathons. He has also written a book entitled *Come Run with Me*.

21) Bruce Lipstadt was born with half a brain. He has an IQ of 123, is married, and is active in sports.

22) Louisa May Alcott's editor once said to her, "You will never write anything with popular appeal." Her books include *Little Women* and many other well known classics.

23) Michael Jordan was cut from his high school basketball team.

24) Wendy Rankin is a quadriplegic who skydives and hang glides.

25) When she was in her early eighties, Millie Hupp skydived.

26) Mugsy Bogues played in the National Basketball Association. He has been the starting point guard for the Charlotte Hornets and also played for other teams. He is 5'2" tall.

27) Of Fred Astaire, his first screen testing director said, "Can't act. Slightly bald. Can dance a little." Mr. Astaire kept that memo over his fireplace in his Beverly Hills home. The point to remember from this is not to let someone else's opinion of you become your reality.

28) An expert said of famous football coach Vince Lombardi, for whom the Super Bowl trophy is named, "He possesses minimal football knowledge and lacks motivation."

Here are some conclusions about the topic of attitudes:

- By choosing our attitudes, we create the environment in which we live—either positive or negative.

- Our attitudes become habitual ways of responding to people, things, and events. We have the freedom to change our attitude(s) anytime we wish to do so. Proverbs 23:7 in the KJV and NKJV says as we think in our hearts, so we are.

- Indeed, it is our attitude about stressful conditions that determines whether or not we experience distress.

# How do we Develop Proper Attitudes?

We need to be other-centered because there is a law of giving. Luke 6:38 says, "Give, and it will be given to you. A good measure, pressed down, shaken together and running over, will be poured into your lap. For with the measure you use, it will be measured to you."

We need to think proper thoughts. Philippians 4:8 says, "Finally, brothers, whatever is true, whatever is noble, whatever is admirable—if anything is excellent or praise-worthy—think about such things."

We must realize that it is necessary for us, by a decisive act of our will, to choose to be joyful and thankful in all circumstances. Likewise, Philippines 2:14 teaches us to do everything without grumbling or arguing.

We must adopt the habit of happiness—simply learn how to be fun to be around. Research has found that fun people are friendly, can laugh at themselves, are outgoing, energetic, hard-working, intelligent, are not always serious, and have a sense of humor.

We are to be enthusiastic—that means having a real zest for life. The word enthusiasm comes from the Greek *en theos* which means "in God." If any group in this life should be enthusiastic, it is we who are Christians because we are in God and God is in us. Enthusiasm can help to produce confidence that God is sovereign, is working in our lives, and impacting the lives of others. Also, enthusiasm is the key to helping others be excited about life.

We must learn to look at problems as opportunities.

We need to know what to say when we wake up in the morning. When I was in Air Force boot camp, there was an individual who woke up each day and said quite loudly, "Praise God for another day in which to excel." As you can imagine, he was the object of derisive comments and not just a few pillows that found their way into his room. Nonetheless, he helped to set the attitude of all of us for the day. I have since adopted and extended his morning proclamation and when I wake up, I say silently to myself (so that I don't wake up my wife,) "Praise God for another day in which to excel in the power of the Holy Spirit." I also pray and ask God to lead, guide, direct, and control everything I say, think, do, and feel so that I can be one of His best ambassadors. I pray the prayer of Jabez (I Chronicles 4:10) asking God to bless me, increase my territory, to keep His hand upon me each step of the way, and keep me from evil so that I cause no pain. Finally, I pray Philippians 4:8 back to Him, asking Him to help me focus on what He wants.

We must establish positive symbols in our lives. Zig Ziglar says that we ought to look at the red, green, and yellow traffic lights that we typically call stop lights as go lights. If we abide by them, we go more safely. He also says that we ought to look at our alarm clocks as opportunity clocks because if we can hear them in the morning, it means we still have an opportunity to get up and be used by God. Zig also suggests that we look at Saturday and Sunday not as weekends, but as strongends to a good week. He also says that we should not look at a loaf of bread as having two ends but as having two beginnings. As silly as these suggestions may sound, they will make a difference in how we view life and what kind of attitude(s) we adopt.

Zig tells us to remember that a good minute is a miniature good hour; a good hour is a miniature good day; a good day is a miniature good week; a good week is a miniature good month; a good month is a miniature good year; a good year is a miniature good life. A good life, then, starts with the attitudes we choose to have.

Finally, we need to remember to base our attitudes on WHO God is—not on our circumstances—and unequivocally accept that He is sovereign.

# Winning the Battle for Hearts and Minds

Jeff Myers

During a Bible study in a wealthy suburb of Indianapolis, I asked a group of high school students, "Was Adolf Hitler wrong in murdering millions of Jews?" They said yes. I asked them why they believed that. Their response was chilling.

"Well, you see," they said, "Adolf Hitler was defeated by the Allies. And in war, like everything else, the victor gets to define reality. The Allies determined that what Hitler had done was wrong. Therefore, he was wrong."

These students all came from fine Christian homes, so there was no excuse for them to have been ignorant of the moral implications of that reply. But they were. Only one student saw the truth: "I think Adolf Hitler would have been wrong, even if he had won the war and brainwashed everyone into believing he was right." This lone student knew how to articulate a moral absolute.

We are engaged today in a battle between worldviews. Ultimately our battle is not against flesh and blood. At stake are the hearts and souls of America's youth, who are falling away from the faith at an unprecedented rate. Our involvement as Christians must go beyond political action.

To effectively fight spiritual battles, we must understand and defend a biblical worldview in every area of life and impart this worldview to the next generation of leaders.

This is why I believe the mission of Summit Ministries to be so important. For more than four decades Dr. David Noebel has been on the front lines of the culture war, and his work has only grown more important with time.

From my perspective as a college professor and leadership consultant, I'd like to reflect on the significance of Dr. Noebel's mission by sharing some of the things I like to talk about when invited to speak at Summit Ministries.

## Three Philosophies that Take People Captive

The Apostle Paul says, "See to it that no one takes you captive, through hollow and deceptive philosophy, which depends on human tradition and the basic principles of this world, rather than on Christ" (Colossians 2:8). Three philosophies deceive young people such as those I met in Indianapolis, and, I suspect, most adults as well.

The first deceptive philosophy is: No one can say what is right and what is wrong. Over the last 20 years Christian students have begun to ask, "Maybe you think adultery, abortion, or homosexuality is wrong. But who are you to say what is right or wrong for everyone else?" According to a poll by George Barna, only 6% of young people said that they believe that truth is absolute.

When I attended a two-week Summit Ministries program fresh out of high school, Dr. Noebel made sure I was prepared to refute this philosophy on my college campus. When one of my professors proclaimed that "There are no absolute truths," I asked him, "Professor, are you sure?"

He said, "Yes, I'm sure."

"Are you absolutely sure?" I queried.

My professor just stared at me, a smile playing on the corner of his lips. He shot back, "You're a very clever young man. If I say there are no absolutes, then that is an absolute statement. Let me revise my remarks. There is one absolute, which is this: There are no absolutes."

I was stunned at the careless illogic of his reply. It was a willful refusal to see the truth. This should not surprise Christians, however. Proverbs 4:19 says, "The way of the wicked is like deep darkness. They do not even know what makes them stumble." Without a moral compass people cannot think well or make rational decisions about what is right and wrong for them or for society.

The second deceptive philosophy is: No one can know anything for sure. My philosophy professor taught this on the first day of class. He asked, "How do you know the sky is blue? Maybe it's green, but society has conditioned you to call it blue." After several such examples, he crowed, "My point is that you can't know anything for sure. You can't even know that you exist."

The postmodern mindset has embraced this philosophy with a vengeance. German philosopher Martin Heidegger said, "In the naming, the things named come into their thinging. Thinging they unfold world, in which things abide, and so are abiding ones." In other words, there is no such thing as objective reality; reality is what each person creates for himself through communication with others.

A number of years ago, I started a program for Summit Ministries that would help students develop leadership skills through a seven-day backpacking and wilderness survival trip. On the last day of each trip, the guides left camp and told students to meet them at the trailhead, using a map and compass. The students were in the middle of nowhere, but they always found their way back. Imagine what would happen, however, if the young man with the compass had an enormous magnet strapped to this back. "I am the North Pole," he'd say. Without a fixed point of reference, those students might still be wandering in the Colorado wilderness!

The third idea that takes people captive is this: The only meaning in life is what you create for yourself. We live in perhaps the most self-centered age in our nation's history. Everyone seems to be saying, "I have a right not to have your existence affect my life." People move from the front porch to the back deck. They stop singing around the piano and start wearing headphones, using music to eliminate interaction rather than create it. The populace cries, "Leave me alone!" and perhaps the ultimate hell is that this wish would be granted.

## Taking Every Thought Captive

These deceptive philosophies are taking young people and adults captive at an astonishing rate. We must reclaim this lost ground by developing a strong, effective biblical worldview. As the Apostle Paul wrote, "We demolish arguments and every pretension that sets itself up against the knowledge of God. And we take captive every thought, to make it obedient to Christ" (2 Corinthians 10:5).

The Bible teaches that to take every thought captive we must first embrace the truth that is found in Jesus Christ. In John 14:6, Jesus said, "I am the way, the truth and the life." This is indeed a deep and philosophical statement. The great philosophers of all time have struggled to answer three questions: What is good? What is true? And finally, what is beautiful?

In Jesus' day, "the way" referred to a moral course of action. By claiming to be the way, Jesus essentially claimed to be the standard for right and wrong. When He said He was "the truth," He was claiming that all reality is defined by the nature and character of God, and that He himself was God made flesh. When He claimed to be "the life," Jesus established himself as the standard for that which was worthwhile, that which was beautiful.

In this simple statement, Jesus revealed himself to be the answer to the philosopher's quest. It is my experience that there is only one pursuit in all of life that yields unending satisfaction: a personal relationship with Jesus Christ.

The second way to take every thought captive is to see the conflicts of our age as a battle between competing views of God. One says that God created us, and that His existence and plan give us purpose. Since we are made in his image, we ought to reflect His nature and character in every sphere of life, including politics.

But the secular elite rejects this view today. They embrace the idea that human beings invented the idea of God to help them cope with life in a "meaningless" universe. This view holds that all religious beliefs are based in fantasy and are thus irrational.

The chasm between these two views is unbridgeable. Those who hold that belief in God is inherently irrational are deeply offended when Christians try to make political, educational, or economic decisions based on their beliefs. They scoff, "Who do these Christians think they are to impose their irrational ideas about some make-believe 'god' on us?"

Sadly, most Christians have been intimidated into surrendering to this secular ideology. Wade Clark Roof in *Spiritual Marketplace* pointed out that 50% of evangelical Christians believe that "all religions are equally good and true." Josh McDowell and George Barna note that 56 percent of evangelical Christian young people said it was possible to get to heaven without a personal relationship with Jesus Christ.

To take every thought captive in our current cultural context, we must become thoroughly acquainted with a biblical worldview. We must learn what God's Word has to say about the issues of the day. Moreover, we must be alert to those who attempt to marginalize and ridicule those who believe in God.

A biblical worldview is not just a view of the world, however. It is a view for the world. The apostle Paul said, "Those who oppose him [the Christian], he must gently instruct, in the hope that God will lead them to repentance" (2 Timothy 2:25-26). I know how enraging it is when secular humanists attempt to deny Christian influence in society. But we are not allowed as Christians to respond in the way of our secular counterparts. Our strategy is to know what we believe, be articulate in explaining it, and graciously persuade those in authority to act in God-honoring ways.

## Time to Persevere

Francis Scott Key, the man who penned the words to "The Star Spangled Banner," was also a defender of the Christian faith. He once wrote, "I do not believe there are any new objections to be raised to the truth of Christianity. Men may argue ingeniously against our faith, but what can they say in defense of their own?"

One great way to challenge the secular elite is by forcing its advocates to defend what they believe. When I speak at Summit I offer students four simple questions they can use to take every thought captive. Here they are, along with examples.

*Question #1: What do you mean by that?*

If someone says, "We should be tolerant of all beliefs," simply ask, "What do you mean by tolerance?" Most people have never considered this question or its implications (i.e. we would have to be tolerant of the beliefs of Adolf Hitler, Chairman Mao, Joseph Stalin, etc.).

Tolerance is actually a very shallow philosophical concept which glosses over the realities of evil and injustice and the need to strive for truth. Asking for a definition will get the person to reconsider whether it is a good idea.

*Question #2: How do you know that is true?*

Next time someone makes a truth claim such as "There is no God," throw them a curve ball by asking, "How do you know that is true?"

If you are up against a non-believer who is accustomed to mocking Christianity without having to defend his own beliefs, this question will stop him cold. By the way, it is important to never use this question in an arrogant manner—the idea is to destroy the idea, not the person.

*Question #3: Where do you get your information?*

If someone says "I cannot believe in God because of all the evil and injustice in the world," ask where he gets his ideas about evil and injustice. Injustice and evil cannot exist unless there is a standard of what is just and good. Where does this standard come from? On what is it based? Is it always true? Just by asking for additional information you can get a good conversation started.

*Question #4: What happens if you are wrong?*

A professor once told me that all cultural practices should be tolerated. I challenged this by giving examples of cannibalism, Nazism, Suttee' (burning a man's wife alive on his funeral pyre), and several other unspeakably evil cultural practices. I ended our conversation by asking, "What happens if you are wrong? Millions of people suffer pain, torture, and death and you cannot stop it because you cannot decide what is right and wrong."

## For Such a Time as This

The Bible tells of a young woman named Esther who was forced to marry a pagan king. Her relative Mordecai discovered that this king had been tricked into a plot to kill all of Esther's people, the Jews. Mordecai pleaded with Esther to appeal to the king by saying, "Who knows but that you have come to a royal position for such a time as this?" (Esther 4:14). This is how we must view our mission today. Rather than fear the world of ideas, we should learn to engage it by operating from a Christian worldview that applies to every area of life.

When Dr. David Noebel first began his work, this idea of cultural engagement was almost unheard of. It isn't anymore, and in large measure we have Dr. Noebel to thank for that. Count me among those who are grateful for his nearly half a century of faithfulness.

# Where is Your Hope?

Chuck Asay

My granddaughter, Emily, when she was 3 or 4 years old, was coloring a picture with her grandmother. She suddenly stopped coloring and let out a deep sigh and said, "I don't know why I'm so cute." I feel a little like Emily, as I'm writing this chapter. I know I'm not "cute," but I don't know why I'm so "blessed" that I get an opportunity every other week in the summer to walk into a room full of hungry-for-ideas young adults at Summit Ministries and throw out some red meat that they seem to enjoy.

It seems I am always invited to speak right after the kids have finished lunch. I suspect the leaders at Summit plug me in

there because I draw funny pictures as I talk, which keeps the kids awake until they get their second wind. Keep in mind that the students have just eaten and probably got about two hours of sleep the night before.

The title of my talk is, "Where is your hope?" which links to 1 Peter 3:15: "Always be prepared to give an answer to everyone who asks you to give the reason for the hope that you have." My talk is about how to engage the enemy, and hopefully equips them with some tools to survive.

I make my living inflicting my opinion on as many people as I possibly can. I get paid to comfort the afflicted and afflict the comfortable...which has become somewhat of a cliché nowadays, but nevertheless is still true. In my political cartoons, I lay out my political views daily in a bunch of newspapers and over the net, which draws fire from the enemy. I think of it as counter-terrorism. We are to be wise as serpents—and who is wiser in this world than Satan—and innocent as doves. The innocent part is what Satan doesn't get. We can't do it either. We can't fake innocence when we know are hearts are desperately wicked. If we are to be innocent, we need Jesus to do that part...and He has promised to do it if we ask Him. "The one who calls you is faithful and he will do it" (1 Thessalonians 5:24).

Spiritual warfare is very real, sometimes dangerous, and always exciting. Most people who view my work and like my ideas probably share the same worldview that I have. Those who get mad at me and respond with letters, e-mail, or phone calls open up an opportunity to discuss worldview divisions. They are mad at me, but I am not mad at them. I love them because God loves them. They just don't understand that we are alike, sinners in need of a savior. They think I'm an idiot, but that's not true either. If they get to know me they'd see I'm OK...not too bright, but not dumb either. It's not me they hate—it's probably just my ideas they don't like. I don't like some of their ideas either.

Ephesians 6:12 says, "For our struggle is not against flesh and blood, but against the rulers, against the authorities, against the powers of this dark world and against the spiritual forces of evil in the heavenly realms."

I see the world as ruled by ideas, not people. There are bad ideas, which result in death, and there are good ideas, which produce life. We need to resist the bad ideas and try to promote the good ideas. In my worldview, the world is ruled, not by people, but by ideas. Where do these ideas come from? From the "...rulers...of evil in the heavenly realms."

In my talks at Summit, I like to show students some of my cartoons and explain how they are aimed at bad ideas or promote good ideas. I then try to lay out my biblical, worldview and explain how it "evolved," which I know is a bad word, but it seems to be more believable to people in this day. If I said my worldview was given to me as a gift from God, they'd think I was some kind of religious fanatic...which I am...but I like to disguise myself as a normal person.

Here are some cartoons I use to explain how the ideas I try to communicate differ from what the world says. I change these cartoons often to keep up with the current events. I then talk about where my ideas come from. The short answer to that is that the good ideas come from God and the bad ideas come from me.

To give them the longer answer, I have to go back to the beginning where the Bible says, "...God created..." (I start by drawing a fish). Right there we enter into controversial waters. We, in the present day, can't teach that concept in our public schools because it is a "religious idea." The word "God" can't be used, unless we are swearing, and we certainly can't say "created." That's not scientific.

As I draw, I talk about how I used to believe that the lizard and fish were related in that the lizard had evolved. We dwell on that idea, on how it contradicts what God says in Genesis.

We go on to talk about the monkey—how it looks a lot like the boy sitting in the front row—and how effective it is that observation has power to draw in folks who swallow the lie hook, line, and sinker.

I then go on to depict what I see in the Bible about God creating man. I pick some poor victim in the audience to represent Adam. I repeat the creation story: how God wants His creation to rule over the earth, and how God commands Adam not to eat the fruit of the tree of the knowledge of good and evil.

It's here where things get interesting. It seems that man did not ask for this...it is God who said, "It is not good that (name of victim) live alone."

I introduce the woman and explain how God messed up. I explain how it was Eve who was tempted and ate the fruit and gave some to (name of victim). Here is where many students find, in a humorous but uncomfortable way, the importance of paying close attention to detail in the Bible. I try to pin all the blame on the girls for messing everything up. We talk about the curse and ask why the man gets the big curse...death.

It all comes to light when we see the rest of Genesis 3:6: "...she took some and ate it. She also gave some to her husband, WHO WAS WITH HER..." We then get into "sin" and how we wind up with having no hope.

I tell the kids a story about a Mexican Chihuahua. It starts out as a joke but leads to the idea that we, who have no hope, but are created in the image of God, have within us a little dog: God spelled backwards. It's just a little dog (we are created in the image of God, you know) but it's no big deal—in our eyes, we can just run over that bit of information. But if we do pay attention to that little thing, we come to see that dogs, no matter how small, can pick up on things we often miss. Dogs can smell blood...and that's what gives me hope.

As I depict the trail of blood in the scriptures, from the animals God used to cover Adam and Eve's shame to the lamb sacrifice in the temple to cover the peoples' sin, it leads to the cross where Jesus took care of our sin. In His blood, I have hope.

## The Call of Abraham

I find my hope back in Genesis 12 in the call of Abram. The Lord speaks to a man who may have been asking the same question. Who knows why God chose Abram to talk to, but what He said to Abram I believe He says to whomever listens. He told Abram to "leave your country, your people and your father's household..."

He might be saying to me (and to you) what he said in Proverbs 3:5-6: "Trust Me...leave your understanding."

The Lord told Abram, "Go to a land I will show you." Notice the Lord doesn't tell Abram where He is going to lead him. He seems to want Abram to just go and trust God to get him there. This is a tough thing for us to do. We want clarity. If we had clarity, why should we need faith? God seems to be looking for faith. It seems the only way I can get by my anxiety of trusting someone I can't see and who is not too interested in giving me verbal directions is to believe He exists and that He will reward those who earnestly seek him (Hebrews 11:6).

Going back to the call of Abram, the Lord says we are to be a blessing along the way. Our journey is not just for us; it's supposed to be for others. Then, there's a promise. God will bless those who bless us and will curse those who curse us. I don't see anything in that call that says we are to curse, do you? It's God who does the cursing. That's important.

We can see the out-working of this call when Jesus sends out the 12, then the 72 in the gospels. Remember what he told them? "Don't take travelers checks, I will provide for your needs through my people (who in turn get blessed)," he said, in a rough paraphrase. "If they don't want you there, just leave and shake the dust off your feet as a testimony against them." I don't see anything there that suggests He told His sent ones to get even. "It is mine to avenge; I will repay" says the Lord in Deuteronomy 32:35.

Have you ever noticed how the bin Ladens of this world seem so angry? There are people all around us who seem to be mad. They see themselves and others as "victims." It seems they are angry because they haven't seen justice. Habakkuk was angry too. He hadn't seen justice and asked the Lord about it. What did God say to him? "Hey, you haven't seen nothin' yet. Wait 'til you see how the Babylonians, who I'm raising up, are going to pound you."

I think a lot of people around Jesus wanted to see justice also. They saw some miracles but not the kind of miracles they wanted to see. They wanted to see the justice of God come down and pound their enemies. Jesus told them that will come later. So they killed Him. What happened after that is what gives us hope.

Others have their hope in leaders...wise leaders. Have you ever noticed how the liberal media portray the democratic nominee as a realistic, intelligent visionary and

his/her opponent as a dangerous, dim-witted ideologue? These people have their hope in government...in the wisdom of leadership. Nationalism is bad, in their eyes—multinationalism is good. Their hope is in the idea that mankind will eventually evolve to a stage where we can live in peace with everyone. It will take time, but WE can do it.

First Corinthians 1:22 says that Jews look for miracles (justice?), Greeks, for wisdom (peace?), but we preach Christ crucified.

Now that's a winning message. No wonder people think we're stupid. But Paul said that's the most important thing I can tell you—that Christ died for sins, that He was buried, and that He rose again on the third day.

When you connect the dots of the disciples shaking the dust from their sandals, you see a demonstration of their faith. They didn't have to carry any anger away from that place. They trusted God to handle it. They didn't believe they could bless the people who blessed them—they believed God would do it.

Justice and peace are good things. We should always strive for it. When people sin against us, we should follow the instructions in Matthew 18. When people want to kill the weak, we should look to the authorities whom God put over us for justice (Romans 13).

But what if they don't act? What do we do with our anger then? It seems we have two choices. We can become revolutionaries and take matters into our own hands and seek justice or we can shake the dust from our sandals and go with Jesus. (He's heading toward Jerusalem, by the way.)

What a freeing concept—to just leave matters we can't handle to God and trust that He is faithful and He will do it (1 Thessalonians 5:24 again).

It seems the end of the sermon on the mount always winds up with us being persecuted. We don't win. We are

WHAT WE PREACH

being set up to fail. Did we sign up for this, Lord? "Welcome to the club," the Lord says. If you want to know who else is in the club, go to Hebrews 11 and read some of their names. Abraham is there among them.

I close the talk with an illustration of the believers on the canvas. The world seems to be in control...but coming again soon is the one who said He had overcome the world.

What a blessing, what joy to be His. It is my hope that all those hungry young adults will choose Him as well. Thank you.

# The Chronicle of
# an Undeception

Michael Bauman

> *"The central myth of the sixties was that [its]*
> *wretched excess was really a serious quest for*
> *new values."*
>
> George Will

## The Tragic Vision of Life

I confess to believing at one time or another nearly all
the pervasive and persistent fantasies of the sixties. In the
words of Joni Mitchell's anthem for the Woodstock nation,
I thought all I had to do was "get back to the land to set my
soul free." I thought that flowers had power, that love could
be free, and that the system was to blame. By 1968, I had
the whole world figured out. I knew the cause of every evil—
America—and I knew the solution to every problem—freedom and tolerance.

If truth be told, of course, I knew nothing, at least nothing worth knowing. I knew how to posture, but not how to
stand. I knew how to protest, but not how to protect. I knew
how to work up an impressive case of moral outrage, but I

didn't know morality. I knew about peace, but I didn't know enough to fight for it. I knew about self-indulgence, self-preservation, self-esteem, and self-expression, but I didn't know about self-sacrifice and self-control.

Worse still, I didn't even know myself. I didn't know what Socrates knew about me—that I entered this world in a state of total and seamless ignorance, and that my ignorance could never be breached as long I remained blissfully unaware of it. I didn't know what St. Augustine knew about me—that the well of my soul was poisoned, and that whatever was down in the well would come up in the bucket. St. Augustine also knew this about my soul: no matter how hard it tried, no matter where it looked, it could never find its rest anywhere but in God. I didn't know what Edmund Burke knew about me—that no government could fix what ailed me, either by the things it did or by the things it did not do. The most any state could do was to help protect me from myself and from others. Most importantly, however, I didn't know that I was Everyman. When I learned that, I stopped being a liberal.

Like almost all dissidents of my generation, I was a protestor without a plan and a visionary without a vision. I had not yet learned that you see only what you are able to see, and I was able to see only the egalitarian, relativistic, self-gratifying superstitions of the secular, wayward left. Please do not think that this was simply a case of prelapsarian innocence. It was not. It was ignorance and it was evil, although I would have denied it at the time.

Only slowly did I come to understand that my fellow dissidents and I had taken for ourselves the easiest and least productive of all tasks, that of denigrator. And only slowly did I come to understand that to destroy is easy, that to build is hard, and that to preserve is hardest of all.

But it was worse even than that, because my fellow dissidents and I were blind to the most obvious truths, especially to what Russell Kirk and others have called the tragic vision of life—the profound realization that evil is not something "out there," it is something "in here." The tragic vision of life arises from the fact that we are flawed—deeply, desperately, tragically flawed—and we cannot be trusted. We are broken at the heart; our defect is life wide and soul deep. Though we are capable of reason, because of our selfish passions and our moral weaknesses we are rarely reasonable. We ourselves are what is chiefly wrong with the world. We are this planet's most malignant and enduring ailment. We have our dignity, to be sure, but we have our horror as well. I can tell you this: I did not wake up until I met the enemy face to face—in the mirror. We all do.

I had to learn to stare squarely into that face in the mirror, into the face of hard, fallen reality, and not to flinch. I did not, in fact I could not, comprehend the tragic vision of life until I learned that the problem of the human heart is at the heart of the human problem. Once I examined with care and honesty the habits of my own heart and those of my dissident friends, I learned that C.S. Lewis was right: to be one of the sons of Adam or the daughters of Eve is both glory enough to raise the head of the lowest beggar and shame enough to lower the head of the highest king. I am a human being. That is my wealth; that is my poverty.

Before that undeception, I was like all of the other cultural and political liberals. I had fallen prey to what Jeane Kirkpatrick identified as the error of misplaced malleability. I thought that human institutions could be reshaped at will to fit the plans already existing inside my head. It cannot be done. Human institutions arise from human action; human action arises from human nature; and human nature is notoriously intractable. Apart from the grace of God, human nature cannot be fixed, no matter how badly it needs fixing. I finally learned that my deepest need was not more freedom. I needed the grace and guidance of God. Until I understood that, I remained shamelessly superficial.

I had to put my insipid and airy romanticism where it belonged, on the burgeoning junk pile of the fatally flawed and conclusively overthrown fantasies to which the human mind seems continually to give rise. Not romanticism but religion, not Byron but the Bible, not poetry but Paul, not Voltaire but virtue, not trends but tradition, not idealism but ideas, not genius but grace, not freedom but faith could cure me. I had to exchange Wordsworth for the Word and revolution for repentance. Thus, while some of the things I valued were useful and good, they were not properly fundamental. I had to put first things first.

The tragic vision of life humbled me. From it I learned that it was not my prerogative to invent wisdom and virtue. That had already been done. My responsibility was to listen to the One who invented them and to those whom He taught. Wisdom and virtue, I had to learn, were not born with my generation, or with Rousseau's, or Matthew Arnold's, or even Eugene McCarthy's. I had to learn in the last half of the twentieth century what was already old news in the days of Jeremiah, the ancient prophet, who wrote,

> Stand at the crossroads, and look,
> and ask for the ancient paths,
> where the good way lies;
> and walk in it, and find rest for your souls.
> (Jeremiah 6:16)

Wisdom is found by walking the "ancient paths." Those "ancient paths" led through the wilderness, through the sea, even through the valley of the shadow of death, and not through Berkeley, not Columbia, not the Village, not Watts, not Haight-Ashbury, not Altamont, and not Woodstock.

The tragic vision of life also taught me that order is the most fundamental of all political and social needs. Because it is, I learned that the police are not pigs. They never were, and are not now, an occupying army intent upon destroying my freedom. Quite the opposite. Imperfect as they sometimes are, the police are the guardians of freedom and the paid protectors of life and property. In the line of duty, some of them even died for me, and for you. The tragic vision of life taught me that you cannot reject authority—whether civil, familial, cultural, or divine—and yet live in an orderly world. When you "off the pigs," (of whatever sort) you give birth to an outlaw culture, not to freedom. To live outside the rules, to live outside authority, to live without the wisdom of the ages and of God, is to court slavery and

death. Enforceable law and law enforcement are require-
ments of the first rank. Because human nature is what it is,
without great volumes of enforceable law, freedom is impossible. As Dean Clarence Manion observed in the very last
line he wrote before his death in 1979, "a society that is not
held together by its teaching and observance of the laws of
Almighty God is unfit for human habitation and doomed to
destroy itself."

When is freedom not enough? Every time truth and
righteousness are at stake. In a fallen world, that is almost
always. Freedom must be exercised according to the dictates of truth and virtue, never the other way round. Freedom must be limited by the demands of justice, love and
revelation. The most important consideration regarding any
action is not "Is it free?," but "Is it good?" When I learned
that, I stopped being a libertarian. Freedom, furthermore,
is an incomplete concept. Whenever someone insists upon
freedom, you must ask "Freedom to do what?" You must
ask that question because freedom, like tyranny, has its
unintended and unforeseen consequences, some of which
are colossally vile. In passing, I name only one—abortion.

From the tragic vision of life I learned that you have to
do what is right whether it suits you or not. In the sixties,
we hardly did anything that did not suit us. I also learned
that the enemy is not the CIA, not the FBI, and not the
GOP; it's the NEA, NOW, NBC, ABC, CBS, CNN, DNC, WCC,
and NPR, indeed the entire grab bag of alphabetized, leftist subverters of culture, of tradition, and of revelation. I
learned that those who deprive themselves of the wisdom
of western tradition are no more free than a baby left alone
by its parents to do as it pleases. I learned that politics is
not about equality, but justice; that personal action is not
about freedom, but righteousness; and that sex is not about
pleasure, but love and privilege and posterity.

Those things and more I learned from the tragic vision of
life. I commend them to you. They taught me that in many
ways the sixties were twisted and misshapen.

The sixties are over, and it's a good thing. The sixties
were a bad idea, if for no other reason than because the

sixties had no ideas, only selfish desires hiding behind the shallow slogans and freelance nihilism emblazoned on psychedelic bumper stickers, slogans like "I dissent, therefore I am." The only things about which we were intellectually modest in the sixties were the claims of objective truth. We seemed unable to wrap our minds around even the most obvious ideas. We seemed unable to realize, for example, that you cannot raise your consciousness until you have one. The sixties were perhaps the most unconscious decade in centuries. It was a time of suffocating intellectual mediocrity, from which our nation has not yet recovered.

## Sixties Redivivus

I can imagine a student reading these remarks and wondering, "This all might be well and good, but what does it have to do with me? I wasn't even alive in the sixties."

My answer is simply this: While the sixties are over, they are not dead, not by a long shot. They live, indeed they thrive, not only in the White House juvenocracy (which is tragic enough), but in the faculty lounges and endowed chairs of nearly every college and university in the United States. Tenured faculty members everywhere have traded their tie-dyed T-shirts and their bell bottom jeans for a cap and gown, if not a cap and bells. Those faculty members are the entrenched purveyors of an unexamined and indefensible hand-me-down Marxism, and of what Allan Bloom called nihilism with a happy ending. They have become paid agents of the very colleges and universities they once tried to burn to the ground, and not because they gave up on the dreams of the sixties. What they failed to do as protesters they have succeeded in doing as professors. Quite possibly they have done it to you, because the entire teaching profession, from the pre-kindergarten level to the post-graduate, has become a political captive of the cultural left. Like roving street gangs prowling the halls of academe, power hungry bands of leftist professors everywhere have instigated countless institutional turf wars, most of which they won. They succeeded in burying the accumulated wisdom of the ages in the name of learning; in overthrowing academic freedom in the name of tolerance; in stifling debate in the name of openness; in exalting egalitarianism above all other ideas in the name of equality; and in segregating and tribalizing the university, the nation, and the culture by gender, by age, by religion, by race, and by sexual preference, all in the name of unity. The schools and colleges that hire and then tenure them commit academic treason. I simply remind you that any intellectual community that is unwilling or unable to identify its enemies cannot defend itself. David Horowitz was exactly right: Those who cherish free institutions, and the culture of wisdom and virtue that sustains them, must stand up boldly against the barbarians already inside the gates.

Because the sixties live, this decade has become irrational, ignorant, and morally illiterate. If the sixties were majestically self-indulgent, this decade is perhaps the most self-congratulatory decade our nation has ever seen, and not because we have succeeded where all other generations have failed, but in spite of the fact that we have failed where all other American generations have succeeded—in learning to learn, in learning to work, in learning to listen, and in learning to worship. This is a decade determined to ignore, if not belittle and malign, beauty, truth, and goodness, three things most moderns foolishly believe are in the eye of the beholder. Our decade is the sworn enemy of revelation and of righteousness. If the threefold mantra of the sixties was "tune in, turn on, and drop out," today's is comprised of that earlier mantra's four silly children, four sentences that no thinking man ever permits himself or herself to utter in the face of a moral challenge, sentences like: "Everything is relative," "There is no right or wrong," "There are no absolutes," and "Who's to say?"

If you cannot now figure out why belief in those four sentences is the death of learning and of virtue, then perhaps for that very reason you can understand why I spend nearly all my time and energy as a professor and as a writer defending the ancient liturgy of the enlightened mind—that right and wrong are matters of fact, not matters of feeling;

that without God there is no good; that justice is not equality; that new is not necessarily better; and that relativism, secularism, and pragmatism are not the friends of truth and goodness. The denizens of modernity probably do not realize and probably do not care that they are the befuddled and bedeviled lackeys of designer truth, of made-to-order reality, and of *ad hoc* morals. If you follow them, you walk into the night without a light and into the woods without a compass. I want to tell you as plainly as I can that their vision of academic tolerance lacks intellectual virtue. It dilutes the high cultural inheritance of the past with the petty and insupportable leftisms of the present.

A moment ago, I imagined a student that might be wondering about the relevance of my semi-autobiographical musings. I also can imagine someone thinking that all I've done since the sixties is simply to change sides in the culture war that rages around us. To think so, however, is to assume that flower power and Christianity are morally equivalent and that hippies rank equally with saints, two false assumptions that, if you make them, show just how much a child of the sixties you really are.

I have often wondered why today feels like a sixties renaissance. I discovered the answer to that question in a college cafeteria and in conversations with some of my students' parents.

First, the parents: I have often noticed my students saying and thinking the same sorts of things their parents say and think when I speak with them. Such things happen because the acorn seldom falls far from the oak tree. That fact is more than a little significant because the parents of today's college students were probably the young men and women of the sixties. Many of the responses my students learned to give to life are responses they learned from their parents. More often than not, those responses are the stock responses of the sixties. In one way, of course, that is good; I want my students to learn all the truth they can from their parents. But insofar as my students' responses mimic the responses of the sixties, they too must learn the lessons I had to learn. They must come to understand, with all the clarity and courage they can muster, the truth of the tragic vision of life: We are, every one of us, morally defective, ethically twisted, and spiritually broken. If my students fail to come to that realization and to act upon it, both they and their world shall suffer.

Second, the cafeteria: I often notice my students echoing some of the things they hear their teachers say. When talking with students in the cafeteria, for example, I sometimes have the eerie feeling that I'm not in the cafeteria at all; I'm in a faculty meeting. I say so because I frequently hear the clear and unmistakable intonations of my colleagues' voices, but coming from other people. Sometimes I even hear my own voice. Again, that's good; I want college students to learn all the truth they can from their professors. But here's the rub: Like me, many of their teachers were children of the sixties; and like me, many of those professors have made only an incomplete break with the mistakes of that era. From their other professors and from me, my students have gotten many of their ideas. Like my students themselves, their ideas have parents. Worldviews and attitudes, just like the people who have them, show marked family resemblances. For that very reason, I often want to ask my students this question: From where do you imagine your rampant relativism and your not-very-carefully-hidden contempt for authority arise? In most cases, when I consider asking such a question, I already know the answer—from the sixties and from the people (like me) who reached their emotional and intellectual maturity at that time.

## Undeception Redivivus?

Here's my point: If you believe in the sixties, or if you believe in today, you believe a lie. As I did, you need an undeception. In order to get it, you need to go back well beyond the sixties, back to a wisdom that is older than time. You need to go back to God and to the wisdom that spoke this universe into existence. You need to go back to the God who made you and redeemed you. Real answers are found nowhere else.

It should not surprise you when I tell you that, if you do what I suggest, you shall meet energetic and determined opposition, sometimes even from those who call themselves the friends of God and of tradition. As Socrates observed long centuries ago, most men do not take kindly to the preacher of moral reform, to the pursuer of the good. There is no telling, he said in the *Gorgias*, what might happen to such a man. But do not let that stop you. Do it anyway. Do it because you need it; do it because it is right; and do it because it ought to be done. Your task will be difficult. It's always easy to be a modernist; it's always easy to go with the spirit of the age. But in the face of the world's downward slide you must be vigilant, strong, perceptive, and courageous. The world needs people like that, people unafraid to turn around and walk back into the light. Our world needs people like that more now than perhaps it ever has because everywhere you look the adversary culture of the sixties has become the dominant culture of today.

Our cultural patrimony is being embezzled from under our very noses. If you think of yourself as a Christian, or as a conservative, or as both, the view from here is haunting: We don't own the public square; we don't own the media; we don't own the arts; we don't own the sciences; we don't own the arena; we don't own the marketplace; we don't own the academy; we don't own anything. We don't even own the Church. It's all owned by the sixties.

Therefore, if, as I did, you find yourself an unwilling or unwitting child of the sixties, I invite you, I exhort you, to turn with an open mind and an open heart to the prophets and apostles in Scripture and to the great poets and sages outside Scripture. They are your only liberation from modernist thralldom and from slavery to your own fallen desires. (Did you know that you can be a slave to your own will?) Put yourself on a quest for eternal truth, and never give up until you find Him.

While you are on this quest, you must always remember that most of the powers that be are of no help to you. Those who loved the sixties own today. The left still hates America, and it still hates what made America possible: faith in God, the sacredness and inviolability of the family and of life, individual responsibility, local and limited government, and traditional morality. The leftists of today are the enemies of heartland values. They want you to keep quiet. They want you to sit meekly in the corner of the room, hands folded and mouth shut. They want you to be nice. They want the friends of beauty, truth, and goodness to speak only when spoken to and, when they do speak, to speak only those things that offend no one. That they have offended you seems not to matter. They want you to stick to the script. They want you to keep your views to yourself and to act as if your views were not true, indeed as if there were no truth. That's what political correctness—or should I say political cleansing?—is all about.

Consider it for just a moment: What kind of man or woman would you be if you let yourself be controlled by the empty criticisms of the rootless left, and what kind of world would you be creating for those who came after you if you neglected to restore realism to human thought and turned your back on the only thing that can make you content, even in dungeons, even in slums, even in the face of death?

My desire for you is that you throw off the vestiges of leftist cultural subversion, that you make yourself a devotee and guardian of the wisdom of the ages, that you become the sworn enemy of nonsense in all its forms, and, most importantly, that you become the faithful and ardent friend of God. Then, and only then, can you be free.

What has been given you as a heritage you must now accept as your quest. If you wish to be wise, you must learn to learn from your ancestors. You must learn to make peace with the wisdom of the ages and with those who gave it, regardless of their sex, their race, or their ethnic background. You must do so because wisdom and truth are not gender-based, race-based, or nation-based. They are thought-based, and thinking is very hard work. Knowledge is not parochial. It is not the private property of any race, gender, era, or ethnic group. It belongs to those determined to get it, to those who seek it resolutely and who will not be denied, no matter how difficult the quest.

In that light, I invite you today to make one of the most important choices of your entire life: Which will you have, truth or rest?

You cannot have both.

# Radical Environmentalism's Assault on Humanity

E. Calvin Beisner

I wish I could tell you how pleased I am to be with you, but I can't. I don't take kindly to bombs and explosions, or cancer or the plague. And these are what you are.

How does that make you feel? Does it build your self-respect? Does it make you glad you're here?

Of course not. And it isn't intended to. It's intended to make you feel *guilty* for being alive. *Guilty* for taking up space, eating up food, using up energy, spewing out pollution, displacing animals and plants on dear Mother Earth—Gaia, as enlightened environmentalists know her. *Guilty,* finally and most importantly, *for being human.* And while it doesn't represent my real position—actually, I consider it a great privilege to share a room with people made in the glorious image of God—it does represent the dominant view of mankind among the definers of the environmentalist movement.

In this chapter, you'll meet some of those people and get to know their worldview and its implications for your life and mine. Then you'll get to see their view contrasted with a Biblical Christian view of man. When we're finished, you'll need to choose between the two.

Let me say at the start that while I oppose the environmentalist movement, and while I believe that many of its claims about man's impact on the environment are false and driven by ideology, not by truthful observation, I do not mean to denigrate all concern for the environment. My dispute is with environmental*ism*, not with legitimate concern for the environment—what we properly call environmental *stewardship*, our responsibility as God's stewards to protect and improve the environment for His glory and our benefit. As we shall see, environmentalism and environmental stewardship are not synonymous.

## Environmentalism vs. Humanity

Humanity is under siege. I refer to the anti-human attitudes expressed by leaders of the population control and environmentalist movements. In 1970, Kingsley Davis wrote contemptuously, "In subsequent history the Twentieth Century may be called either the century of world wars or the century of the population plague,"[1] an attitude that fueled his suggesting, seven years later, that population be reduced by promoting the breakdown of the family, "very high divorce rates, homosexuality, pornography, and free sexual unions"—with easy access to abortion.[2]

Davis is not alone in hating people. In an article in *The Animals' Agenda*, a magazine published by the Animal Rights Network and portraying itself as moderate, Sydney Singer writes, "For an animal rights activist, it's easy to become disgusted with humankind. Humans are exploiters and destroyers, self-appointed world autocrats around whom the universe seems to revolve." Condemning the use of animals in medical research that has contributed to cures or effective treatments for once fatal diseases, he adds, "It is often hard to feel compassion for humans in their pain and fear as they brutalize other animals....

[1] Kingsley Davis, "The Climax of Population Growth," *California Medicine* 113 (November 1970): 33-39.
[2] Kingsley Davis, "Population Policy and the Theory of Reproductive Motivation," *Economic Development and Cultural Change* 25 (Supplement, 1977): 176.

In the face of speciesist rationalizations for animal exploitation, which frame the issue in terms of animal suffering or human suffering, it's hard not [to] take sides and fight for the animals." And no wonder; Singer, like most other animal rights advocates, equates human beings with animals: "When the ethical issue of active euthanasia arises concerning a terminal patient who is asking to be killed, I find myself thinking about the millions of dogs and cats 'euthanized' each year in pounds."[3] Singer was a medical student when he wrote the article. You might pray for his patients. Dr. Jack "the Dripper" Kevorkian might have competition. Indeed, he might have more than Singer to compete with. Singer and his wife Tanya, under the pseudonym Screaming Wolf, published the book *A Declaration of War: Killing People to Save Animals & the Environment* in an attempt to enlist the help of others who might rather kill people than animals.[4] But even Singer and Kevorkian can hardly compete with Ingrid Newkirk, of People for the Ethical Treatment of Animals (PETA), who was cited in *The Washington Post* as saying, "Six million people died in concentration camps, *but six billion broiler chickens will die this year in slaughter houses!*"[5]

If putting people on the level of animals isn't bad enough, how about putting them on the level of trees? The West German Green Party's Carl Amery said in 1983, "We, in the Green movement, aspire to a cultural model in which the killing of a forest will be considered more contemptible and more criminal than the sale of 6-year-old children to Asian brothels."[6] Michael W. Fox, one of the chief gurus of

---

[3] Sydney Singer, "The Neediest of All Animals," *The Animals' Agenda* (June 1990): 50-51.
[4] Ron Arnold, *EcoTerror: The Violent Agenda to Save Nature: The World of the Unabomber* (Bellevue, WA: Free Enterprise Press, 1997), 147. (Note: I added this sentence to this lecture on August 13, 1997.) Also, Sydney and Tanya Singer, *A Declaration of War* (Grass Valley, CA: Patrick Henry Press, 1991).
[5] Emphasis added; cited in the Regnery Gateway Fall/Winter 1993 book catalogue, 2; in advertisement for Kathleen Marquardt's, with Herbert M. Levine and Mark LaRochelle, *Animalscam: The Beastly Abuse of Human Rights* (Washington: Regnery Gateway, 1993).
[6] Cited in Dixy Lee Ray, with Lou Guzzo, *Trashing the Planet: How Science Can Help Us Deal with Acid Rain, Depletion of the Ozone, and Nuclear Waste (Among Other Things)* (Washington: Regnery Gateway, 1990), 169.

the radical environmentalist and animal rights movements, writes in his book *Returning to Eden* that man "is the most dangerous, destructive, selfish and unethical animal on earth."[7]

David Brower, of Friends of the Earth, considers "other people's children" pollution and therefore an environmental concern. Said he, "Childbearing [should be] a punishable crime against society, unless the parents hold a government license....All potential parents [should be] required to use contraceptive chemicals, the government issuing antidotes to citizens chosen for childbearing."[8]

Not to be left behind in this attack on reproductive freedom, Paul Ehrlich, author of *The Population Bomb* and *The Population Explosion*, writes, "Several coercive [methods of birth control] deserve serious consideration, mainly because we will ultimately have to resort to them, unless current trends in birth rates are revised." He suggests deindustrialization (since the wealth made by industries makes providing for children easier), liberalized abortion, and tax breaks for sterilized couples.[9]

Where is the outcry against Big Brother in the bedroom? Whatever happened to the liberals' vaunted rights to privacy and reproductive freedom?

But Amery, Brower, and Ehrlich are mild compared with Les Knight, founder of VHEMT (pronounced "vehement")—the Voluntary Human Extinction Movement. "The hopeful alternative to the extinction of millions of species of plants and animals," he says, "is the voluntary extinction of one species: *Homo sapiens*—us. When every human makes the moral choice to live long and die out, Earth will be allowed to return to its former glory. Each time one of us decides not to add another of us to the burgeoning billions already squatting on this ravaged planet, another ray of hope shines through the gloom....A baby condor may not

[7] Michael W. Fox, *Returning to Eden* (New York: Viking, 1980); cited in Robert James Bidinotto, "Environmentalism: Freedom's Foe for the '90s," *The Freeman* vol. 40, no. 11 (November 1990), 409-420, p. 412.
[8] David Brower, cited in Rael Jean Isaac and Erich Isaac, *The Coercive Utopians* (Washington: Regnery Gateway, 1985); also in Ray, *Trashing the Planet*, 169.
[9] Cited in Ray, 168.

be as cute as a baby human, but we must choose to forgo one if the others are to survive." Knight, by the way, got a vasectomy eighteen years ago to ensure that *he* wouldn't reproduce.[10] Cheers!

If restraints on reproduction don't work, we can always turn to killing people outright. Norwegian philosopher of ecology Arne Naess, one of the formative voices of environmentalism, suggested an ideal world population of 100 million.[11] One wonders what he would do with the other 5 billion of us! In reviewing Bill McKibben's *The End of Nature*, National Park Service biologist David Graber wrote,

> Human happiness, and certainly human fecundity, are not as important as a wild and healthy planet. I know social scientists who remind me that people are part of nature, but it isn't true. Somewhere along the line—at about a million years ago, maybe half that—we quit the contract and became a cancer. We have become a plague upon ourselves and upon the Earth....Until such time as Homo Sapiens should decide to rejoin nature, some of us can only hope for the right virus to come along.[12]

Graber didn't need to wait long. The Earth First! newsletter suggests, "If radical environmentalists were to invent a disease to bring human populations back to sanity, it would probably be something like AIDS. It has the potential to end industrialism, which is the main force behind the environmental crises."[13]

One might expect radical feminists, so quick to defend reproductive freedom in their "right to abortion," to oppose

---

[10] *New Age Journal* (September/October 1991), reprinted in *Reader's Digest* (April 1992), 147.

[11] Cited in Evan Eisenberg, "The Call of the Wild," *New Republic* (April 30, 1990), 31. Naess apparently thinks so little of human beings that he cares little whether there are a hundred million or a billion of them, since elsewhere he suggests an ideal population of a billion; see Petr Borrelli, "The Ecophilosophers," *The Amicus Journal* (Spring 1988) 32-3.

[12] Cited in Virginia Postrel, "The Green Road to Serfdom," *Reason* (April 1990),24.

[13] Cited in *Access to Energy* 17:4 (December 1989).

the population control movement. Think again. The real animus of their defense of abortion is not love of freedom but hatred of mankind. No less authoritative a radical feminist spokesman than the lesbian Riane Eisler, who in 1984 addressed Congress on "Population: Women's Realities, Women's Choices,"[14] wrote:

> The population crisis...lies at the heart of the seemingly insoluble complex of problems futurists call the *world problematique.* For behind soil erosion, desertification, air and water pollution, and all the other ecological, social, and political stresses of our time lies the pressure of more and more people on finite land and other resources, of increasing numbers of factories, cars, trucks, and other sources of pollution required to provide all these people with goods, and the worsening tensions that their needs and aspirations fuel.[15]

The fear of population growth is so strong as to provoke positively apocalyptic visions. Consider this, from *Life* magazine in 1965:

> A British scientist recently calculated that with the population of the world now about 3 billion and doubling every 37 years, we will reach the ultimate terrestrial limit of 60 million billion humans in somewhat less than 1,000 years. At that state, people will be jammed together so tightly that the earth itself will glow orange-red from the heat.[16]

No wonder that, as we pulled into a parking space before checking into a hospital for the birth of our first child, my wife and I noticed a bumper sticker on the car beside us

[14] Riane Eisler, "Population: Women's Realities, Women's Choices," *Congressional Record,* 98th Cong., 2d sess., 1984.

[15] Riane Eisler, *The Chalice and the Blade: Our History, Our Future* (San Francisco: Harper & Row Perennial Library, 1987), 174-175, second emphasis added.

[16] "Population Explosion and `Anti-Babyism,'" *Life* 58:16 (April 23, 1965), 6.

saying, "Beam me up, Scotty. This planet sucks!" Doesn't this mad scientist realize that long before the world became that crowded and its temperature rose that high love-making would lose all its appeal?

Now, I could explain why such projections of future population are nonsense, the statistical games of those with an axe to grind. I have done so in my book *Prospects for Growth*.[17] But what I would rather do now is to suggest why a Biblical understanding of man necessitates very different attitudes.

First, however, I need to familiarize you with three important and overlapping segments of the environmentalist movement—the Green political movement, the Deep Ecology movement, and the animal rights movement. In the process, I'll flesh out for you the radical environmentalist worldview.

## The Greens

Arising in Europe, the Greens are the politically sophis-ticated environmentalists. They are also socialists. "March-ing under the banners of 'Green politics' or 'Social Ecology,' they profess at least a nominal concern for human values and modern culture. But their goal," wrote Robert Bidinotto in an excellent critical article, "is a socialist, redistribution-ist society, which they claim is nature's proper steward and society's only hope."[18]

---

[17] E. Calvin Beisner, *Prospects For Growth: A Biblical View of Population, Resources, and the Future* (Westchester, IL: Crossway Books, 1990), 44-48.

[18] Bidinotto, 410. We should take care not to oversimplify the socialism of the Green parties, however. They have arisen out of the Left-libertarian movements in Europe, and "Left-libertarian parties oppose the priority given to economic growth in public policy making, an overly bureaucratized welfare state, and restrictions placed on participation which confine policy making to the elites of well-organized interest groups and parties. They favor imposing limits on the institutions that modern conservatives and socialists prefer for allocating social costs and benefits: markets, because they orient human preferences toward the pursuit of material commodities, devalue social community, and endanger the supply and protection of nonmarketable collective goods, such as an intact environment; bureaucracies, because they subject individuals to centralized controls, establish a hegemony of professional expertise undercutting political participation, and organize social interaction according to impersonal rules. From the left-libertarian

The Greens tend to be pragmatic and *publicly* less radical than their allies in the Deep Ecology and animal rights movements. They work through the political process, particularly legislatures and international treaties (like the global climate treaty being negotiated through the United Nations and signed in Rio de Janeiro recently). They also have gained influential positions in "respectable" environmentalist groups like the Natural Resources Defense Council, the Environmental Defense Fund, the Sierra Club, the Wilderness Society, the Worldwatch Institute, the Union of Concerned Scientists, and even the federal Environmental Protection Agency.[19]

One of their chief tactics—shared with other environmentalists—is the insurance policy ruse. First, they promote a major environmental scare, usually using no science, bad science, or ambiguous science. When later data prove their dreadful scenarios extremely unlikely, they argue, "Well, but we can't be *sure* something won't happen. Doesn't it make sense to insure against it now rather than to wait until all the data are in, since by that time it may be too late to avert the disaster?"

Popular environmental scare-monger Jonathan Schell, author of *The Fate of the Earth*, makes explicit the extent to which such enviro-political advocacy departs from the traditional course of objective science:

> In the past, action usually awaited the confirmation of theory by hard evidence. Now, in a widening sphere of decisions, the costs of error are so exorbitant that we need to act on theory alone—which is to say on prediction alone....[Scientists must] disavow the certainty and precision that they normally insist

point of view the formal rationality and efficiency of markets and bureaucracies deprives people of choosing a life-style that maximizes autonomy and solidarity." Herbert Kitschelt, *The Logics of Party Formation: Ecological Politics in Belgium and West Germany* (Ithaca and London: Cornell University Press, 1989), 9-10. In other words, the Left-libertarian Green parties tend to endorse a decentralized, debureaucratized socialism while adopting all of the traditional socialist critiques of capitalism.

[19] Bidinotto, 410.

on....Scientists need to become connoisseurs and philosophers of uncertainty....[T]he incurable uncertainty of our predicament, far from serving to reassure us, should fill us with unease and goad us to action.[20]

Perhaps the first victim of the environmentalist movement has been the coolly rational quest for truth that has marked scientific endeavor for centuries in the West. For the sake of promoting the environmentalist agenda, says Stephen Schneider of the National Center for Atmospheric Research, scientists "have to offer up scary scenarios, make simplified, dramatic statements, and make little mention of any doubts we might have," cautiously deciding the "right balance [between] being effective [i.e., in promoting a political agenda] and being honest. I hope," he adds wistfully, "that means being both."[21] This subterfuge underlies the determined push for new laws that might strangle our economies, harm our lives and health, and destroy our liberties in the name of averting global warming and ozone depletion and reducing acid rain, species extinction, rain forest destruction, and other alleged pending catastrophes. The problem with the insurance policy ruse is that it attempts to force us to buy insurance at an unknown but extremely high price against a risk of unknown but extremely low probability of an unknown but probably very slight degree of harm—with no assurance that the insurance will pay off.

## The Deep Ecologists

Allied with the Greens but using different tactics are the devotees of "Deep Ecology." Often pantheists—who believe that God is everything—and sometimes explicitly embracing such Eastern religions as Hinduism and Buddhism,[22] the

---

[20] Jonathan Schell, "Our Fragile Earth," *Discover* (October 1989), 50; cited in Bidinotto, 417.
[21] Cited in Schell, 47; cf. Bidinotto, 417.
[22] See, for example, Steven Rosen, "Ahimsa: Animals and the East," *The Animals' Agenda* (October 1990), 21-5.

Deep Ecologists are spiritual and religious in their attitudes toward environmental issues. Some actively seek to revive such pagan ways as Druidism, witchcraft, Native American religions, and—among feminists—goddess worship. Drawing from both the Eastern religions and Darwinian science, they tend to find man's identity with the rest of nature in his ascent through the evolutionary chain of being. Thus, "One itinerant environmentalist conducts 'workshops' in which participants are urged to remember their alleged evolutionary history by rolling on the ground and imagining what their lives were like as dead leaves, slugs, and lichens."[23]

Deep Ecologists tend to reject the pragmatic, political approach of the Greens, favoring direct action through groups like Greenpeace, Earth First!, Sea Shepherds, Rainforest Action Network, People for the Ethical Treatment of Animals, the Animal Rights Network, and the Animal Liberation Front.

While the Greens cloak their eco-disaster claims in science, the Deep Ecologists depend more on mysticism and intuition. Arne Naess, the Norwegian philosopher of ecology who would like to rid our planet of 98 percent of its people, is one of the chief framers of the Deep Ecology worldview and the coiner of the phrase *deep ecology*.[24] He specified that his work consists not "of philosophical or logical argumentation" but is "primarily intuitions."[25] Just how intuitive this worldview—which Naess calls "ecosophy"—is may be illustrated by his student and translator David Rothenberg's description of one of Naess's lectures in Oslo: "After an hour he suddenly stops, glances quickly around the stage, and suddenly leaves the podium and approaches a potted plant to his left. He quickly pulls off a leaf, scurries back to the microphone, and gazes sincerely at the audi-

---

[23] Bidinotto, 410; citing Lindsy Van Gelder, "It's Not Nice to Mess with Mother Nature," *Ms.* (January/February 1989), 60.
[24] Arne Naess, "The Shallow and the Deep, Long-range Ecology Movements: A Summary," *Inquiry* 16:95-100.
[25] David Rothenberg, "Introduction: Ecosophy T: from intuition to system," in Arne Naess, *Ecology, Community and Lifestyle: Outline of an Ecosophy*, trans. and rev. David Rothenberg (New York: Cambridge University Press, 1989), 2.

ence as he holds the leaf in the light so all can see. `You can spend a lifetime contemplating this', he comments. `It is enough. Thank you.'"[26] (Don't feel bad if you don't get Naess's message. The problem isn't with you.)

The focus on intuition in the Deep Ecology movement explains, in part, why feminism allies itself with environmentalism, Deep Ecology, and animal rights. Feminism rejects science outright—or redefines it—because science operates in a manner not sufficiently sensitive to "feminine thought patterns" because it is a fundamentally "masculine" discipline. "Science's insistence on being tough, rigorous, rational, impersonal, and unemotional is intertwined with men's gender identities," says feminist and animal rights theorist Carol Adams, author of *The Sexual Politics of Meat: A Feminist-Vegetarian Critical Theory.*[27]

At Deep Ecology's root is the insistence that "all life is fundamentally one." From this principle flows a new vision of Self-realization—with a capital *S*: "a bold attempt to connect the general statement that `all life is fundamentally one' with our individual needs and desires." Here all distinction between God and the world collapses in the vision of the one Self that encompasses not only all of life but all of everything.[28]

Naess insists, "Economic growth as conceived and implemented today by the industrial states is incompatible with" sound ecology. Consequently, "the implementation of deep changes...requires increasingly global action in the sense of action across every border, perhaps contrary to the short-range interests of local communities."[29] Here is the root of Deep Ecology's alliance with socialism and the movement toward a one-world government that would abolish national sovereignty.

It is crucial to recognize that Deep Ecology explicitly rejects any distinction between man and nature. Naess

[26] Rothenberg, "Introduction," in Naess, 1.
[27] Kim Bartlett, "Of Meat and Men: A Conversation with Carol Adams," *The Animals' Agenda* (October 1990), 13.
[28] Rothenberg, "Introduction," 8, 9.
[29] Naess, 31.

complains that while "Shallow Ecology" fights "against pollution and resource depletion," its central objective is "the
health and affluence of *people....*" In contrast, Deep Ecology involves "rejection of the man-in-environment image in
favour of *the relational, total-field image.*"[30] In other words,
man's needs and desires are not to be considered as in any
sense higher than those of the rest of nature, for man is
nothing more than a part of nature. Nature does not exist
*for* man.

Naess sees and embraces the logical implication of his
views: "*Biospherical egalitarianism—in principle....*To the
ecological field worker, *the equal right to live and blossom* is
an intuitively clear and obvious value axiom. Its restriction
to humans is an anthropocentrism with detrimental effects
upon the life quality of humans themselves."[31] Or as Earth
First! founder David Foreman puts it, "...man is no more
important than any other species....It may well take our
extinction to set things straight."[32]

## The Animal Rights Movement

If "all life is fundamentally one," as Naess insists—in
concert with scientific naturalism and the other evolutionary religions: Hinduism, Buddhism, and the contemporary
New Age Movement—then no one part of life has any greater
claim on life and health than any other. Consequently,
as animal rights philosophers John Harris and Stanley
and Roslind Godlovitch put it, "...there can be no rational
excuse left for killing animals, be they killed for food, science or sheer personal indulgence."[33]

The logic is inescapable. But it is also unlivable, for
without consuming life, human life cannot continue. Naess
stepped back from the abyss when he proclaimed "*Biospherical egalitarianism—in principle*," adding, "The `in prin-
ciple' clause is inserted because any realistic praxis [i.e.,

[30] Naess, *Ecology, Community and Lifestyle*, 28.
[31] Ibid.
[32] Bidinotto, 414.
[33] Harris, Godlovitch, and Godlovitch, *Animals, Men and Morals*; cited in
Bidinotto, 412.

staying alive] necessitates some killing, exploitation, and suppression."[34] So he permits killing/eating animals.

That won't do for the animal rights crowd. To them, such inconsistency is mere "human chauvinism," as David Greanville puts it.[35] The more common label is *speciesism*, a word coined in 1973 and made popular by philosopher Peter Singer's book *Animal Liberation* in 1975. What is speciesism? It is, according to Singer, "a prejudice or attitude of bias toward the interests of members of one's own species and against those of members of other species." For proponents of animal rights, speciesism is so self-evidently wrong that "it should be obvious that the fundamental objections to racism...made by Thomas Jefferson...apply equally to speciesism. If possessing a higher degree of intelligence does not entitle one human to use another for his own ends, how can it entitle humans to exploit nonhumans for the same purpose?"[36] Speciesism is to animals what racism is to racial minorities, sexism to members of the opposite sex, and anti-Semitism to Jews: an unjustifiable prejudice against those unlike oneself.

It is crucial to see the root of this view in evolutionism. In the preface to his book, Singer had written,

> We commonly use the word "animal" to mean "animals other than human beings." This usage sets humans apart from other animals, implying that we are not ourselves animals—an implication that *everyone who has had elementary lessons in biology knows to be false.* In the popular mind the term "animal" lumps together beings as different as oysters and chimpanzees, while placing a gulf between chimpanzees and humans, although our relationship to those apes is much closer than the oyster's.[37]

[34] Naess, 28.
[35] David Patrice Greanville, "Holocaust at the Animal Shelter," *The Animals' Agenda* (January/February 1990), 44.
[36] Peter Singer, *Animal Liberation: A New Ethics for Our Treatment of Animals* (New York: Random House/New York Review Book, 1975), 7.
[37] Singer, *Animal Liberation*, xiii.

Agreeing with the "environmental ethic" set forth by UCLA historian Lynn White Jr. in 1967—"the equality of all creatures, including man"[38]—Singer builds his whole argument for animal rights and against speciesism on this assumption of essential equality between human and other animal life forms, an equality as morally significant as the equality of Blacks and Whites and of men and women. If the fundamental equality of Blacks and Whites makes racism immoral, and the fundamental equality of men and women makes sexism immoral, then the fundamental equality of humans and other animals makes speciesism immoral.

There is grave danger in this line of argument. The assumption that common biological evolution necessitates *equal* treatment does not define *right* treatment. While Singer argues from biological equality to the conclusion that we should treat animals as we treat humans, one could as readily argue from biological equality that we should treat humans as we treat animals. Animal rights philosopher Patrick Corbett asks, "Is it not perverse to prefer the lives of mice and guinea pigs to the lives of men and women?" No, he answers, because "if we stand back from the scientific and technological rat race for a moment, we realize that, since animals are in many respects superior to ourselves, the argument collapses."[39] What Corbett neglects is that "animals are in many respects superior to ourselves" means the same as "people are in many respects inferior to animals," and if that is so then there is no reason to expect people to behave differently from—or better than—animals.

Evolutionary egalitarianism—the belief that all animals are equal because all are part of the evolutionary continuum—lies at the root of racism, which sees certain races as lower on the evolutionary scale than others and therefore properly to be treated more like animals than the higher races. Never forget that the full title of Charles Darwin's *The Origin of Species* was *The Origin of Species By*

[38] Lynn White Jr., "The Historical Roots of Our Ecologic Crisis," *Science*, March 10, 1967; reprinted in *The Environmental Handbook*, ed. Garrett De Bell (New York: Ballantine Books, 1970); cited in Bidinotto, 411.
[39] Patrick Corbett, "Postscript," in *Animals, Men and Morals*, by J. Harris and S. and R. Godlovitch (Taplinger Publishing, 1972), cited in Bidinotto, 412.

*Means of Natural Selection, Or the Preservation of Favored* **Races** *in the Struggle for Life.* Richard Hofstadter, in *Social Darwinism in American Thought,* showed conclusively "that Darwinism was one of the chief sources of racism and of a belligerent ideology which characterized the last half of the 19th century in Europe and America...."[40] When Hitler applied Darwinism to morality, he concluded, "There is absolutely no other revolution but a *racial* revolution. There is no economic, no social, no political revolution. There is only the struggle of *lower races* against the *higher races.*"[41] Marx considered Darwin's *Origin of Species* a scientific basis for his theory of the class struggle and wanted to dedicate an edition of *Das Kapital* to Darwin. Evolutionary biology applied to ethics has led historically not to humane treatment of beasts but to beastly treatment of humans.

Perhaps this explains why Earth First! activists pound spikes into trees to discourage loggers from cutting them down and sawmill operators from milling them: when the power blades hit the hidden spikes, the blades can explode, threatening serious injury or death to operators. Perhaps it explains why Sea Shepherds activists boast of sinking twelve whaling ships—at considerable risk to the ships' crews.[42] Perhaps it explains why one animal rights activist—a woman—was convicted for attempting to murder, with two pipe bombs filled with nails, the president of U.S. Surgical Corporation, which uses animals to teach doctors surgical procedures.[43]

---

[40] Raymond F. Surburg, "The Influence of Darwinism," in *Darwin, Evolution, and Creation,* ed. Paul A. Zimmerman (St. Louis: Concordia, 1959), 196. "Darwin and Nietzsche were the two philosophers studied by the [Nazis] in working out the philosophy set forth in Hitler's *Mein Kampf.* In this work Hitler asserted that men rose from animals by fighting. It was the contention of the Fuehrer that this struggle, where one being feeds on another...has continued from time immemorable and must continue until the most highly advanced branch of humanity dominates the whole earth." Surburg, 196.

[41] Cited in David Noebel, *Understanding the Times: The Story of the Marxist/ Leninist, Secular Humanist, and Biblical Christian Worldviews* (Manitou Springs, CO: Summit Press, 1991), 831; citing George C. Roche, *A World Without Heroes* (Hillsdale, MI: Hillsdale College Press, 1987), 248.

[42] Bidinotto, 415.

[43] *Baron's,* March 5, 1990, cited in Bidinotto, 412. See John G. Hubbell, "The `Animal Rights' War on Medicine," *Reader's Digest* (June 1990), 70-76.

This whole way of thinking actually trivializes racism
by putting speciesism on the same level with it. If I were a
Black, I'd be worried about anyone who said that speciesism was as bad as racism.

Alas, the animal rights movement is blind to this sinister
flip side of the coin of evolutionary ethics. The assumption
that man's treatment of man, not animals' treatment of animals, should be the standard of man's treatment of animals
is at least as anthropocentric as the insistence that people
have rights that animals don't. And it is more condemnable
because it is so hypocritical. At the bottom of the contents
page of every issue, *The Animals' Agenda* proudly asserts
that it "makes every effort to ensure that products and
services advertised herein are consistent with the *humane*
ethic" (emphasis added). Here is anthropocentric speciesism
with a vengeance! Why should we favor "the *humane* ethic"
over "the *beastly* ethic" if human beings are essentially
equal to animals? Indeed, if we are bombs, the plague, "the
most dangerous, destructive, selfish and unethical animal
on earth,"[44] why speak of a "humane ethic" at all?

The practical implication of the animal rights movement
is that mankind, which alone bothers to respect anybody's
rights, must become extinct, while all other species continue feasting merrily on each other. Bidinotto draws the
inference clearly:

> Any intelligible theory of rights must presuppose
> entities capable of defining and respecting moral
> boundary lines. But animals are by nature incapable
> of this. And since they are unable to know, respect,
> or exercise rights, the principle of rights simply can't
> be applied to, or by, animals. Rights are, by their
> nature, based on a homocentric (man-centered) view
> of the world.
>
> Practically, the notion of animal rights entails
> an absurd moral double standard. It declares that
> animals have the "inherent right" to survive as *their*

[44] Michael W. Fox, *Returning to Eden* (New York: Viking, 1980); cited in Bidinotto, 412.

nature demands, but that man doesn't. It declares that man, the only entity capable of recognizing moral boundaries, is to sacrifice his interests to entities that can't. Ultimately, it means that *only* animals have rights: since nature consists entirely of animals, their food, and their habitats, to recognize "animal rights" man must logically cede to them the entire planet.[45]

Let me summarize the environmentalist worldview:

1. All life—including man—is one.

2. Man is part of nature, not above it.

3. Because man uses nature—living and non-living nature—as if he were not part of it, he is a plague on the Earth.

4. Man's effects on nature are that he uses up resources and pollutes the environment.

## A Biblical Christian View of Man and Nature

Well, what are we to say to all this?

Apart from a commitment to the Bible as God's Word, we cannot respond at all. Granted the truth of the evolutionary worldview that underlies every aspect of environmentalism, environmentalism's conclusions are logically inescapable.

But the Bible *is* God's Word, the evolutionary worldview is *false*, and so is all that is logically derived from it. So what does the Bible say?

Consider Psalm 8:3-8, one of the definitive scriptures on the doctrine of man. King David writes, "When I consider Your heavens, the work of Your fingers, the moon and the stars, which You have ordained, what is man that You are mindful of him, and the son of man that You visit him? For You made him a little lower than *God*"—harking back to

[45] Bidinotto, 412.

Genesis 1:26, which tells us that God made man in His own image and after His likeness—"and You have crowned him with glory and honor. You have made him to have dominion over the works of Your hands; You have put all things under his feet, all sheep and oxen—even the beasts of the field, the birds of the air, and the fish of the sea that pass through the paths of the seas."

The Bible, alongside its doctrine of human sin, has a profoundly high view of mankind and his destiny. Yes, we are dead in trespasses and sins, sons of disobedience, by nature children of wrath. We are a frightful piece of wreckage. But we are the wreckage of something gloriously magnificent, something that God Himself "crowned...with glory and honor." And in the resurrected Son of God we see perfectly revealed what we are destined to be.

The Apostle Paul wrote that, in the curse after Adam's sin, God subjected creation to corruption "in hope; because the creation itself also will be delivered from the bondage of corruption into the glorious liberty of the children of God" (Romans 8:20-21). Paul saw that the redeeming and delivering work of Christ was not restricted to the salvation of the souls of the elect, but included the restoration to glory of the physical universe as well.[46]

The amazing leaps in economic productivity and prosperity stemming from the application of the Christian worldview through the scientific and technological advances propelled by the Reformation are but a foretaste of the restoration of creation foretold by Paul and entailed by the incarnation, death, and resurrection of Christ.

Now, that is a big chunk of theology, but it will become clearer if we back up for a moment and consider Genesis 1:26: "Then God said, `Let Us make man in Our image.'"

If you were just starting to read the Bible for the first time, what would you already know that would help you understand what was meant by the image of God in man?

---

[46] This must not be taken to imply universal salvation of all mankind. Nothing could be further from the truth. Scripture clearly affirms that those who reject the saving gospel of Christ will be forever lost, damned to eternity in torment (e.g., Matthew 25:46).

You would know what you had read in Genesis 1:1-25. "In the beginning God *created* the heavens and the earth"—so the image of God includes creativity. "Then God said, `Let there be"—and behold! look at the list! Light, a firmament, and oceans, and dry land, and grass, and herbs, and trees, and stars, and sun, and moon, and birds, and sea creatures, and land creatures! And He instructed all the living things to multiply and fill their various niches in the world. So the image of God includes a wonderful love of variety and life and fruitfulness.

So, if you were just starting out reading the Bible, what would you think God's image was? Chiefly, creativity. And that, my friends, is the first great distinction between the environmentalist view of man and the world and the Biblical view. Recall that environmentalism sees human population growth as "the population *bomb.*" What do bombs do? They explode, of course! So we are "the population *explosion.*" And what do explosions do? They destroy things. Environmentalism starts off on the wrong foot, denigrating mankind, denying the image of God in man. It sees man chiefly as consumer, not producer; destroyer, not creator. It therefore concludes that he is polluting the Earth.

The Bible has a different vision. It sees population growth as a blessing, not a curse. Not the *explosion* of population, but the *blossoming.* We are not the population bomb but the population bloom. People aren't pollution, they're the solution.

This different vision begets a different prediction: that people, because God made them in His image to be creative and productive, because He gave them *creative minds* like His, can actually *make* more resources than we consume. So the Biblical view of man and the universe predicts that, as we apply our minds to raw materials, resources will become *less* scarce, not more. And that is precisely what we find when we look at history.[47]

The image of God in man has other implications, too. First, while environmentalism says that man is part of nature and must not rule over it for his own benefit, God,

---

[47] Beisner, 114-117.

when He made man, specifically said, "Let Us make man in Our image, according to Our likeness; *let them have dominion* over the fish of the sea, over the birds of the air, and over the cattle, over all the earth and over every creeping thing that creeps on the earth" (Genesis 1:26).

Second, while environmentalism grieves over human population growth, the Bible celebrates it, saying, "Then God *blessed* them, and God said to them, `Be fruitful and multiply; fill the earth and subdue it" (Genesis 1:28); it doesn't say, "Then God *cursed* them and said, `Be fruitful and multiply.'" While the animal rights movement says that man must not eat animals, God said to Noah after the flood, "And the fear of you and the dread of you shall be on every beast of the earth, on every bird of the air, on all that move on the earth, and on all the fish of the sea. They are given into your hand. *Every moving thing that lives shall be food for you. I have given you all things, even as the green herbs*" (Genesis 9:2-3).

Third, while radical environmentalism insists that animals have rights and therefore we must not eat them, the Bible calls them "natural brute beasts *made to be caught and destroyed*" (2 Peter 2:12)—that is, not wastefully, but for food and other good purposes, like medical research and clothing. Whereas the animal rights movement condemns killing animals to make furs for human apparel, God Himself did it first, after Adam and Eve sinned (Genesis 3:21). Remember this: environmentalism insists that man is part of nature. The Bible says, "The heaven, even the heavens, are the LORD's, but the earth He has given to the children of men" (Psalm 115:16).

Fourth, environmentalism views nature as good and perfect as it is—except for man (and here alone environmentalism seems to admit a difference between man and nature). Now, the Bible does say, after the creation narrative, "Then God saw everything that He had made, and indeed it was very good" (Genesis 1:31). But it also says that after Adam sinned, God said, "Cursed is the *ground* for your sake" (Genesis 3:17). God subjected creation "to futility" and "the bondage of corruption" (Romans 8:20-

21), and He is using redeemed man to reverse the effects of His curse (Romans 8:18-21). So a Biblical view of man and nature admits that pristine nature is *not* better than nature improved by the good stewardship of the redeemed.

Environmentalism wants to reduce human population and preserve nature untouched by human hands. It ignores the curse and man's call, as God's steward, to reverse its effects. As Stewart Brand put it in *The Whole Earth Catalogue*, "We have wished, we ecofreaks, for a disaster or for a social change to come and bomb us into the Stone Age, where we might live like Indians in our valley, with our localism, our appropriate technology, our gardens, our homemade religion—guilt-free at last!"[48]

In contrast, God calls us to restore the Earth from the curse, to multiply its resources and their productivity for His glory and our benefit. He does not call us to preserve it just as we find it. To put the call into Biblical terms, God calls us to transform the Earth from a wilderness, which throughout Scripture signifies God's curse, into a garden, which signifies His blessing.

[48] Cited in Dixy Lee Ray, letter for Accuracy in Media (May 1992), 3.

# Engaging Popular Culture
### Analyzing Worldviews in Movies

Chuck Edwards

---

*"Who are you?...Then, who am I?...Was nothing real?"* The Truman Show

*"Only try to understand...there is no spoon."* The Matrix

## What's your PCQ?

We live in unprecedented times. Never before have there been so many persuasive avenues of influence begging for our attention. To see what I mean, look at the various ways popular culture gains a foothold in your life:

- Television
- Newspapers/Magazines
- Novels
- Radio/CDs
- Movies/Music videos/DVDs
- Computer/video games

- The Internet

To objectify the influence popular culture has on you, count the number of media "conduits" you currently access on a regular basis and write the number in the margin. This number is what Kenneth Myers calls your "Pop Culture Quotient."[1] Now consider the total number of hours each week you spend on these activities and write that number. This gives you some idea of the sheer volume of information coming your way, twenty-four hours a day, seven days a week, over your entire life.

To gain some perspective on this number, go back just three generations, to the time of your great-grandparents. How many of the above cultural avenues were available during their formative years? When your great-grandparents where growing up, the greatest influence in forming their beliefs and character would have been their immediate or extended family, their small local church, the neighborhood school (whose teachers probably knew your entire family by name), going to an occasional theatrical production (maybe a traveling show once or twice a year), and reading the local newspaper and classic novels. This means that the major role models for young people were adults who for the most part knew who they were and cared for them and the community in which they lived.

Now consider this generation. Today's youth are learning about life from people who live hundreds of miles away, don't know them by name, and don't have a vested interest for their safety and welfare. And it needs to be kept in mind that today's cultural conduits are more than just entertainment—they're education. How do we know this? Influential people in popular culture tell us! For example, Muppet creator Jim Henson is credited as saying, "Television is teaching whether you want it to or not." Also, James Cameron, who won an Academy Award for Best Director for his 1997 film, *Titanic*, said in an interview, "We have a great responsibility. Whatever we make will become the truth, the visual

[1] Kenneth A. Myers, *All God's Children and Blue Suede Shoes* (Wheaton, IL: Crossway Books, 1989). See his introduction.
[2] Quoted in "Titanic Stuff," by Corie Brown and David Ansen, http://www. geocities.com/EnchantedForest/Dell/9305/tistuff.html.

reality that a generation will accept."[2]

## Pop Culture 101

Francis Schaeffer explained that the philosophies of intellectuals filter down to the general public through the arts, becoming what we call "popular culture." Thus, popular culture is the expression of the prevailing worldview of the writers, producers, and directors of blockbuster movies, best-selling novels, "top-forty" songs, and highly rated television shows, as well as those who work in the visual arts and advertising.

For the most part, those who are at the top of their field—writing scripts, directing programs, and belting out songs—do not share views or practices compatible with Christianity. According to one survey of over one hundred of the most influential television writers and producers in Hollywood, 93% seldom or never attend worship services, 97% believe in a woman's right to abort her pregnancy, only 16% strongly agree that adultery is wrong, and only 5% strongly agree that homosexuality is wrong.[3]

For a glimpse behind the scenes of what it is like working in Hollywood, listen to Dean Batali, a Christian who was the script writer for the initial two seasons of *Buffy the Vampire Slayer,* as well as Co-Executive Producer of *That 70's Show,* and others. He says,

> Christians...are hugely misunderstood by most Hollywood writers. I have worked with more than fifty writers on various shows. Of those fifty, I have met only three others besides myself who even go to church—and I am the only one who would describe himself as an evangelical Christian. Most of them simply do not know that people like me exist....One writer literally once said to me, 'I'm so glad I know you, because now I know that all Christians aren't freaks.' But that writer still thinks that the rest of

[3] See Michael Medved, *Saving Childhood,* (New York: Harper Collins, 1998).
[4] "Voiceover: An Interview with Dean Batali," http://www.whedon.info/article.php3?id_article=750&img=

Christians are freaks.[4]

To many in Hollywood, Christians are a little freaky. As another example, take Gene Roddenberry, creator of *Star Trek*. Roddenberry grew up in the South attending church as a youth. According to his own account, Roddenberry rejected Christianity as a young teen because it seemed to him to be nonsense. In 1986 he joined the American Humanist Association (the leading humanist organization in the country) and in May, 1991, Roddenberry was awarded their *Humanist Arts Award*. He had this to say about religious people, "For most people, religion is nothing more than a substitute for a malfunctioning brain."[5]

How does the attitude of Roddenberry, and others in his profession, play itself out in what we see on TV? Let's look at one example: sexual content. According to a Kaiser Family Foundation study in 2001, "...sexual content *increased* from half of all shows in 1998 to two-thirds in 2000."[6] That's an incredible increase in the span of only two years. To cite just one example, when *Dawson's Creek* first aired in 1997, one reporter noted that in some schools, the show was the talk of the fourth grade. Weekly episodes included explicitly sexual dialogue and a fifteen-year-old character having a passionate affair with his teacher, then lying to protect her. During its six seasons it pushed the envelope farther than anyone thought it could, portraying everything from open marriages to gay adoptions.

Numerous reports indicate that this kind of programming is influencing our children, who are dressing and acting in sexually provocative ways at increasingly younger

[5] Quoted in www.tektonics.org/sciencemony.htm.

[6] Kaiser Family Foundation, "Sex on TV 2001: Executive Summary," 2. http://www.kff.org/kaiserpolls/loader.cfm?url=/commonspot/security/getfile.cfm&PageID=13822.

[7] For details on how viewing sexual images on TV affects children and teens, see the following studies: M.S. Calfin, J.L. Carroll, and J. Schmidt, "Viewing music-video tapes before taking a test of premarital sexual attitudes," *Psychological Reports,* 72 (1993), 475-481; L.E. Greeson, and R.A. Williams, "Social implications of music videos on youth: An analysis of the content and effects of MTV," *Youth and Society,* 18, (1986), 177-189; L.M. Ward, R. Rivadeneyra, "Contributions of Entertainment Television to Adolescents' Sexual Attitudes and Expectations," *The Journal of Sex Research,* No. 3, Vol. 36 (1999), 237; and J. Brown, "Mass media influences on sexuality." *The Journal of Sex Research.* No. 1, Vol. 39 (1992), 42.

ages.[7] According to one study, pressure to have sex has become a "big problem" for 49% of 12-to-15 year olds and 33% of 8-to-11 year olds. Dr. Jane Brown, journalism professor at the University of North Carolina, Chapel Hill, observed on NPR's *Talk of the Nation,* "If you believe *Sesame Street* taught your four-year-old something, then you better believe MTV is teaching your 14-year-old something, because the influence doesn't stop when we come to a certain age."[8]

## The Cultural Commission

In light of the onslaught of anti-biblical bias and displays of immorality, what should be the response of a follower of Jesus Christ? Christians can't settle for being passive consumers of pop culture. Instead, we are called by God to be discerning shapers of culture. Being culture shapers is not optional for a believer. The biblical basis for this is found in the Cultural Commission as given to Adam and Eve in Genesis 1:28. After creating the universe, earth, the garden, and mankind, God gives man and woman the responsibility to care for and develop what he had created. This involves every aspect of creation, from naming animals to establishing civil government (see Genesis 9:6 where God commands man to rule over his fellow man by bringing to justice those who commit evil).

This theme of influencing culture continues into the New Testament. Jesus, in Matthew 5:13-16, referred to his followers as society's "salt" and "light"—that which flavors and preserves the social order. Based on Jesus' salt and light metaphor, if our culture is tasteless and wicked, it is because Christians are not doing their job! We cannot blame non-believers if our society is deteriorating. Non-Christians are simply living according to their view of life. Therefore, it is up to those of us who understand the truth to live it out on every level of society, from the boardroom to the classroom to the courtroom, and even the movie set.

---

[8] "Talk of the Nation," National Public Radio. February 9, 2004. "Decency, indecency and community standards."

There is no area of society that is outside God's concern.

Only believers, living in the power of Christ's Spirit, can provide a positive model for the culture at large and bring health and healing to our sin-soaked world. This means that Christians need to be discerning when it comes to popular worldview messages. We need to "take every thought captive" to Jesus Christ and not be "taken captive" by deceitful philosophies (see 2 Corinthians 10:5 and Colossians 2:6-8). Cultural discernment and engagement are part of our Christian calling.

## Learn to Discern

Discernment is the ability to distinguish between good and evil (Hebrews 5:14). Discernment also involves making wise choices. As we face the trials of living in a "post-Christian" culture that is increasingly hostile to biblical teaching, we should ask God to give us this kind of wisdom (James 1:5).

The "Wisdom Literature" of the Bible instructs us in making judgments between alternative choices (Proverbs 3:21-24). We are to think hard as well as humbly, using godly principles and common sense to make the best decisions concerning how to engage today's culture. This implies that in many areas of life the choice is not always black and white. Often we must choose between the good and the best.

Discernment enables the Christian to avoid two undesirable extremes: what Christian screenwriter Brian Godawa describes as *cultural anorexia* and *cultural gluttony*.[9] Cultural anorexia is avoiding everything in popular culture. People who take this approach only see the negative influences of popular media and may express their concerns in the following ways:

"TV corrupts the values of society."
"There is too much sex and violence."
"Movies are worldly and a waste of time."

[9] Brian Godawa, *Hollywood Worldviews* (Downers Grove, IL: InterVarsity Press, 2002).

However, this is not the tone of the New Testament. Jesus prayed to the Father, "I do not ask that you take them out of the world, but to keep them from the Evil One" (John 17:15). And the Apostle Paul advised the Corinthian believers, "I have written you in my letter not to associate with sexually immoral people—not at all meaning the people of this world who are immoral...In that case you would have to leave this world" (1 Corinthians 5:9-10). Avoiding those around us and their cultural expressions is not a viable option for the believer.

On the other hand, cultural gluttons are not discerning about the negative aspects of popular culture and indiscriminately consume everything the culture offers. People with this approach may say things like:

"I just want to be entertained."
"You shouldn't take it so seriously."
"It's only a movie!"

The problem with Christians who hold this view is that they fail to realize that the arts are as much about education—expressing a worldview perspective—as entertainment. Jesus admonished such believers not to "love the world or anything in the world. If anyone loves the world, the love of the Father is not in him. For everything in the world—the cravings of sinful man, the lust of his eyes, and the boasting of what he has and does—comes not from the Father but from the world" (1 John 2:15-16).

A third alternative for the Christian is to *engage the culture*. This means "interacting redemptively" with non-believers by understanding the culture and using this understanding as a bridge to God's truth.

Paul models this kind of cultural engagement when he spoke before the leaders of Athens (Acts 17:16-34). Here we find that Paul was a student of his culture; he did not try to isolate himself from it. In fact, he had studied the religious worldviews of his day, even "carefully" observing their idols. In his speech before the Athenian leaders, he was able to quote their own pagan poets and philosophers (apparently from memory). It's interesting that Paul did not quote from the Bible during his presentation. He realized that his listeners, as pagans, would brush off his comments if he used the Jewish Scriptures as his authority. Instead, he discerned what was true in their pagan worldview and used that as a starting point to present what they had missed concerning God's attributes, man's true nature, and God's redemptive plan through Jesus Christ.[10]

In another context, Paul explained to the believers in Rome about this approach to sharing the gospel. He affirms that the truth about God is revealed in the external world (Romans 1:20) as well as written on the hearts of men (Romans 2:14-15). This means that we can use everyday observations about how God designed the world to make our case with our non-Christians neighbors and the larger community. We are applying the Cultural Commission as we attempt to shape the culture by participating in local, state, and federal government, serving on school boards, running a business, interacting with co-workers, or taking part in other civic/community organizations and services. Obviously, this approach is not intended to lead a person all the way to trusting Christ as Savior. For evangelism, we follow Jesus' Great Commission by presenting the Gospel, based on a clear presentation of Paul's outline in 1 Corinthians 15:1-5. And this is where using the Bible confirms our words as we present the facts of our need for forgiveness through accepting Jesus' death and resurrection as payment for our sins.

A word of caution is in order here. I would like to clarify that I am not advocating watching *everything* on TV or the movies, or listening to any song. "Slasher" movies are definitely off limits, as are most MTV music videos and much rap and hip hop (because of the gratuitous course language,

---

[10] If you take issue with this approach, I suggest you reread Acts 17:16ff carefully and notice how Paul progresses with his argument to his pagan audience. For example, Paul begins by complimenting his audience on their religiosity. In contrast, when Paul is addressing a Jewish audience, those who feared God and revered the Scriptures, he uses Scripture to validate that Jesus was the Christ (see Acts 17:1-4).

violence, and sexual images). Yet, not all violence, sex, and course language should be ruled out per se. It depends on what is portrayed and how it is handled. The Bible describes a number of very violent incidents, yet God placed those in the Bible to show the sinfulness of fallen man or to provide instruction for us. For example, read the gory detail provided in the incident of Ehud's murder of King Eglon (Judges 3:16-26). In a similar way, films such as *Schindler's List, Braveheart,* or *Saving Private Ryan* portray graphic brutality, yet the context of the story, taken as a whole, is redemptive. In other words, the violence needs to be shown in order for the audience to appreciate the greater lesson. Only with the backdrop of the ugliness of sin can a hero really be heroic![11]

The point is that we need to use discernment when it comes to our viewing and listening choices. Getting back to Paul's example in Acts 17, in Athens he *carefully studied* the prevailing pagan religion and understood well their worldview, yet he did not go so far as to embrace their practices, such as going to the temple prostitutes or sacrificing to their gods. Paul models the kind of balance we need as we engage the culture of our day.

## Film: Beyond Entertainment

How do we develop the discernment exhibited by the Apostle Paul? We begin like Paul, by looking carefully at our culture. For instance, when my daughters were in high school, we would occasionally watch a movie together on Saturday night. Afterwards, I'd initiate a discussion on the message of the movie. The girls would say, "Oh, Dad, do we have to talk about it. That ruins it!" My response was, "Girls, if the screenwriter, director, and producer are simply out to *entertain* us, then we can sit back, relax, and allow our emotions to be moved. *However,* if they are also out to *educate* us, then we have to engage our minds."

And as it turns out, Hollywood screenwriters, directors,

[11] For an excellent commentary on how the Bible treats immorality, see Bryan Godawa's Appendix, *Sex, Violence & Profanity in the Bible,* in his book, *Hollywood Worldviews* (Downers Grove, IL: InterVarsity Press, 2002).

and producers *are* out to educate us. How do I know that? They tell us! For example, George Lucas clearly understands his role as a film writer and director. He revealed in an interview, "I've always tried to be aware of what I say I my films because all of us who make motion pictures are teachers...teachers with very loud voices."[12]

Or take David Franzoni, the main writer and producer of *Gladiator* and *King Arthur*. He said in an interview, "That's the whole point of writing to me: to change the world through your art." What is Franzoni's vision for the world? He goes on to explain that *Gladiator* "is about a hero who has morality, but that morality is a secular morality that transcends conventional religious morality..."[13] According to Franzoni, Christian morality is out and "secular" morality is in—meaning a morality that is not derived from the God of the Bible. This is made clear in both films.

As it turns out, these men know exactly what they are doing. They are in the education business! Now, obviously, as artists and craftsmen, they also are concerned with their medium of expression—film—and they take great pains to present their ideas in an entertaining way, or else no one would pay to see their work. Thus, while money is the bottom line when it comes to major motion pictures, it's not the only line, and we must not forget the central place of the worldview message that is the basis for the story being presented. Filmmakers are first and foremost storytellers.

## Worldview Thinking Begins With God

To drive home the point that watching movies is a worldview matter, take another example. By writing and directing *The Matrix* trilogy, Larry and Andy Wachowski captured the imagination of this generation. In a 1999 *Time Magazine* interview, the brothers reveal why they write stories for film:

We're interested in mythology, theology, and to a cer-

12 www.pbs.org/wnet/americanmasters/database/lucas_g.html.
13 Quoted in John Soriano, "WGA.ORG's Exclusive Interview with David Franzoni," WGA, www.wga.org/craft/interviews/franzoni2001.html.

tain extent, higher level mathematics. All the ways human beings try to answer bigger questions, as well as The Big Question...If you are going to do epic stories you should concern yourself with those issues. People might not understand all the allusions in the movie, but they understand the important ideas. We wanted to make people think, engage their minds a bit.[14]

The Wachowski brothers want people to think about "the big question"—the foundational worldview question "What about God?" This is the starting point for everyone's worldview, and how that question is answered has implications for every other area of life!

To see how this works, consider how the question of God is central to *The Truman Show,* the 1998 hit comedy directed by Peter Weir and starring Jim Carrey and Ed Harris. Truman, played by Carrey, is a man who has lived his entire life confined within an enormous Hollywood studio, never realizing his every move was seen live by millions of television viewers around the world, all the time. Everyone in his life is an actor, playing the part of wife, neighbors, and friends, yet Truman is playing himself. (Talk about the ultimate reality show!) But Truman begins to suspect all is not as it appears on his soundstage world, and he determines to walk off the set.

In the final scene, Truman makes his way in a boat across the "ocean" and locates a set of stairs at the edge of the set leading to an exit door. As Truman opens the door, the voice of the show's director, Christof (Harris), comes booming down from the clouds. Startled by this strange event, Truman asks three questions. The first is, "Who are you?" The clear implication is, "Who are you, God?" How do we know this is the message? In addition to the visual clue of the camera angle pointing up into the clouds, the viewer is led to conclude Truman is referring to God by the way Christof answers, "I'm the creator (and he pauses for a half-

[14] Richard Corliss, "Popular Metaphysics," *Time Magazine* (April 19, 1999).

second for emphasis before continuing) of a television show that gives happiness and meaning to millions." There is no getting around it—this scene leads the audience to understand that Christof is playing "God" in the life of Truman.

By the way, here's the world's shortest lesson in "Film Appreciation 101—no extra charge. *Everything in a movie is done for a certain effect.* For example, at the end of this scene, when Truman opens the exit door we see only darkness on the other side. This was done on purpose. Think about it for a minute. The screenwriter could have written this scene any way he wanted to. On the other side of the door, there could be bright sunshine, tall trees, green grass, chirping birds, guys going by on skate boards! Instead, the doorway was dark. What does darkness represent? While darkness can symbolize several things, such as evil (the bad guys wear black hats!), in this scene it signifies the unknown. Since Truman has never experienced the "real" world, the screenwriter visually reinforces this idea by having him step into darkness. Again, every detail of the movie is significant: what is said and how it is said, the camera angle, the set design, the choice of color used for the set and costumes, the lighting, even what's on the other side of a doorway. Therefore, the discerning viewer must pay close attention to the details to understand the message of the movie.

Getting back to Truman, he next asks, "Then who am I?" And after pondering Christof's response, enlightening Truman on his televised existence, Truman inquires, "Was nothing real?" As it turns out, everyone on the planet is interested in the answers to Truman's questions. That's because these questions are foundational to understanding the meaning of life.

Added to these central questions are seven others that, taken together, form our total world and life view. These questions divide among ten major disciplines of study. Here is a list of the ten disciplines and key question(s) associated with each one:

1. Theology: Is God real and what is God like?
2. Philosophy: What is the nature of reality and how can we know what is true?
3. Biology: What is the origin of life?
4. Psychology: What is the nature of man?
5. Ethics: What is morally right and wrong?
6. Sociology: How should society be structured?
7. Law: What is the foundation of law?
8. Politics: How should government be structured?
9. Economics: What is the best system for maintaining a living?
10. History: What can we learn from the past and where is history headed?

As the Wachowski brothers affirm, if these are the issues that give life meaning, then any good story will revolve around one or more of them, and the discerning viewer will ponder the answers provided in the story as it is presented on the silver screen.

## Worldview Message in Movies

There are various ways to evaluate movies, such as tracing the growth of the main character, picking out the theme or themes, critiquing the cinematography, or judging the quality of the acting. However, when it comes to understanding and engaging the culture, the best approach is to discern the key worldview issue being addressed by asking three questions:

1) What is the key worldview question being addressed?
2) How is this question answered?
3) How does the answer given in the movie compare with a Biblical worldview?

By way of illustration, take George Lucas' classic film series, *Star Wars*. In the 1977 original episode, *A New Hope*, there is a scene where Obi-wan Kenobi is talking with Luke Skywalker and brings up the topic of "The Force." When Luke looks puzzled, Obi-wan explains, "The Force is what gives the Jedi his power. It's an energy field created by all living things. It surrounds us and penetrates us and binds the galaxy together." As it turns out, in this one episode there are four specific scenes where Obi-wan teaches Luke (and the viewers) about various aspects of the Force. More than mere entertainment, the viewer is given a Cosmic Humanist answer to the question, "What is God like?"

Not only does Lucas teach theology in his films, but he also provides an answer to the philosophical question, "How do I know what is true?" This is portrayed in a later scene where Obi-wan teaches Luke to use a light saber. After a few futile attempts at deflecting the laser beams from a rotating sphere, Obi-wan instructs Luke to try again, but with a shield over his eyes. "This time," says the Jedi Master, "let go your conscious self and act on instinct...Your eyes can deceive you, don't trust them...Stretch out with your feelings." Luke slowly catches on to the idea of using the Force instead of his sight, as Obi-wan responds, "You see, you can do it...You've taken your first step into a larger world." This "larger world" is the idea that knowledge is gained through feelings instead of conscious thoughts, another mainstay of the Cosmic Humanist worldview.

Luke eventually learns his lesson of epistemology (the study of knowledge). As we watch the film's climatic battle scene, Luke guides his X-wing fighter to its target and destroys the Death Star after hearing Obi-wan's voice urging him to "Use the Force, Luke. Let go, Luke. Luke, trust me...Remember, the Force will be with you always." Obi-wan's last sentence is noteworthy in that his comment echoes Jesus' final words to his disciples as found in Matthew 28:20. George Lucas apparently draws from Christianity as well as Buddhist philosophy in order to create his cosmic myth for this generation.

Worldview themes permeate all six of the *Star Wars* episodes. To cite just one more example, during an extended scene in Episode V, *The Empire Strikes Back*, Jedi master

Yoda finds an opportune time to further instruct Luke in the ways of the Force. Luke had crashed his X-wing fighter into a swamp, so after some initial training on levitating small rocks, Yoda tells Luke to try his hand at raising the ship out of the muck. Luke tries, but fails. Sitting down exhausted and defeated, Luke experiences what we might call a teachable moment, and, by extension, the audience becomes teachable as well, since at this point in the film the viewer is identifying with Luke's character! In true Eastern guru fashion, Yoda enlightens his young apprentice with these words, "For my ally is the Force," Yoda intones, "and a powerful ally it is. Life breeds it, makes it grow. Its energy surrounds us and binds us. Luminous beings are we, not this crude matter. You must feel the force around you, here between you, me, the tree, the rock, everywhere, yes, even between land and ship." Then, to prove his point, Yoda uses the Force to levitate the ship out of the swamp.

In this scene two key questions are answered. First, we learn something about the nature of God (theology). God is simply the energy that permeates everything, including man and machines. And second, we are given information about ourselves (psychology). Yoda explains that Luke is a luminous being. What is luminosity? Light. What is light? Energy! The implication is that if Luke is energy and the ship is energy, than he can use his energy (The "Force") to connect with the ship's energy, and, voila, levitate it at will. Quite simply, everything that exists is part of the god-Force.

Of course, all of this New Age god-talk was inserted into the movie on purpose. Irvin Kerchner, the director of Episode V, *The Empire Strikes Back*, admitted, "I wanna introduce some Zen here because I don't want the kids to walk away just feeling that everything is shoot-em-up, but that there's also a little something to think about here in terms of yourself and your surroundings."[15] And in an interview with Bill Moyers, Lucas divulges his real purpose in writing the science fiction epic. He says,

[Star Wars is] designed primarily to make young

15 *Rolling Stone* Magazine (July 24, 1980), 37.

people think about the mystery. Not to say, "Here's the answer." It's to say, "Think about this for a second. Is there a God? What does God look like? What does God sound like? What does God feel like? How do we relate to God?"[16]

What is interesting about Lucas' declaration that he is not offering "the answer" is the fact that throughout all six movies he is demonstrating exactly the opposite! He *is* offering an answer to the questions of what God is like and how we relate to Him. As we have seen, we are told in numerous ways by various characters that God is an impersonal energy "Force" that pervades the universe and has a "dark side." Irvin Kershner and George Lucas have a worldview and that view is being presented in full Technicolor and Dolby Surround Sound.

## Compare Worldviews

Once we have discovered the worldview issues presented in a movie, we can then compare them with a Biblical worldview. An analysis of what Lucas teaches us about God, knowledge, and man turns out to be in stark contrast to Biblical concepts. The Bible explains that God is a personal being who is wholly righteous. Knowledge is gained by engaging our minds, not letting go and trusting our feelings. We are created in God's image—as personal beings—with physical bodies, not just bundles of energy.

It's important to take the analysis of any film full circle. If we don't go through this process to the point of contrasting a Biblical worldview, we walk away from watching a film with the message of the movie remaining in the back of our minds. Now I'm not suggesting that everyone who walks out of a theater after watching *Star Wars* is going to say, "I now believe God is impersonal energy with a dark side." It's not

---

[16] "Of Myth and Men: A Conversation between Bill Moyers and George Lucas on the meaning of the Force and the true theology of *Star Wars*," *Time Magazine* (April 26, 1999), 93.

that blatant. It's more subtle.

It works like this. If you take in a message without analyzing it, that idea gets tucked away until a later time when you hear another similar message. Each time this idea is reinforced, it becomes a stronger and we become more open to it. Then, if we are confronted with a persuasive presentation of that view, we are susceptible to accepting is as truth.

This actually happened to a friend of mine. While taking an abnormal psychology course in college, the professor assigned reading in three New Age texts. My friend had never been taught to discern the difference between Biblical principles and New Age ideas, and was swayed by the mystical rhetoric of his reading assignments and the professor's persuasive reinforcement. The result—he jettisoned his Christian faith and became deeply involved in the New Age movement.

The Apostle Paul warns us to not be captured by deceptive philosophies (Colossians 2:8). Becoming discern-ing viewers of popular worldview expressions as depicted in film puts us in a better position to "take every thought captive to the obedience of Christ" (2 Corinthians 10:5).

## Living in the Real World

Let's look at another example of worldview messages in movies. In the Kung fu science fiction film, *The Matrix*, high-tech hacker Neo is rescued from a computer-generated world (the Matrix) where "machines" have dominated mankind.[17] Neo is brought back to "the real world" by a leader named Morpheus. As part of Neo's training to save humanity from its slavery to Artificial Intelligence, he is introduced to the virtual reality "loading program." Coming to grips with this new understanding, Neo touches a chair and asks, "This isn't real?" To which Morpheus responds, "What

[17] I am not endorsing this R-rated movie, but I include it because many cultural analysts consider this film to be a similar cultural lighting rod for the current generation that *Star Wars* was in the 1970s. The story not only informs, but also reflects the worldview of this generation. If that is the case, Christians would do well to analyze what it is about this film that young people find so fascinating and to use that insight for building a bridge over which to lead them to the truth.

is real? How do you define 'real?' If by 'real' you mean what you can feel, smell, taste, and see, then reality is simply electrical impulses interpreted by your brain."

At this point in the film, entertainment becomes education by answering a key philosophical question, "What is real?" Morpheus' response is a classic definition of naturalism, the idea that nature is the only reality. To see this more clearly, we only need to consider a different possible answer to Neo's question. According to a Christian worldview, for example, nature (what you can touch, smell, taste, and see) is real, and so is the supernatural realm (what cannot be touched, smelled, tasted, or seen), including God. Since the supernatural dimension is left out of Morpheus' definition, the educa-tion that takes place during this scene is of a distinctly non-biblical nature.[18]

But the film goes further. The Wachowski brothers are playing with our minds when it comes to our understanding of the nature of reality. Later in the story, another answer to the philosophical question is given when Neo enters the Oracle's apartment and notices a boy bending a metal spoon using only the power of his mind. The boy tells Neo, "Don't try to bend the spoon. That's impossible. Only understand the truth." Neo asks, "The truth?" The boy responds flatly, "That there is no spoon. Then you'll come to realize that it is not the spoon that bends, but it is only yourself." The boy's statement reflects a classic Hindu/Buddhist conception of reality—what we think we see is an illusionary world. There is no objective world, only the reality of our mental state.

As it turns out, the writers and directors of *The Matrix*, Larry and Andy Wachowski, are candid about their purpose in bringing up this subject, "We think the most important sort of fiction attempts to answer some of the big questions. One of the things that we had talked about when we first

---

[18] I understand that Morpheus framed his answer as a question, and that much could be said about the meaning of his words and the overall worldview found in *The Matrix*. My purpose here is not to explore these larger issues, but simply to point out that a worldview is being expressed and Morpheus does, indeed, give a definition, even if that definition is not fully explained until later in the film.

had the idea of The Matrix was an idea that I believe philosophy and religion and mathematics all try to answer. Which is, a reconciling between a natural world and another world that is perceived by our intellect."[19] In the same interview, the Wachowski brothers admit Zen Buddhism plays a major role in their understanding of religion.

As pop culture commentator Roberto Rivera observes, "You can see Zen's fingerprints everywhere, including the way Morpheus talks to Neo. Instead of answering Neo's questions in a straightforward manner, he insists on [Buddhist-style] koans such as, 'I can only show you the door, you must walk through,' and 'when the time comes, you won't need to dodge the bullet.' Or my favorite, '[the Oracle] didn't lie, she told you exactly what you needed to hear.'"[20]

These are just a few examples, but they help us see the wide array of worldview ideas being presented through major motion pictures.

## Responding to Pop Culture

When defending a biblical worldview in the marketplace of ideas—whether it takes the form of a letter to the editor of the local paper or a face-to-face dialogue with a neighbor—we as Christians must keep two things in mind. According to 2 Timothy 2:24-26, we must present the truth in order set free those who have been captured by deceptive philosophies, and secondly, we are to be kind and gentle in the process. Both our content and our character are important.

How can we use the prevailing culture to help others understand God's truth? Here's an example of what it can look like. In an interview with Bill Moyers, filmmaker George Lucas said, "The conclusion I've come to is that all

[19] Interview with Larry and Andy Wachowski, Nov. 6, 1999. Online article at www.dvdwb.com/matrixevents/wachowski.html.
[20] Roberto Rivera, "So, What is The Matrix? Rethinking Reality." Online article at www.boundless.org/1999/departments/atplay/a0000115.html.
[21] "Of Myth and Men: A Conversation between Bill Moyers and George Lucas on the meaning of the Force and the true theology of *Star Wars*," *Time Magazine* (April 26, 1999), 92.

the religions are true."[21] As it turns out, this conviction is shared in the wider population, even among many Christians. According to George Barna, 48% of those surveyed who claim to be "born again" agree that "Christians, Jews, Muslims, Buddhists, and others all pray to the same God, even though they use different names for that God."[22]

In our rush to be non-judgmental, many Americans may choose to believe "all the religions are true." However, worldview analysis shows that this idea is actually a logical impossibility. The first law of logic, the law of non-contradiction, states specifically what we know intuitively: Two things cannot be the same and different at the same time and in the same way. In other words, something cannot be both true and false at the same time. When we apply the law of non-contradiction to the religions of the world, we find that Hindus, Buddhists, Jews, and Muslims deny what Christians affirm: that Jesus is God incarnate, the third person of the Trinity. Either Jesus is, in fact, a member of the Trinity, or He is not. If He is not, then Christians are wrong about their belief. On the other hand, if Christians are right, then all the other religions are wrong. It cannot be both ways. While it is possible all the religions of the world are false, it is a certainty that they cannot all be true.

So the first step in setting free those who have been captured by this kind of New Age theology is to point out the illogic of the idea. Some may counter that logic and rational thought cannot be trusted, that we must instead trust our feelings. To counter this objection, ask this simple question: "Did you just make a rational statement concerning what can be trusted?" Since the answer is "yes," you can point out their statement is self-refuting—they made a rational statement claiming rational statements cannot be trusted.

Logic cannot be denied. God has designed our minds to operate rationally, so even when someone rejects rationality, we can use it to our benefit to shed light on the reality of clear thinking.[23] Once again, this affirms the reality of

---

[22] George Barna, *What Americans Believe*, (Ventura, CA: Regal Books, 1991), 212.
[23] This statement does not deny the fallen nature of man, and I understand the theological debate as to whether man's intellect is fallen and to what extent. Yet,

the biblical view of God.

When it comes to the nature of God and reality, the Christian worldview offers confidence not found in Cosmic Humanism. Hebrews 11:1 explains that biblical faith is not based on intuition or subjective feelings, but upon "evidence" and "substance." In contrast to the idea that "all roads lead to God," the historical evidence maps out only *one* road leading to God, and it passes through the life, teachings, death, and resurrection of Jesus Christ. *This* we can know with certainty (John 8:31-32; Colossians 2:2; 2 Peter 1:16-18; 1 John 5:20).

## Counter-Cultural Christians

As noted earlier, Paul engaged the philosophers of his day. He understood his role in the battle of the gods as he declared the pagan objects of worship to be mere metal and mortar, a simple man-made image compared with the Creator of heaven and earth and all living things.[24] And this God held the keys to judgment and the resurrection to eternal life.

In our own day, nothing has changed. The followers of Jesus Christ are still facing the self-styled prophets, champions, and philosophers of foreign gods. Whether they worship the impersonal god within or the earth itself, as mortal man they stand arrayed to do battle with the God of the Bible.

Yet the answer to all of life's questions is ultimately found in whose God is real. The main problem today is a theological issue. It always has been and will continue to be. If we as Christians are genuinely concerned about the world we are leaving for our children, grandchildren, and great-grandchildren, then we must engage the culture

we are repeatedly told in the Scriptures to use our minds. In Isaiah 1:18 God tells the people to come and reason together, and in Romans 12:1-2 the Apostle Paul admonishes believers to "renew" their mind. These passages, and others like them, make no sense if our minds are totally devoid of the ability to reach logical conclusions. It is evident that, as part of our God-image, God has built into our minds rational thought that depends on the laws of logic for its very rationality.
[24] See Acts 17:22-34.

now. We can no longer wait in our cities of refuge. Those who seek to destroy us are mounting the walls and have broken down the gates. We must go on the offensive. We must figure out where the enemy of God's righteousness is strongest, and confront the false ideas that bring so much misery, sickness, and sorrow to each generation.

We come armed with the truth, we go in love, and we seek those who will turn their hearts and minds to the Savior. Jesus met the physical needs of those around Him, but he also confronted the false ideas that had shaped his culture. God's truth will ultimately prevail. Yet in the meantime, we are not to hold the fort, but are called to go on the defensive.[25] Understanding how our neighbors think and incorporating the language they know best—as illustrated through popular culture—provides Christians with the means to renew society based on godly principles.

### Resources:

- *Engaging Popular Culture: Worldviews in Movies and Music* is an entertaining and educational multi-media presentation featuring movie clips and song lyrics revealing significant themes that shape our culture. It also discusses biblical guidelines for encouraging Christians to be discerning when it comes to their entertainment choices. Presented by Chuck Edwards, the set contains four DVDs. Visit www.summit.org for more information.

- Brian Godawa, *Hollywood Worldviews* (Downers Grove, IL: InterVarsity, 2002)

[25] In Matthew 28:19-20, Jesus commissioned his followers to "Go ..."

# Pro-Life 101
## Making Abortion Unthinkable

Scott Klusendorf

Dr. Noebel gets it.

To make abortion unthinkable, Christian students need more than sermons that condemn abortion—they need tools of thought to defend their pro-life convictions.

It's easy to see why he's right.

Imagine that you're a senior in high school. Soon you'll be heading off to college or out into the work place—experiencing, maybe for the first time, an environment that is hostile to your Christian faith. How do you handle it? Do you know where you stand on issues like abortion and why? Can you carefully think through your position and graciously present your view using arguments a nonbeliever will accept? To thrive as a pro-life Christian on hostile turf, you need more than Bible verses; you need confidence that the pro-life view is rationally superior to the abortion-choice view that will be rammed down your throat if you are not equipped to engage.

In short, you need a crash course in pro-life apologetics. And that's exactly what students at Summit get.

**THE CASE FOR LIFE**

Pro-life advocates contend that elective abortion unjustly takes the life of a defenseless human being. This simplifies the abortion controversy by focusing public attention on just one question: Is the unborn a member of the human family? If so, killing him or her to benefit others is a serious moral wrong. It treats the distinct human being, with his or her own inherent moral worth, as nothing more than a disposable instrument. Conversely, if the unborn are not human, elective abortion requires no more justification than having a tooth pulled.

Pro-life advocates defend their views using science and philosophy. Scientifically, we argue that from the earliest stages of development, the unborn are distinct, living, and whole human beings. True, they have yet to grow and mature, but they are whole human beings nonetheless. Leading embryology textbooks affirm this.[1]

Philosophically, there is no morally significant difference between the embryo you once were and the adult you are today. As Stephen Schwarz points out, using the acronym SLED, differences of size, level of development, environment, and degree of dependency are not relevant in the way that abortion advocates need them to be.[2]

*Size*: True, embryos are smaller than newborns and adults, but why is that relevant? Do we really want to say that large people are more human than small ones? Men are generally larger than women, but that doesn't mean they deserve more rights. Size doesn't equal value.

*Level of development*: True, embryos and fetuses are less developed than you and I. But again, why is this relevant? Four year-old girls are less developed than 14 year-old ones. Should older children have more rights than their

---

[1] See T.W. Sadler, *Langman's Embryology*, 5th ed. (Philadelphia: W.B. Saunders, 1993), 3; Keith L. Moore, *The Developing Human: Clinically Oriented Embryology* (Toronto: B.C. Decker, 1988), 2; Ronand O'Rahilly and Pabiola Muller, *Human Embryology and Teratology*, 2nd ed. (New York: Wiley-Liss, 1996), 8, 29.

[2] Stephen Schwarz, *The Moral Question of Abortion* (Chicago: Loyola University Press, 1990), 18. SLED test was initially suggested by Schwarz, but is modified and explained here by Scott Klusendorf.

younger siblings? Some people say that self-awareness makes one human. But if that is true, newborns do not qualify as valuable human beings. Remember: Six-week old infants lack the immediate capacity for performing human mental functions, as do the reversibly comatose, the sleeping, and those with Alzheimer's Disease.

_Environment_: Where you are has no bearing on _who_ you are. Does your value change when you cross the street or roll over in bed? If not, how can a journey of eight inches down the birth-canal suddenly change the essential nature of the unborn from non-human to human? If the unborn are not already human, merely changing their location can't make them valuable.

_Degree of Dependency_: If viability makes us valuable human beings, then all those who depend on insulin or kidney medication are not valuable and we may kill them. Conjoined twins who share blood type and bodily systems also have no right to life.

In short, although humans differ immensely with respect to talents, accomplishments, and degrees of development, they are nonetheless equal because they all have the same human nature.

## MAKING ABORTION UNTHINKABLE: FIVE ESSENTIAL TASKS
### Task #1: Clarify the Issue

The abortion controversy is not a debate about privacy or trusting women to make their own responsible choices. For example, does the right to make one's own responsible choices include the rights of parents to abuse children in the privacy of the home? Therefore, if the unborn are human like other children (a point I will argue in a moment), killing them in the name of privacy is a clear moral wrong. Hence, the abortion debate is really about one question: What is the unborn? Is he or she a member of the human family? Everything comes back to that one question.

Let me be clear. I am vigorously "pro-choice" when it comes to women choosing a number of moral goods. I support a woman's right to choose her own health care provider, school, husband, job, religion, and career, to name a few. These are among the many choices that I fully support for the women of our country. But some choices are wrong, like killing innocent human beings simply because they are in the way and cannot defend themselves.

## The Problem: Hidden Assumptions

Advocates of elective abortion generally believe that the unborn are not fully human. But instead of proving this conclusion with facts and arguments, many people simply assume it within the course of their rhetoric. We call this "begging the question" and as Francis J. Beckwith points out, it's a logical fallacy that lurks behind many arguments for abortion.[3] For example, arguing that abortion is justified because a woman has a right to control her own body assumes there is only one body involved—that of the woman. But this is precisely the point abortion advocates try to prove. Hence, they beg the question. Or, take the claim that no one knows when life begins, therefore abortion should remain legal. But arguing that abortion must remain legal through all nine months of pregnancy because life begins at an unknown point assumes that life does not begin until birth—the exact point abortion advocates try to prove. This is a clear case of begging the question.

## The Fix: Trot Out a Toddler

Here's how to clarify things. If you think a particular argument begs the question regarding the status of the unborn, ask yourself if this justification for abortion also works as a justification for killing toddlers. If not, the argument assumes the unborn are not fully human. Now, it may be the case that the unborn are not fully human and abortion is therefore justified. But this must be argued with evidence, not merely assumed by one's rhetoric. Suppose, for example, a friend justifies elective abortion this way: "Women have a right to make their own decisions. What goes on in the bedroom is their business and no one else's."

[3] Francis J. Beckwith, *Politically Correct Death: Answering Arguments for Abortion Rights* (Grand Rapids: Baker Books, 1993) p. 59.

When you hear this, don't panic: trot out a toddler.

> Pro-lifer: You say that privacy is the issue. Pretend that I have a two-year old in front of me (hold out your hand at waist level to illustrate this). May I kill him as long as I do it in the privacy of the bedroom?
>
> Abortion-advocate: That's silly—of course not!
>
> Pro-lifer: Why not?
>
> Abortion-advocate: Because he's a human being.
>
> Pro-lifer: Ah. If the unborn are human, like the toddler, we shouldn't kill them in the name of privacy anymore than we'd kill a toddler for that reason.
>
> Abortion-advocate: You're comparing apples with oranges, two things that are completely unrelated. Look, killing toddlers is one thing. Killing a fetus that is not a human being is quite another.
>
> Pro-Lifer: Ah. That's the issue, isn't it? Are the unborn human beings, like toddlers? That's the one issue that matters.
>
> Abortion-advocate: But many poor women can't afford to raise another child.
>
> Pro-lifer: When human beings get expensive, may we kill them? Getting back to my toddler example, suppose a large family collectively decides to quietly dispose of its three youngest children to help ease the family budget. Would this be okay?
>
> Abortion-advocate: Well, no, but aborting a fetus is not the same as killing children.

Pro-lifer: So, once again, the issue is, What is the unborn? Is the fetus the same as a human being? We can't escape that question, can we?

Notice that you've not yet argued for the humanity of the unborn. You'll do that later. For now, all you are doing is framing the issue around one question: What is the unborn? That is the crux of the debate and it clarifies many of the toughest questions.

Abortion-advocate: But what about a woman who's been raped? Every time she looks at that kid she's going to remember what happened to her. If that's not hardship, what is?

Pro-lifer: I agree that we should provide compassionate care for the victim and it should be the best care possible. That's not at issue here. It's your proposed solution I'm struggling to understand. Tell me, how should a civil society treat innocent human beings that remind us of a painful event? (Pause and let the question sink in.) Is it okay to kill them so we can feel better? Can we kill a toddler who reminds her mother of a rape?

Abortion-advocate: No, I wouldn't do that.
Pro-lifer: I wouldn't either. But again, isn't that because you and I both agree that it's wrong to kill innocent human beings, even if they do remind us of a painful event?

Abortion-advocate: But you don't understand how much this woman has suffered. Put yourself in her shoes. How would you feel?

Pro-lifer: You're right. I don't understand her feelings. How could I? How could anyone? I'm just asking if hardship justifies homicide. Can we, for instance, kill toddlers who remind us of painful events? Again,

my claim here is really quite modest. If the unborn
are members of the human family, like toddlers,
we should not kill them to make someone else feel
better. It's better to suffer evil rather than inflict it.[4]
Personally, I wish I could give a different answer, but
I can't without trashing the principle that my right to
life shouldn't depend on how others feel about me.
In the end, sometimes the right thing to do is not the
easy thing to do. What's right always comes back
to the question, What is the unborn? We can't get
around it.

**Task #2: Make a Case for Life Using Science & Philosophy**

Pro-life advocates defend their claim for the humanity of
the unborn with science and philosophy. That is, they offer
public reasons for their views, not merely religious ones.
Hence, pro-life arguments should not be excluded from the
public square, though some secular critics would like them
dismissed from the abortion debate altogether.

Scientifically, we know that from the earliest stages of
development, the unborn are distinct, living, and whole
human beings.[5] Prior to advocating abortion, former
Planned Parenthood president Dr. Alan Guttmacher was
perplexed that anyone, much less a medical doctor, would
question these basic scientific facts. "This all seems so
simple and evident that it is difficult to picture a time when
it wasn't part of the common knowledge," he wrote in his
book *Life in the Making.*[6]

Ronald Bailey of *Reason* magazine insists that we gain
no real knowledge from these scientific facts. Bailey argues
that embryonic human beings are biologically human only
in the sense that every cell in the body carries the full

[4] Peter Kreeft, *The Unaborted Socrates* (Downers Grove: InterVarsity Press, 1983)
[5] See T.W. Sadler, *Langman's Embryology*, 5th ed. (Philadelphia: W.B. Saunders,
1993), 3; Keith L. Moore, *The Developing Human: Clinically Oriented Embryology*
(Toronto: B.C. Decker, 1988), 2; Ronand O'Rahilly and Pabiola Muller, *Human
Embryology and Teratology,* 2nd ed. (New York: Wiley-Liss, 1996), 8, 29.
[6] A. Guttmacher, *Life in the Making: the Story of Human Procreation* (New York:
Viking Press, 1933), 3

genetic code, meaning that each of our somatic (bodily) cells has as much potential for development as any human embryo. Put simply, Bailey would have us believe that there is no difference in kind between a human embryo and each of our cells.[7]

This is bad biology. Bailey is making the rather elementary mistake of confusing parts with wholes. The difference in kind between each of our cells and a human embryo is clear: An individual cell's functions are subordinated to the survival of the larger organism of which it is merely a part. The human embryo, however, is already a whole human entity. Robert George and Patrick Lee say it well. It makes no sense to say that you were once a sperm or somatic cell. The facts of science make it clear that you were once a human embryo. "Somatic cells are not, and embryonic human beings are, distinct, self-integrating organisms capable of directing their own maturation as members of the human species."[8]

Dr. Maureen Condic, Assistant Professor of Neuro-biology and Anatomy at the University of Utah, points out that embryos are living human beings "precisely because they possess the single defining feature of human life that is lost in the moment of death—the ability to function as a coordinated organism rather than merely as a group of living human cells." Condic explains the important dis-tinction between body parts and whole human embryos:

> The critical difference between a collection of cells and a living organism is the ability of an organism to act in a coordinated manner for the continued health and maintenance of the body as a whole. It is precisely this ability that breaks down at the moment of death, however death might occur. Dead bodies may have plenty of live cells, but their cells no longer function together in a coordinated manner.[9]

[7] Ronald Bailey, "Are Stem Cells Babies? *Reason,* July 11, 2001.
[8] Robert George and Patrick Lee, "Reason, Science, and Stem Cells," *National Review OnLine,* August 20, 2001.
[9] Maureen L. Condic, "Life: Defining the Beginning by the End," *First Things,* May 2003.

From conception forward, human embryos clearly function as whole organisms. "Embryos are not merely collec-
tions of human cells, but living creatures with all the properties that define any organism as distinct from a group of
cells; embryos are capable of growing, maturing, maintaining a physiologic balance between various organ systems,
adapting to changing circumstances, and repairing injury.
Mere groups of human cells do nothing like this under any
circumstances."[10]

*Bad science: Three common objections*

Twinning

Cloning advocates sometimes claim that because an
early embryo may split into twins (up until 14 days after
conception), there is no reason to suppose that it's an individual human being prior to that time. Hence, early embryo
research (prior to day 14) is morally permissible. The flaw
in this argument is easy to spot. How does it follow that
because an entity may split (or even recombine) that it was
not a whole living organism prior to the split? As Patrick
Lee points out, we can take a flatworm, cut it in half, and
get two flatworms.[11] Would advocates of destructive embryo
research argue that prior to the split, there was no distinct
flatworm? I agree that twinning is a mystery. We don't know
if the original entity dies and gives rise to two new organisms or if the original survives and simply engages in some
kind of asexual reproduction. Either way, this does nothing to call into question the existence of a distinct human
organism prior to splitting.

Miscarriage

Cloning advocates cite the high number of miscarriages
as proof that a) embryos are not individual human organisms, and b) destructive research is morally permissible.
Suppose miscarriages are common: How does this fact

[10] Ibid.
[11] Illustration taken from Patrick Lee, *Abortion and Unborn Human Life*
(Washington D.C.: Catholic University Press in America, 1996), 93.

refute the claim that embryos are human beings? Many third-world countries have high infant mortality rates. Are we to conclude that those infants who die early were never whole human beings? Moreover, how does it follow that because nature may *spontaneously* abort an embryo that I may *deliberately* kill one? Admittedly, these miscarriages are tragic events. But as journalist Andrew Sullivan points out, just because earthquakes happen doesn't mean massacres are justified.[12]

Ignorance

Philosopher David Boonin discounts the pro-lifer's claim that the newly conceived zygote is a distinct, living, and whole human organism. How can this be, he argues, when we don't know the precise moment during the conception process at which the new zygotic human being comes into existence?[13] Here Boonin is both right and wrong. True, we don't know exactly when during the conception process that the zygote comes to be. Some embryologists argue that it happens when the sperm penetrates the ovum while others point to syngamy, when the maternal and parental chromosomes cross over and form a diploid set. But as Beckwith points out, although Boonin raises an important *epistemological* question (When do we know that sperm and egg cease to be and a new organism arises?), he's mistaken that his skepticism successfully undermines the pro-lifers strongly supported *ontological* claim that the zygote is a distinct, living, and whole human being: "It may be that one cannot, with confidence, pick out the precise point at which a new being comes into existence between the time at which the sperm initially penetrates the ovum and a complete and living zygote is present. But how does it follow from this acknowledgment of agnosticism that one cannot say that zygote X is a human being?" Boonin, writes Beckwith, "commits the fallacy of the beard: Just because I cannot say when stubble ends and a beard begins, does not mean

---

[12] Andrew Sullivan, "Only Human," *The New Republic*, July 19, 2001.
[13] David Boonin, *A Defense of Abortion* (Cambridge: Cambridge University Press, 2003), 37-40.

I cannot distinguish between a clean-shaven face and a bearded one."[14]

Moreover, Boonin's skepticism cuts both ways and serves to undermine his own case. Abortion advocates typically claim that until a fetus has value-giving properties such as self-awareness, rationality, and sentience, it does not have a right to life. But since when can we know the precise moment that those properties come to be in the fetus? That is, at what *exact* point in the pregnancy does the unborn become rational enough to warrant a right to life? No one can say, though abortion advocates suggest that it's somewhere between 24 weeks to 30 weeks. Despite their lack of certitude on these questions, few abortion advocates are willing to surrender their views. However, if the pro-life position is refuted by a lack of certitude, so is the pro-abortion one.[15]

*Humans without rights?*

Abortion advocates like Mary Anne Warren claim that a "person" is a living entity with feelings, self-awareness, consciousness, and the ability to interact with his or her environment. Because a human fetus has none of these capabilities, it cannot be a person with rights.[16] Warren makes two assumptions here, neither of which she defends. First, she doesn't say why anyone should accept the idea that there can be such a thing as a human being who is not a human person. What's the difference? I've never met a human who wasn't a person, have you? Second, even if Warren is correct about the distinction between human being and human person, she fails to tell us *why* a person must possess self-awareness and consciousness to qualify. In other words, she merely *asserts* that these traits are necessary for personhood, but never says why these alleged value-giving properties are value-giving in the first place.

[14] Francis J. Beckwith, *Defending Life: A Moral and Legal Case Against Abortion Choice* (New York, NY: Cambridge University Press, 2007).
[15] Ibid.
[16] Mary Anne Warren, "On the Moral and Legal Status of Abortion," in *The Problem of Abortion,* Joel Feinberg, ed. (Belmont, CA: Wadsworth, 1984).

In his article "Why Libertarians Should be Pro-Choice Regarding Abortion," philosopher Jan Narveson makes points similar to Warren's.[17] His larger purpose is to tell us who is and is not a subject of libertarian rights. He argues that humans have value (and hence, rights) not in virtue of the kind of thing they are (members of a natural kind or species), but only because of an acquired property, in this case, the immediate capacity to make conscious, deliberate choices. Because fetuses lack this acquired property, they have no rights. A woman's choice to abort, then, does not negatively effect the fetus or deny it fundamental liberties.

But this can't be correct. Again, newborns, like fetuses, lack the immediate capacity to make conscious, deliberate choices, so what's wrong with infanticide?[18] What *principled* reason can Narveson give for saying, "No, you can't do that?" Peter Singer in *Practical Ethics* bites the bullet and says there is none, that arguments used to justify abortion work equally well to justify infanticide.[19] For example, if the immediate capacity for self-awareness makes one valuable as a subject of rights and newborns, like fetuses, lack that immediate capacity, it follows that fetuses and newborns are both disqualified. You can't draw an arbitrary line at birth that spares newborns. Hence, infanticide, like abortion, is morally permissible.

Abraham Lincoln raised a similar point with slavery, noting that any argument used to disqualify blacks as possessing rights applies equally to disqualify many whites.

> You say 'A' is white and 'B' is black. It is color, then: the lighter having the right to enslave the darker? Take care. By this rule, you are a slave to the first man you meet with a fairer skin than your own.

---

[17] Article is posted on Narveson's website at http://www.arts.uwaterloo.ca/~jnarveso/abortion.htm

[18] Conor Liston and Jerome Kagan, "Brain Development: Memory Enhancement in Early Childhood," *Nature* 419, 896 (2002). See also Ronand O'Rahilly and Pabiola Muller, *Human Embryology and Teratology,* 2nd ed. (New York: Wiley-Liss, 1996), 8.

[19] Peter Singer, *Practical Ethics* (Cambridge, UK: Cambridge University Press, 1997), 169-171.

You do not mean color exactly—You mean the whites are intellectually the superiors of the blacks, and therefore have the right to enslave them? Take care again: By this rule you are to be a slave to the first man you meet with an intellect superior to your own.

But you say it is a question of interest, and, if you can make it your interest, you have the right to enslave another. Very well. And if he can make it his interest, he has the right to enslave you.[20]

In short, if humans have value only because of some acquired property like skin color or self-consciousness and not in virtue of the kind of thing they are, then it follows that since these acquired properties come in varying degrees, basic human rights come in varying degrees. Do we really want to say that those with more self-consciousness are more human (and valuable) than those with less? As Lee and George point out, this relegates the proposition that all men are created equal to the ash heap of history.[21] Philosophically, it's far more reasonable to argue that although humans differ immensely with respect to talents, accomplishments, and degrees of development, they are equal because they share a common human nature. Humans have value simply because they are human, not because of some acquired trait that they gain or lose during their lifetimes. If you deny this, it's difficult to say why objective human rights apply to anyone.

*Natural rights versus legal rights*

Put differently, pro-life advocates, echoing Lincoln, argue that we must distinguish between *natural* rights and *legal* ones. Natural rights are those rights that you have simply because you are human. The are grounded in your

---

[20] *The Collected Works of Abraham Lincoln*, vol. II (Rutgers University Press, 1953), 222.
[21] Robert P. George, "Cloning Addendum," *National Review OnLine*, July 15, 2002; Patrick Lee, "Human Embryos and Fetuses are Subjects of Rights." (See note #2 above.)

human nature and you have them from the moment you begin to exist.[22] For example, you have a natural right not to be harmed without justification and a natural right not to be convicted of a crime without a fair trial. Government does not grant these basic rights. Rather, government's role is to protect them. In contrast, legal (or positive) rights are those rights you can only acquire through accomplishment or maturity. These rights originate from the government and include the right to vote at your eighteenth birthday and to drive on your sixteenth. But your natural right to live was there all along. It comes to be when you come to be.

To cash this out further, I do not have a legal (positive) right to vote in the next Canadian election for the simple reason that I am not a Canadian citizen. But just because I lack the right to vote in Canada does not mean I lack the right to basic protections whenever I visit that country. Likewise, just because a fetus may not have the positive right to drive a car or vote in the next election does not mean he lacks the *natural* right not to be harmed without justification. Elective abortion unjustly robs the unborn of his or her natural right to life, as Hadley Arkes explains:

> No one would suggest that a fetus could have a claim to fill the Chair of Logic at one of our universities; and we would not wish quite yet to seeks its advice on anything important; and we should probably not regard him as eligible to vote in any state other than Massachusetts. All of these rights and privileges would be inappropriate to the condition or attributes of the fetus. But nothing that renders him unqualified for these special rights would diminish in any way the most elementary right that could be claimed for any human being, or even for an animal: the right not to be killed without the rendering of reasons that

[22] Hadley Arkes, *Natural Rights and the Right to Choose* (Cambridge: Cambridge University Press, 2002), 13-14.
[23] Hadley Arkes, *First Things: An Inquiry into the First Principles of Morals and Justice* (Princeton: Princeton University Press, 1986), 366.

satisfy the strict standards of "justification."[23]

## Do women have a natural right to abort?

Secular liberals insist that abortion is a fundamental human right the State should not infringe upon. In reply, I borrow a question from Hadley Arkes and ask, "Where did that right to an abortion come from?" In other words, is it a natural right that springs from our nature as human beings or is it a positive (legal) right granted by government? If the latter, the abortion advocate cannot really complain that she is wronged if the State does not permit her to abort. After all, the same government that grants rights can take them away. On the other hand, if the right to an abortion is a natural right—a right one has in virtue of being human— then the abortion-advocate had that right from the moment she came to be, that is, from conception![24] Thus, we are left with this amusing paradox: According to the logic of many abortion-advocates, unborn women do not have a right to life while in the womb, but they do have a right to an abortion. Absurd! In short, liberals cannot tell us where rights come from or why anyone should have them. As Arkes points out, they have talked themselves out of the very natural rights upon which their freedoms are built.

## Inclusive or exclusive?

Sadly, opponents of the pro-life view believe that human beings that are in the wrong location or have the wrong level of development do not deserve the protection of law. They assert, without justification, the belief that strong and independent people deserve the protection of law while small and dependent people do not. This view is elitist and exclusive. It violates the principle that once made political liberalism great: a basic commitment to protect the most vulnerable members of the human community.

We can do better than that. In the past, we used to discriminate on the basis of skin color and gender, but now,

[24] Hadley Arkes develops this paradox in detail in *Natural Rights and the Right to Choose*. I owe the observation to his excellent analysis.

with elective abortion, we discriminate on the basis of size, level of development, location, and degree of dependency. We've simply swapped one form of bigotry for another.

In sharp contrast, the position I have defended is that no human being, regardless of size, level of development, race, gender, or place of residence should be excluded from the moral community of human persons. In other words, the pro-life view of humanity is inclusive, indeed wide open, to all, especially those that are small, vulnerable, and defenseless.[25]

### Task #3: Make Abortion-Choicers Defend Their Claims

Not long ago, an abortion-choice blogger who goes by the name "Dadahead" (hereafter, DH) took me to task on his blogspot, alleging that my pro-life metaphysics were deeply suspect—and largely undefended.[26] Given the seriousness of the charge, I was eager to see how DH defended his own metaphysical claims.

Throughout his post, DH chides pro-lifers for not establishing that the human fetus is a person. "They've given us no reason why we should accept this metaphysic," he writes. "Like most metaphysics, it is basically a mixture of nonsensical and unsupported claims."

Like his own unsupported claims? Fact is, nowhere in his own essay does DH defend his own metaphysical assumption that there can be such a thing as a human being that is not a person. Why should anyone believe that? Nor does he defend his claim that personhood is an accidental property rather than something intrinsic to the human subject. I wonder: Other than the embryos and fetuses he'd like to arbitrarily exclude, has he ever met a human non-person? Have any of us? That's the problem with so-called personhood arguments: They're *ad hoc*, arbitrary, and prove too much. For example, abortion-choicers Mary Ann Warren, Michael Tooley, and Peter Singer all concede that any argument used to disqualify the fetus as a

---

[25] I'm indebted to Frank Beckwith for the wording of this paragraph.
[26] http://dadahead.blogspot.com/2005/07/wingnut-metaphysics.html

person works equally well to disqualify the newborn.

Simply put, there is no way to avoid the metaphysics involved in the abortion dispute, though DH would like us to think he's above it all. Both views—pro-life and abortion-choice—are asking the exact same question: What makes humans valuable in the first place? Metaphysical neutrality on that question is not a workable option.

Indeed, as Beckwith explains, the nature of the abortion debate is such that all positions on abortion presuppose a metaphysical view of human value, and for this reason, the pro-choice position is not entitled to a privileged philosophical standing in our legal framework.[27] At issue is not which view of abortion has metaphysical underpinnings and which does not, but which metaphysical view of human value is correct—pro-life or abortion-choice?

The pro-life view is that humans are intrinsically valuable in virtue of the kind of thing they are. True, they differ immensely with respect to talents, accomplishments, and degrees of development, but they are nonetheless equal because they all have the same human nature. Their right to life comes to be when they come to be (conception). DH's own abortion-choice view is that humans have value (and hence, rights) not in virtue of the kind of thing they are, but only because of an acquired property such as self-consciousness or emotional awareness. Because the early fetus lacks the immediate capacity to exercise these properties, it is not a person with rights. Notice that DH is doing the abstract work of metaphysics. That is, he is using philosophical reflection to advance a disputed view of human persons—namely, the idea that humans are valuable by function, not nature. Hence, DH's attempt to disqualify the pro-life view from public policy based on its alleged metaphysical underpinnings works equally well to disqualify his own view.

Here's the question he ought to ponder: Which metaphysical worldview better explains human dignity and human equality? Is it the one that grounds human value

---

[27] Francis J. Beckwith, "Law, Religion, and the Metaphysics of Abortion: A Reply to Simmons." *Journal of Church and State* 43.1 (Winter 2001): 19-33.

in our common human nature or the one that grounds it
in accidental traits that come and go within the course of
one's life-span? That's the real issue at stake with abortion and so far, DH has given us little reason to suppose
that his own metaphysics can explain why *anything* should
have a right to life. Indeed, when it comes to human beings,
he never tells us why certain value-giving properties are
value-giving in the first place. Sure, he eventually appeals
to consciousness, but isn't that just question-begging, since
the issue is whether one has a right to life even if one is not
conscious?

As I've said in many previous posts, I don't think abortion advocates like DH can account for basic human equality. Robert George is correct: If humans have value only
because of some acquired property like consciousness
or self-awareness and not in virtue of the kind of thing
they are, then it follows that since these acquired properties come in varying degrees, basic human rights come in
varying degrees. Do we really want to say that those with
more self-consciousness are more human (and more valuable) than those with less?[28] As stated earlier, it's far more
reasonable to argue that although humans differ in terms
of their functional abilities, they are nonetheless equal
because they share a common human nature. Humans
have value simply because they are human. All other explanations fail to account for human equality and dignity.

I suppose DH could reply that pro-lifers are simply
begging the question by starting from our intuitions that
human beings have intrinsic (or transcendent) value simply
because they are human. But doesn't this objection cut
both ways? While pro-lifers assume that human value is
intrinsic, DH assumes that it's an acquired property—a
moral claim for which he provides no compelling argument.
He seems to just assume it. Yes, every philosophical argument needs a starting point and ours is the self-evident
truth that humans by nature are subjects with rights. We're
in good company: Thomas Jefferson and the rest of the
American Founders built our constitutional republic on the

───────────────

[28] George, "Cloning Addendum," ibid.

exact same premise. So my question for DH is simply this: Why is your starting point more persuasive than ours? Of course, he's free to deny our self-evident claim all he wants, but only at a terrible cost. Without it, he'll have great difficulty explaining why natural human rights—including a basic right to have an abortion—exist for anyone.

Toward the end of his post, DH finally blurts out what's really bugging him:

> So what the anti-choice movement is trying to do is impose the normative implications of their pet metaphysical theory (highly influenced by their pet religious ideology) on the rest of society, without giving us any reason to believe that their theory is, you know, true.

Question: Is DH saying it's wrong for pro-lifers to do that? If so, who is he to impose *that* "pet" rule on us without first giving us reasons why it's, you know, true? And if he's not saying we're wrong to impose our views, then why is he correcting us with his own metaphysical presupposition—one he nowhere defends—which essentially says religious truth claims don't count as real knowledge? (I don't think pro-lifers are wrongly imposing their views—a point I made in an earlier post.)

Moreover, DH is just plain wrong that pro-life advocates provide no defense for their metaphysics. Sure they do. The problem is DH takes no time to actually engage pro-life arguments; he simply dismisses them as "religious ideology." However, his dismissal does not constitute an argument and it ignores the sophisticated reasons pro-life philosophers use to support their case. Even at the popular level, DH can't bring himself to engage a basic pro-life argument—one based on science and philosophy. To review, pro-lifers contend that from the earliest stages of development the unborn are distinct, living, and whole human beings. True, they have yet to grow and mature, but they are whole human beings nonetheless. Leading embryology textbooks affirm this. Philosophically, pro-lifers agree with Schwarz that there is no morally significant difference between the embryo you once were and the adult you are today. Differences of size, development, and location are not relevant in the way that abortion advocates need them to be. For example, everyone agrees that embryos are small—perhaps smaller than the dot at the end of this sentence. But since when do rights depend on how large we are? Men are generally larger than women, but that hardly means they deserve more rights. Size does not equal value. Pro-lifers don't need Scripture to tell them these things. There are truths even atheists and secular libertarians can, and sometimes do, recognize.[29] Yet nowhere in his post does DH present a principled argument explaining why pro-lifers are mistaken on these points.

True, DH is correct to say that pro-life metaphysics are "endorsed by some of the world's most popular religious institutions." Ah, but once again, the sword cuts both ways. According to the Religious Coalition for Reproductive Choice, the vast majority of religious denominations—including The Presbyterian Church USA, United Methodists, United Church of Christ, Evangelical Lutheran Church in America, Episcopal, Unitarian Universalist, and most Jews—hold the exact same metaphysical view DH does concerning the status of the unborn—namely, that embryos and fetuses are not valuable human beings. Many of these groups specifically cite Scripture to make the case that abortion should remain legal through all nine months of pregnancy. (I've written elsewhere on why this appeal to Scripture is flawed.) Put simply, if the pro-life view is suspect because of it's alleged connection to the metaphysics of religion, so is the pro-abortion one.

## Task #4: Clarify Misstatements of Fact

*Illegal abortion*

No sooner did justice Sandra Day O'Connor announce

---

[29] See, for example, Godless Pro-lifers at http://godlessprolifers.org/ and Libertarians for Life at http://l4l.org/

her retirement when the National Organization for Women published this on its homepage: "These are the faces of women who died because they could not obtain safe and legal abortions. If *Roe v. Wade* is overturned, these pictures could include your daughter, sister, mother, best friend, granddaughter. Don't let George W. Bush and the U.S. Senate put another anti-abortion justice on the Supreme Court."[30]

The argument goes like this: If laws are passed to protect the unborn, women will once again be forced to procure dangerous illegal abortions. Besides, we are told, the law can't stop all abortions, so why not keep the practice legal?

Although the argument has strong emotional appeal, it fails logically for several reasons. First, it begs the question. That is, unless you begin with the assumption that the unborn are not human, you are making the highly questionable claim that because some people will die attempting to kill others, the state should make it safe and legal for them to do so. Why should the law be faulted for making it tougher for one human being to take the life of another completely innocent one? Should we legalize bank robbery so it is safer for felons? As abortion advocate Mary Anne Warren points out, "The fact that restricting access to abortion has tragic side effects does not, in itself, show that the restrictions are unjustified, since murder is wrong regardless of the consequences of forbidding it." Again, the issue isn't safety. The issue is the status of the unborn. (You should always start and end with that question.)

Second, the objection that the law cannot stop all abortions is silly. Laws cannot stop all cases of rape—should we legalize rape? The fact is that laws against abortion, like laws against rape, drastically reduce its occurrence. A sophisticated analysis by Syska, Hilgers, and O'Hare indicates that prior to *Roe v. Wade* (1973), there were at most 210,000 illegal abortions per year while more conserva-

[30] http://www.now.org/press/07-05/07-01b.html
[31] Barbara J. Syska, Thomas W. Hilgers, M.D., and Dennis O'Hare, "An Objective Model for Estimating Criminal Abortions and Its Implications for Public Policy," in *New Perspectives on Human Abortion*, ed. Thomas Hilgers, M.D., Dennis J. Horan, and David Mall (Frederick, MD: University Publications of America, 1981), 78.

tive estimates suggest a mean of 98,000 per year.[31] Within eight years of legalization, abortion totals jumped to over 1.3 million annually! True, no law can stop ALL illegal behavior, but that's not the point. At issue is the status of the unborn: Are they human beings? If so, we should legally protect them as we would any other group unjustly harmed.

Third, women aren't forced to have illegal abortions—they choose to have them. Yes, pro-lifers mourn the loss of any woman who dies needlessly, but I refuse to accept the premise that women MUST seek illegal abortions. Greg Koukl writes, "A woman is no more forced into the back alley when abortion is outlawed than a young man is forced to rob banks because the state won't put him on welfare. Both have other options."[32]

Finally, the claim that thousands died annually from back-alley abortions prior to 1973—when Roe. v. Wade legalized abortion in the U.S.—is just plain false. Dr. Mary Calderone, former medical director for Planned Parenthood, wrote in 1960 that illegal abortions were performed safely by physicians in good standing in their communities. True, this doesn't prove no woman will ever die from an illegal abortion, but it does put to rest NOW's claim of high mortality rates for the years prior to legalization. Here's Calderone's quote in its full context:

> Fact No. 3—Abortion is no longer a dangerous procedure. This applies not just to therapeutic abortions as performed in hospitals but also to so-called illegal abortions as done by physicians. In 1957 there were only 260 deaths in the whole country attributed to abortions of any kind. In New York City in 1921 there were 144 abortion deaths, in 1951 there were only 15; and, while the abortion death rate was going down so strikingly in that 30 year period, we know what happened to the population and the birth rate. Two corollary factors must be mentioned here: first,

32 Greg Koukl, "I'm Pro-Choice" at http://www.str.org/site/News2?page=NewsArt icle&id=5313.

chemotherapy and antibiotics have come in, benefiting all surgical procedures as well as abortion. Second, and even more important, the conference estimated that 90 per cent of all illegal abortions are presently being done by physicians. Call them what you will, abortionists or anything else, they are still physicians, trained as such; and many of them are in good standing in their communities. They must do a pretty good job if the death rate is as low as it is. Whatever trouble arises usually comes after self-induced abortions, which comprise approximately 8 percent, or with the very small percentage that go to some kind of non-medical abortionist. Another corollary fact: physicians of impeccable standing are referring their patients for these illegal abortions to the colleagues whom they know are willing to perform them, or they are sending their patients to certain sources outside of this country where abortion is performed under excellent medical conditions. The acceptance of these facts was such that one outstanding gynecologist at the conference declared: "From the ethical standpoint, I see no difference between recommending an abortion and performing it. The moral responsibility is equal." So remember fact number three; abortion, whether therapeutic or illegal, is in the main no longer dangerous, because it is being done well by physicians.[33]

Meanwhile, the Centers for Disease Control report that 39 women died from illegal abortion in 1972, the year prior to legalization.[34] Admittedly, this number is understated, but as abortion-choice ethicist Daniel Callahan points out, the claim of 5,000 to 10,000 deaths per year is out of the question. Callahan's own survey of available data suggests a more reasonable figure of 500 deaths annually.

[33] Mary S. Calderone, "Illegal Abortion as a Public Health Problem," *American Journal of Public Health*, July 1960.
[34] *Morbidity and Mortality Weekly Report*, Centers for Disease Control Surveillance Summaries, 9/4/92: 33.

But again, the argument from illegal abortions only has force if abortion-choice critics assume that the unborn are not human beings. Remember: If you think a particular argument begs the question regarding the status of the unborn, simply ask if this justification for abortion also works as a justification for killing toddlers or other humans. If not, the argument assumes the unborn are not fully human. Again, it may be the case that the unborn are not fully human and abortion is therefore justified. But this must be argued with evidence, not assumed with rhetoric.

*Rape*

Earlier, I explained why appeals to rape (as a justification for abortion) are question-begging—that is, they assume that the unborn are not human. But the appeal to rape is flawed in another way that has nothing to do with one's attitude toward women or the morality of abortion. It's flawed because it is not entirely truthful.

Here's why. The "pro-choice" position is not that abortion should be legal only when a woman is raped, but that abortion is a fundamental right she can exercise for any reason she wants during all nine months of pregnancy. Instead of defending this position with facts and arguments, many disguise it with an emotional appeal to rape. But this will not make their case. The argument from rape, if successful at all, would only justify abortion in cases of sexual assault, not for any reason the woman deems fit. In fact, arguing for abortion-on-demand from the hard case of rape is like trying to argue for the elimination of all traffic laws because a person might break one rushing a loved one to the hospital.[35] Proving an exception does not prove a rule.

To expose their smokescreen, I ask abortion advocates the following question: "Okay, I'm going to grant for the sake of discussion that we keep abortion legal in cases of rape. Will you join me in supporting legal restrictions on abortions done for convenience, which, as your

---

[35] Beckwith uses this example in *Politically Correct Death,* 69.

studies show, make up the overwhelming percentage of abortions?"[36]

The answer is almost always no, to which I reply, "Then why did you bring rape up except to mislead me into thinking you support abortion only in the hard cases?"

Again, if abortion-advocates think that abortion should be a legal choice for all nine months of pregnancy for any reason whatsoever, including sex-selection and convenience, they should defend that view with facts and arguments. Exploiting the tragedy of rape victims is intellectually dishonest.

## Task #5: Give them something to Think About

True, secular students are skeptical of anything related to abortion that smacks of religion. No problem—in this chapter, I've shown how to give them biblical truth without chapter and verse. To review, we've argued *scientifically* that from the earliest stages of development, the unborn are distinct, living, and whole human beings. True, they have yet to grow and mature, but they are whole human beings nonetheless. Leading embryology textbooks affirm this.

Philosophically, we've shown there is no morally significant difference between the embryo you once were and the adult you are today. Differences of size and development are not relevant in the way that abortion advocates need them to be. In short, although humans differ immensely with respect to talents, accomplishments, and degrees of development, they are nonetheless equal because they share a common human nature. When I made these same points at the University of North Carolina Law School last October, a female professor responded (in front of her students): "I did not come to this talk with the same pro-life views you hold. In fact, I came here today expecting an emotionally charged religious presentation. Instead, you gave one of the most

---

[36] Dr. Warren Hern, America's leading abortionist, writes, "The impression of clinical staff is that all but a few women seek abortions for reasons that can broadly be defined as socioeconomic, and many cite strictly economic reasons." Warren Hern, *Abortion Practice* (Boulder, CO: Alpenglo Graphics, 1990), 10, 39.

compelling arguments I have ever heard. Thank you." True, she didn't fall on her knees and confess Christ on the spot. But now she's begun wrestling with biblical truth. To use a baseball example provided by Greg Koukl, you don't have to hit a home run with every conversation. Sometimes just getting on base is enough. And you'll certainly do just that whenever you clarify the moral logic of the pro-life view.

Finally, it's amazing how people will tolerate a strong pro-life presentation if you make your case graciously and incisively. Kindness goes a long way and often pays off with changed lives. Consider this email from fifteen-year-old Brittany, received after I spoke to an assembly of 1,000 high school students in Baltimore:

> *Dear Scott,*
> *Yesterday you came and talked to my high school about pro-life. It made a big difference on how I thought about abortion. I was totally for abortion and I thought that pro-life was just plain stupid. I have totally changed my mind after I listened to the pro-life point of view. Upon watching the short video clip of aborted fetuses, I felt my stomach turn and I thought, "How could anybody do this? How could anyone be so cruel and self absorbed as to kill an unborn baby who doesn't have a say in that decision?" Then I thought, "Oh my gosh, I think that!" I was totally ashamed at how selfish I had been. Before the assembly, I didn't want to listen to what you had to say. I was going to nap during your speech...until I saw that video. Now, I am totally changed forever. Keep doing what you do!*

Always stress grace. Give hope to those wounded by abortion. Ask God to fill your heart with love for students struggling to know right from wrong. Then speak the truth in love. Your listeners can take it.

# A Christian View
# of Government[1]

H. Wayne House

*State absolutism and its spirit of titanic government
now seem rampant on every continent.*[2]

Carl F.H. Henry, 1964

*The God of Abraham has withdrawn his conscious
Presence from us and another god whom our fathers
knew not is making himself at home among us. This
god **we** have made[3] and because we have made him,
we can understand him; because we have created
him, he can never surprise us, never overwhelm us
nor astonish us, nor transcend us.*[4]

A.W. Tozer

---

[1] Portions of this chapter are found in the author's essays "The Christian's Duty of Civil Disobedience to the Government," in *The Christian and American Law* (Grand Rapids: Kregel Publications, 1998), 142-152; and *Christian Ministries and the Law: What Church and Para-Church Leaders Should Know* (Grand Rapids: Kregel Publications, 1999), 34-37.

[2] Carl F.H. Henry, *Aspects of Christian Social Ethics* (Grand Rapids: Eerdmans, 1964), 12.

[3] Cf. Hab 1:5-11

[4] A.W. Tozer, *The Knowledge of the Holy* (New York: HarperSanFrancisco, 1978).

In order to set forth a Christian view of government, I must first make clear that I am proposing one understanding of Christian thought on government, rather than *the* Christian view. There are fine Christian scholars who would differ partly or wholly with my perspective. Second, to understand a Christian perspective of government we must understand how government relates to the rule of God, its basis and form, how this differs from a pagan view of government, and also how Christians have viewed the relationship between the church and the state over the centuries. Third, we will look at how Scripture presents governmental authority, its obligations and its limits. Last of all, we will give biblical teaching on the responsibilities of Christians to the government, personally and politically.

## THE RELATIONSHIP OF GOD TO GOVERNMENT
### Christian View of Government

*The Basis of Government Authority is Divine Ordination*

All governments rule by force, maintaining their power over those under the control of the governing forces by what is known as "police power." The matter of rule and power, however, are different from whether the governmental action is legitimate, that is, whether it has a right or authority to rule. This issue becomes the matter of utmost importance for one wanting to discover a Christian view of government. For example, Christians acknowledge the sovereign rule of God in the world, while the Constitution of the United States says that government derives its just power from the governed and states at the beginning of our founding compact the words WE THE PEOPLE. Whether the Christian should recognize this form of government is important as followers of Jesus seek to interact with their world.

Peter Gilchrist has argued that "It is...inconsistent with the Scripture to consider that human government derives its legitimate authority ultimately from a 'social compact,' or from 'the consent of the governed,' or even 'the will of the majority."[5] Gilchrist is correct if one requires specific scriptural declarations for a representative government as the United States, or other forms of democratic rule found in many countries of the globe. May we, though, find within Scripture and the natural law the basis for one—or differing—forms of acceptable government that may give legitimacy to republics, democracies, or even autocracies? May one form a poliology,[6] a theology of the state, from the pages of the Bible, if not in specific text, then, at least, within the principles of authority and jurisdiction authored by God within the natural realm?

I believe that the Scripture gives to us a brief insight to the beginning of human government, the formation and operation of the government of Israel and pagan nations around Israel, and glimpses into God's perspective on the duty of believers to governmental authority in the pages of the New Testament. These provide assistance in knowing how governments should function under God's rule, and how Christians should relate to these governments while continuing to submit to the lordship of Jesus.

*Alternative Forms of Human Government May Be Legitimate*

The governing of governmental rulers is by divine authority (to be developed later in this chapter); human government is then a divinely ordained institution. It is, however, precisely because the state is a *divine* institution (that is, ordained by God) that its authority is not absolute. Biblically speaking, government does not derive its authority from the consent of those it governs, in spite of what documents may say. A constitutional democracy, such as the United States, is a preferable form of government in most instances, but one must realize that it is God who gives government legitimacy. That a government does not *need* to be democratic in nature to be divinely ordained may

---

[5] Peter R. Gilchrist, "Government," *The International Standard Bible Encyclopedia*, ed. C.W. Bromiley (Grand Rapids: Eerdmans, 1982), 545.
[6] This is a term I have coined, speaking of the Greek term *polis*, meaning state or city, and *logos*, word or study.

be seen in the Roman state ("an antidemocratic theory of power"[7]) that existed when Paul penned Romans 13. For a person who has only known forms of democratic government, there appears to be no legitimate alternative, but one must remember that even democratic governments can bring forms of tyranny, self-interest, and other evil acts while a constitutional monarchy, or even benevolent dictatorships may bring considerable peace and righteousness—as was known in the days of the good kings of Judah and Israel, a constitutional monarchy such as the kingdom of Tonga (with which I have had personal experience)—not to mention the future reign of Jesus the Messiah on earth.

## The Government is a Servant of God

Scripture clearly implies that the state is God's minister and has no inherent power or authority. The state is a servant, not a sovereign. It is a minister of God for human benefit. When government fails to acknowledge its proper source of authority and seeks to become a law unto itself it makes man the absolute standard of right and wrong and so relativizes law.[8]

Weak governments have two possible results. Either they allow lawless people to set their own standards of conduct, bringing about anarchy, or they react to societal chaos or crisis by erupting into full-blown totalitarianism, exercising complete control over a country's social life.

## Satan is Neither the Creator nor Sustainer of Government

Scripture is clear that Satan influences government and that he rules the sinful world system (John 12:31; Daniel 8:16). It is equally true that "the Most High is sovereign over the kingdoms of men and gives them to anyone he wishes"

---

[7] Wayne Boulton, "The Riddle of Romans 13," *The Christian Century,* Vol 93, No. 28, (Sept. 15, 1976): 760.

[8] Cf the words of Thomas Jefferson on walls of the Jefferson Memorial. "And can the liberties of a nation be thought secure when we have removed their only firm basis, a conviction in the minds of the people that these liberties are of the gift of God–that they are not to be violated but with His wrath?" Thomas Jefferson, 1783.

(Daniel 4:17). Proverbs 21:1 tells us that "the king's heart is in the hand of the Lord; he directs it like a watercourse wherever he pleases."

So then, though I do not question that Satan influences unregenerate political leaders and societies, I do deny that the devil has authority apart from that specifically allowed to him by God. God allows Satan to exert authority only as far as it furthers His plans. Our God does not tremble on His heavenly throne, wringing His "hands" and worrying about what Satan will do next. It is the Lord Jesus Christ who controls the events and course of history, not Satan.

Since Satan does influence ungodly men and nations, Christians should seek to become a leavening, countervailing influence in government and society.[9] For the Christian, there can be no dividing line between "sacred" and "secular." Jesus Christ is Lord of all. Christians should proclaim this truth and live in light of it.

## Pagan View of Government

*Rulers are Divine Rather than Under God*

The Jewish philosopher Philo records a meeting between a delegation of Alexandrian Jews and the Roman Emperor, Gaius. The Jews denied charges that they failed to give thanksgiving offerings for the emperor's recovery during an illness early in his reign. They swore that they often sacrificed on Gaius' behalf, claiming that they "had offered twice daily for the emperor since the time of Augustus." The emperor replied, "What is the use of that? You offered sacrifices for me, it is true; but you offered none *to* me." He then called them "pitiable fools" because they did not recognize his "divine nature."[10]

The story of Gaius and the Jews illustrates a view of the state that has profoundly influenced events in the twentieth century. In ideologies like Nazism and Marxism, the state

---

[9] R.D. Culver, *Toward a Biblical View of Civil Government* (Chicago: Moody Press, 1974), 57.
[10] F.F. Bruce, *New Testament History* (Garden City: Doubleday & Co., 1980), 253.

embodies all virtue and truth, with references to God or a god only used to meet some end of the state's goals. These systems deny the reality of a personal-infinite God; thus humanity in the form of the state becomes the center of all things. The individual's worth is negligible compared to the value of the mass of humanity represented by the state.

It is ironic that Marxist-Leninist theory predicts the state will wither away. Once a truly communist society evolves, the theory goes, no coercive government is needed. Everyone will share in the products of everyone's toil, and there will be plenty and prosperity for all.[11] Holding such beliefs, Marxists fail to understand the basic nature of fallen man.

Friederich Georg Hegel, an important influence on Karl Marx, wrote that the state is "god walking on earth."[12] State-worship generally accompanies "emperor"-worship. Even as the state embodies its people, so a revered and emulated leader (or group of leaders) embodies the state. Lenin, Stalin, Hitler, Mao tse Tung, Castro, and Quddafi all emerged as unquestioned leaders, the will of the people incarnate.

## The Government Deserves the Allegiance Owed Only to God

No matter in which state functions the government abandons its divine commission—whether it acknowledges the existence of the true God or not—it usurps God's authority and denies Him dominion in the life of a nation. Accordingly, the leaders of such a government do not answer any longer to God, but proclaim themselves as lords of the citizenry. This state of affairs is true in reference to American government. As the United States drifts from its Judeo-Christian heritage, and as the government becomes ever more pervasive in American life, it could ultimately insist on full allegiance from the people, an allegiance belonging only to God. American government seems to have

[11] G.M. Carter, *The Government of the Soviet Union* (New York: Harcourt, Brace, Jovanovich, 1972), 6.

[12] Alfred Meyer, *Communism* (New York: Random House, 1967), 22.

begun viewing itself as master, not servant. Agencies—without any reference to God's laws—are seeking to regulate more and more spheres of public and private life, files of data on its citizens are expanding, and bureaucracy increasingly asserts its authority. While these trends may have begun with good intentions, they reflect a dangerous tendency to deny deity to the Creator and claim it for Uncle Sam.

## Christian Theories on Church and State Relationships

In historical Christian thought, there are four broad perspectives on how the government and the church relate to one another. Of these four models, three recognize the authority of God over government and the duties of the Christian to have an impact on government, though the extent of this Christian involvement varies in each view. However, the the final view, Anabaptism (in its more radical forms), goes so far as to raise questions about God's creation of and control over the state.

### Roman Catholic

Catholic theologians have generally recognized a difference between the Church and the State—the two kingdoms (to use Luther's terminology)—but have usually viewed the Church as the greater of the two. The reasoning for the Church as greater than the state largely rests on the perspective of Augustine. He argued for the superiority of the Church, since it is eternal and the state is temporal, and because the Church must answer to God for the conduct of the state.

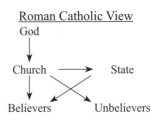

Roman Catholic View

## Lutheran

Luther viewed the State as being responsible to restrain evil. Believers belong to both kingdoms, the Church and the State, and have responsibilities to each. Luther believed that believers relate to the first kingdom, the Church, by faith, and to the second kingdom, the State, by reason.

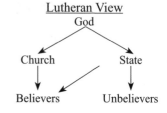

Luther did not believe that Christians had the right to use the State to promote Christianity. Christians who were in government should use Christian principles in government only inasmuch as the principles could also be justified by reason. Even a prudent but evil ruler is to be preferred to an imprudent but virtuous ruler, since the latter may bring ruin to the State while the former at least may resist evil.

## Calvinistic or Reformed

Calvin believed that the State's authority came directly from God and not through the Church. The Christian is a citizen of both kingdoms, being under the authority of both the State and the Church.

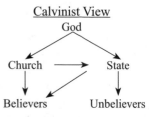

The State's authority, however, is limited to the areas of authority given to it by God; if the State steps beyond its authority, its acts are without legitimacy. In such a case, believers owe a higher duty to God than to the State and should resist. The Church is to affect the world by its biblical principles and, Calvin reasoned, may properly use the vehicle of the State to accomplish this purpose.

*Anabaptist*

Many of the early Anabaptists (and some of their descendants) believed that the State was part of the evil world system ruled by Satan. Thus Christians were to do everything possible to remove themselves from it and its affairs; this included not permitting Anabaptist members to vote, hold public office, serve in the armed forces, or be involved in government in any other way. Christians, generally, were to obey the State,

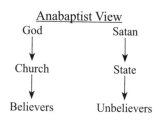

but the State had no real authority over Christians, nor did the Church have any authority over unbelievers.

Certainly the above is a generalization of the various views, with persons over the centuries within these perspectives deviating from these categorizations, but they do give a sense of the differing conflicts between church and government during the medieval, Reformation, and contemporary periods.

## BIBLICAL PRINCIPLES OF GOVERNMENT
### Responsibilites of the State

Why has God appointed the State His "minister" and "servant" (Romans 13:4-6)? Why should government exist? Much of the answer to these questions is found in Romans 13:1-7, the major New Testament passage on the believer's relationship to government. Unlike the statements on government made by Jesus in the Gospels (especially Matthew 22:15-22 and parallels Mark 12:13-17 and Luke 20:20-26), this passage occurs in a letter giving instruction to a local church. It is more extensive than the passages in 1 Peter 2:13-17, 1 Timothy 2:1-2, or Titus 3:1, and goes into more detail regarding the function of government and the Christian's response to it. Like all passages of Scripture containing vital teaching directly applicable to contempo-

rary life, Romans 13 must be understood in its context.
Notice that Paul deals with this subject following his call
to present our bodies as a living sacrifice (12:1) and not to
be conformed to this age (12:2). This means that a proper
attitude toward government is part of the believer's priestly
service to God. In addition, a Christian attitude toward government will be distinct from that of unbelievers under the
authority of Satan (cf. Ephesians 2:2).

In Romans 12:17 the apostle discusses the Christian's
relationship to those outside the church (notice the "all
people" in vv 17-18). He discourages an attitude of revenge
and encourages believers as far as possible to seek peace
and harmonious relations with everyone, summing up
with "do not be conquered by [the] evil, but conquer [the]
evil with [the] good." After these admonitions Paul immediately begins to discuss the relationship of the Christian to
government in Romans 13:1-7. This discussion is not an
abrupt change of subject, but leads from chapter twelve
without any distinct break. Paul uses some of the same terminology as in 12:17-21. Notice especially the words "evil,"
and "good" (12:17, 21; 13:3, 4); "pay" (or "repay," 12:17, 19;
13:7); "revenge" (or "revenger," 12:19; 13:4); and "wrath"
(12:19; 13:4, 5).

The state's fundamental role is to provide for good social
order. Romans 13:1-7 emphasizes that government pre-
vents social collapse and enforces social justice. Perry C.
Cotham[13] claims that the bedrock responsibility of government is the prevention of anarchy. How can government
fulfill its mandate? According to Romans 13, it can be done
by punishment of "the wrongdoer" so that the one who
pursues good conduct has nothing to fear. With all this in
mind, I offer this definition of the proper purpose of government: *God ordains human government to uphold social
order by promoting social justice and freedom.* This definition
limits government's role in society.

One of the problems in interpreting the Pauline view of
government in Romans 13:1-7 is whether its teaching may

---

[13] Perry C. Cotham, *Politics, Americanism and Christianity* (Grand Rapids: Baker
Book House, 1976).

be directly applied to modern government. Most commentators refer the passage to the Roman Empire, citing the phrase "the [authorities] which exist" (13:1b). The peculiar thing is that the same commentators (e.g., Murray, Cranfield, Newman, and Nida) exposit the passage as if it were universally applicable: "The apostle is...[not writing an essay on casuistic theology but]...setting forth the cardinal principles pertaining to the institution of government and regulating the behaviour of Christians."[14] It is likely that the entire passage deals with government in general, while the phrase "the [authorities] which exist" is used by Paul to apply these general principles to his readers and their situation within the Roman Empire. While not obvious in the translations, the first two mentions of authority in verse one are indefinite, while the third is definite. This can be seen in a stiff English translation: "Everyone must submit himself to governing authorities, since authority does not exist apart from God. Yet *the* [authorities] which do exist have been appointed by God." Romans 13:1-7 should therefore be understood as spelling out the *principles* of government in general and the believer's relation to it.

These *principles* are my present concern. When one understands the reasons for government, he can determine whether it is faithfully carrying out its God-given mission. Government can foster a just and free society in two primary ways: By punishing criminals and by promoting public good and political freedom. This is the "essence of good government."[15]

*Punish Criminals*

Romans 13:4 declares that the state "bears the sword" as "God's servant, an agent of wrath to bring punishment on the wrongdoer." The apostle Peter says much the same when he writes that governmental authorities are sent by God "to punish those who do wrong, and to commend those

[14] John Murray, *The Epistle to the Romans* (Grand Rapids: Eardmans, 1997), 150.
[15] Donald Guthrie, *New Testament Theology* (Downers Grove: InterVarsity Press, 1983), 948.

who do right" (1 Peter 2:14) Thus, force is legitimate for maintaining law and order.[16]

I must emphasize that crime is not only personal, but societal. If an intruder illegally enters a person's home and steals valuables, he has committed a criminal act. A just government will punish that act. But criminal activity may occur on the suprapersonal level. If a corporation knowingly pollutes a river with toxic waste, this too may be criminal. If a farmer withholds just wages from his laborers or if a shopkeeper subjects his employees to dangerous work conditions, he may also be guilty of wrongdoing. Governments are also obliged to protect their citizens from the attacks of international criminals. Although the Bible does not authorize governments to act against just anyone they dislike, it does direct them to protect their own lands. "At root," George Ladd comments, "it makes little difference whether this force is exercised through local police punishing wrongdoers within the community, or in international terms through armies enforcing justice among nations."[17]

Still, the state is not commanded to punish *all* evil. It has no right to punish someone for an unkind thought or wrong attitude. It must be concerned with punishing evil which endangers the existence of an organized society. Only actions which damage the social structure are punishable. The German theologian Helmut Thielicke writes that "the state, when it restrains evil, is not aiming at sin itself...but simply contesting the excesses of selfishness. It resists the selfishness which is inimical to order."[18] The state executes God's wrath on that sin which disrupts social order. In doing so, it deters crime and punishes criminals.[19] An obvious corollary is the upholding of justice. The government punishes criminals because it is unjust for them to harm either individuals or society. The promotion of justice is the underlying theme of Romans 13:4.

[16] See G.E. Ladd, "The Christian and the State," *Command* (March, 1982): 13.
[17] Ibid.
[18] Helmut Thielicke, *Ethics: Politics*, Vol 2 (Philadelphia: Fortress Press, 1969), 252.
[19] Alan Johnson, *Romans: The Freedom Letter*, Vol 2 (Chicago: Moody Press, 1977), 86.

*Promote Public Good and Political Freedom*

Paul says, "Do what is right, and he (the magistrate) will commend you." The apostle does not so much speak of obtaining specific reward—a letter of commendation, financial gifts, etc.—but of social approval. ". . .the idea of reward is not implicit in the term," writes Murray.[20] "The praise could be expressed by saying that good behavior secures good standing in the state, a status to be cherished and cultivated."[21] The law-abiding citizen has nothing to fear from his government. The government will allow him to live in peace and freedom.[22]

Many commentators point out that Paul does not discuss whether an evil government may encourage evil actions. "The presentation seems to take no account of the possibility that government may be tyrannical and may reward evil and suppress good,"[23] notes Everett Harrison. Why? Paul's silence probably means he was dealing with the "norm," with the state that fulfills the ideal for government.[24] However, Paul does not call for absolute obedience to everything the state demands, nor for a willingness to comply at any cost for the sake of security. He deals instead with the mandate God gives to government and the way a government *should* function. This is upheld by Romans 13:6b, "for they are God's servants, attending to this very thing." "This very thing" probably does not refer to collection of taxes, but goes back to verse 4, "he is God's servant to you for [the] good." Putting this together with the fact that the participle "attending" can be understood as meaning "if" or "when," the phrase may be translated "when they do what they should do."[25] This would mean that the state is God's servant, provided it acts in accordance with God's

---

[20] Murray, 151.
[21] Ibid.
[22] Ladd, 13.
[23] E.F. Harrison, "Romans," in *The Expositor's Bible Commentary*, vol 10, ed. F.E. Gaebelein (Grand Rapids: Zondervan, 1976), 137.
[24] Ibid., 138.
[25] Barclay Newman and Eugene Nida, *A Handbook on Paul's Letter to the Romans,* (Reading, UK: United Bible Societies, 1994), 248.

law. The statement in verse 3b ("do [the] good and you will have praise from it [the authority])" implies a state acting as it should, that is, in accord with God's law.

The responsibility of the state to act in harmony with God's law creates a difficult biblical/political problem. The problem is: how can a state which is pagan (as in the ancient world) or "pluralistic" (as in modern western society) be expected to uphold the law of God? This problem is further complicated by the fact that the New Testament does not set down a code of civil law for the state. The role of the state is expressed in Romans 13 and other passages in the broad terms of "good" and "evil." Paul's definition of these terms must be based on the law of God as revealed in the Old Testament. This immediately raises another question: how could a pagan state know or a pluralistic state enforce Old Testament law? A quotation from Calvin may bring the issue into sharper focus: "The law of the Lord forbids killing; but, that murders may not go unpunished, the Lawgiver himself puts into the hand of his ministers a sword drawn against all murders."[26]

Virtually all societies do, and have, enforced civil sanctions against murder. (Surely such aberrations as cannibalism, genocide, and abortion do not negate this general principle.) Why is it that pagan and pluralistic societies enforce "the law of the Lord" when they either do not have the Bible or reject it as a basis for law? The apostle Paul gives a clue to this in Romans 2:14-15, "For even the Gentiles who do not have the Law do naturally the things contained in the Law, they have become a law to themselves (not having the Law), who demonstrate the work of the Law written on their hearts...." It is only because of this "law written on their hearts" (presumably the human conscience) that civil authorities do good and punish evil apart from a conscious policy of applying biblical law in the civil sphere. To rely on the secular conscience for the framing and enforcing of just laws, however, is a risky proposition. Not only is it possible, as Paul says, for the conscience to be "seared" (1

---

[26] John Calvin, *Institutes of the Christian Religion* (Louisville, KY: Westminster John Knox Press, 1960), 1497

Timothy 4:2) and therefore insensitive to the law written on the heart, but in fact the unbelieving world in general is under the control of Satan (Ephesians 2:1-3). It seems better, when possible, for society as a whole to be under the restraining influence of God's moral law.

This leads to two other important questions: is not Old Testament law a unique code of regulations given to Israel to observe as a witness to God's character? And was not this law done away with in Christ (granted that the ceremonial code governing priesthood, sacrifices, etc., was fulfilled in Christ)? In addition, the general and specific laws governing Israel's relationship to God (generally called the first table of the Law) cannot and should not be enforced by a government which quite properly avoids restricting the free exercise of religion in a democratic and pluralistic society. This leads to the second table of the Law, dealing with interrelationships between humans created in God's image. (I am not advocating a theonomist-Christian reconstructionist view).[27]

The objection to using this part of the Old Testament as the basis for civil law today may take the following form: God dealt with Israel as a religio-civil state. Israel was an earthly nation, even though Israel was more than a nation. The Church, on the other hand, is the mystical body of Christ with a fully spiritual and heavenly calling. Israel as a state was given a body of civil law to enforce. The church was given the law of love. While this is good biblical theology, as a basis for civil law it is a cop-out. It will not do for Christians to leave the secular state to base its laws solely on the non-Christian conscience, whether determined by elected leaders or the "whims of a 51% majority."[28] What is more, to argue that because we live in a "pluralistic society" Christians ought to argue *against* biblical standards as a basis for civil law is downright ludicrous! This is *not* to suggest that the state should overtly push unique and

---

[27] See H. Wayne House and Thomas Ice, *Dominion Theology: Blessing or Curse?* (Portland, OR: Multnomah Press, 1988), for a refutation of a reconstructionist view of government.

[28] Francis Schaeffer, *The Church at the End of the 20th Century* (Downers Grove, IL: Inter-Varsity Press, 1970), 83.

specific Christian laws and theology. So then, when Old Testament Scriptures, principles, and illustrations are used here, I am attempting to apply creatively biblical standards to the mutual responsibilities of the established state and Christian citizens.

Nothing in the New Testament would specifically say that the government is to provide religious freedom, but there are implications of this truth. Believers in Christ should pray "for kings and all those in authority, that we may live peaceful and quiet lives in all godliness and holiness" (1 Timothy 2:2). We should pray for our leaders so that we can practice our faith unmolested. This implies that freedom of religion—and by inference, a variety of other freedoms (e.g., speech, assembly)—should be guaranteed by the government. So then, by implication, government ought to promote political freedom (1 Timothy 2:2, cf. Jeremiah 34:13,17; Leviticus 25:10). Man, like God, is capable of making free choices within the context of his character. To prohibit responsible exercise of this ability is to dehumanize God's creation. It is therefore a logical, Scriptural inference that government should allow citizens to make morally and socially responsible choices. I am not advocating "total" freedom, which results in anarchy. Instead, I would advocate the exercise of freedom within the confines of Judeo-Christian ethics—the type of freedom promoted by the United States Constitution. Supporting this is a vital function of civil government.

### The Nature of Governmental Authority

God, as said at the beginning of this essay, has given authority to the state (Romans 13:1; Daniel 2:21), but this authority derives from a higher power and hence is subordinate and non-absolute. But "when power becomes an end in itself and seeks its own glorification, transgressing the divinely appointed bounds of good order, it becomes demonic."[29] Government has legitimate areas of authority. Criminal justice (both personal and corporate), military

[29] Ladd, 14.

defense, and the promotion of freedom, order, and justice are all delegated by the Bible to government. It follows that governmental authority is limited by biblical revelation. Once government oversteps those bounds—should it interfere with the life of the church or demand compliance with unjust laws, for example—it exceeds its God-ordained boundaries.

## Biblical Authority Pattern

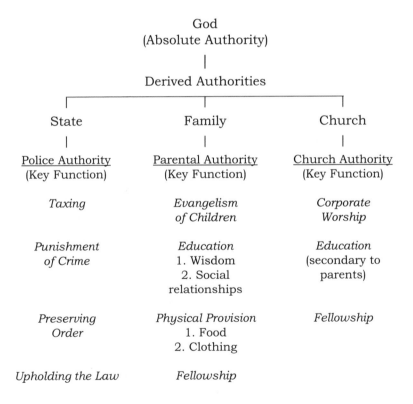

God
(Absolute Authority)

Derived Authorities

| State | Family | Church |
|---|---|---|
| Police Authority (Key Function) | Parental Authority (Key Function) | Church Authority (Key Function) |
| *Taxing* | *Evangelism of Children* | *Corporate Worship* |
| *Punishment of Crime* | *Education* 1. Wisdom 2. Social relationships | *Education* (secondary to parents) |
| *Preserving Order* | *Physical Provision* 1. Food 2. Clothing | *Fellowship* |
| *Upholding the Law* | *Fellowship* | |

## Cultural Authority Pattern

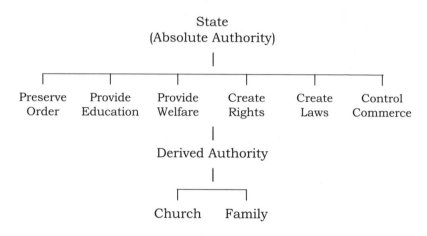

*The Proper Sphere of Government*

Jesus said to "give to Caesar what is Caesar's, and to God what is God's" (Luke 20:25). Therefore, Caesar must be rendered some very specific things—government has particular areas of jurisdiction. There *are* limits. What does Scripture say about those limits?

First, as we have seen, the state is under God and is responsible to Him for its actitivities. When the state behaves unjustly, inefficiently, or oversteps its biblical role, it rebels against its divine Sovereign.

Second, civil government should not regulate the church (however, I am not saying that the state should not support Judeo-Christian values, fulfill its biblical mandate, or admit its dependence on God).

Third, since the state and church are different institutions of God and have different responsibilities under God, the church should not formally regulate the state. The church's mission is not to govern the world, but to evangelize it and help meet its needs. To accomplish this, the government should act biblically and responsibility. The Bible does not directly argue the issue of separation of church and state. In the Old Testament, at least from the time of Moses down to the Babylonian Captivity, Israel was God's constituted nation. They were to be holy as a nation in order to be a witness to the pagan nations of the Lord's character. This necessitated a natural connection between the state and the ceremonial functions of religious life. Indeed, to speak of "church" and "state" as if they were separate entities may well have confused the Old Testament believer, for whom no real analogy to such a distinction existed. It is surprising, then, in this context to note that a definite "no trespassing" policy was enforced between civil and religious leadership.

In 1 Samuel 13, Saul, growing impatient in his wait for Samuel, decided to offer sacrifices himself. That impetuous act earned him the wrath of God. In trying to fulfill a role designated for a religious leader, Saul overstepped his sphere of authority and was judged; God deposed him. On the other hand, we read in 1 Chronicles 26:20 that the Levites had specific charge over the treasury of the Temple and over the gifts devoted to God. Their sphere was religious, and they were not to control government.

After the Babylonian Captivity the situation was different. The civil authority under which Israel then lived was accustomed to enforcing the establishment of pagan religion. This led to a *de facto* separation of Israel's spiritual life from state control. Faithful Jews under these conditions exercised two main options. Daniel and his friends resisted government commands to engage in pagan worship during the time of the Babylonian and Persian empires. Later under Persian, Greek, and Roman rule an uneasy truce between the pagan state and Israel allowed the Jews their "peculiar observances."

It is into this situation that the church was born. The principle given by the Lord ("Give to Caesar what is Caesar's and to God what is God's") implied a distinction of spiritual and civil responsibilities. While the Roman empire may have looked on the young Christian church as a mere sect of Judaism (which the Judaistic establishment regarded as a heretical cult), clearly Christ and the apostles viewed it as a radically different organism. It was the body of Christ, a new kingdom with a king who ruled from heaven. No earthly state could regulate the spiritual life of such a kingdom. Nor would the subjects of such a kingdom desire to establish it in place of the existing state while their citizenship and their true King were in heaven. The political implications of this new kingdom are summarized by Penner: "The New Testament enjoins no civil laws for the Christian, neither is the church called upon to form an autonomous state. It is assumed that the Church will subsist under the secular state."[30] Or, to put it in the most succinct words of Calvin: "[the apostles'] purpose is not to fashion a civil government, but to establish the spiritual kingdom of Christ."[31]

Two points are critical in the previous discussion: I am not advocating a secular/sacred dichotomy. Nor do I suggest that government must always disregard religious disorder. Christians are to be committed to Jesus Christ as Lord over all of life. This includes the way Christians respond to government. When the state demands worship or violation of the laws of God, it must be disobeyed (Acts 5:29). But when the state operates biblically in its proper sphere of authority, we must obey (Romans 13:1-7). We serve but one Lord, and He has instituted human government.

## Limits on Law Enforcement

It is civil government's role to punish crime. The Bible gives *principles* for the type of punishment to be given and the manner in which it should be applied. First, it may punish only the guilty. The cities of refuge prescribed in the Old Testament for those accused of killing others were designed to prohibit the family and friends of the accused from taking the law into their own hands. If someone was falsely accused, he could stay in a city of refuge until proven innocent (Numbers 35:9-28). No one could be slain

[30] Penner, quoted in H. Wayne House, *The Christian and American Law* (Grand Rapids: Kregel Publications, 1998), 151.
[31] Calvin, *Institutes*, 1500.

for another's sin (Deuteronomy 24:16). The law demands a fair trial. Evidence alone can convict the accused (Deuteronomy 17:6-7). There can be no "kangaroo courts."

Second, punishment must fit the crime. The oft-misquoted "eye for an eye" principle was given to prohibit excessive punishment. If someone broke another's arm, he could not be executed in return (Exodus 21:18-25). The principle extended to war. Norman Geisler writes that "Abraham's battle against the kings of Genesis 14 lends support to the principle that unjust national aggressors should be resisted."[32] Scripture directs that wars must be fought in a just manner (Deuteronomy 20:10-17; Amos 1:13-15) for just purposes (implied both by Deuteronomy 32:35, where the Lord condemns revenge as a motive, and by the just nature of God, who ordains government).

## Limits on Social Involvement

Every evangelical should embrace the personal and corporate responsibility Christians have to help the needy. The story of the church today should be the story of the Good Samaritan. But the indisputable necessity of evangelical social action is not the concern here. The question is the role of the *government* in social programs.

Most evangelicals hold one of two positions. One group agrees with James E. Johnson when he states:

It would be a sad development indeed if evangelical Protestantism were to become identified with a rigid opposition to the developing welfare situation in America. This kind of negativism would mean that evangelicals would be excluded from involvement in one of the most powerful movements in American history...[E]vangelicals should support welfare programs...because there are no live options available in today's complex society for meeting economic

---

[32] Norman Geisler, *Ethics: Alternative and Issues* (Grand Rapids: Zondervaan, 1971), 171.
[33] James E. Johnson, "The Christian and the Emergence of the Welfare State," *Protest & Politics*, ed. R.G. Clouse (Greenwood, SC: The Attic Press, 1968), 115-16.

needs.[33]

A second group believes that coercive charity (i.e., government taking from one person to give it to another) is hypocritical and unjust, and that government welfare is a threat to both the free-enterprise system and personal initiative. They therefore reject government social involvement.[34] Advocates of this view contend that law enforcement ought to be the essential role of government. They believe that any other function is illegitimate in that it violates biblical limits placed on governmental jurisdiction and results in an unjust, compulsory charity.

Who is right? Both groups believe that God cares for the poor. Proverbs 19:17 tells us that "he who kind to the poor lends to the Lord." One of the charges God brought against Israel was that the poor were refused "justice in the courts" while being forced to "give you grain" (Amos 5:11). Clearly, both individuals and nations are responsible to treat the economically disadvantaged with justice and sensitivity.

I would suggest that the most effective way to help the poor is not through direct social welfare programs. There are several reasons for this. Prior to 1935, more than half of all welfare came from private charity. Now the figure is less than one percent.[35] The welfare system has grown to enormous proportions. Although it has helped in isolated individual cases, the system in general has failed.

First, a great many poor remain poor. Black economist Thomas Sowell wrote in 1981 that "the amount necessary to lift every man, woman, and child in America above the poverty line has been calculated, and it is one-third of what is in fact spent on poverty programs."[36] Why, then, does poverty continue? Because "much of the transfer ends up in the pockets of highly paid administrators, consultants, and staff as well as higher-income recipients of benefits from programs advertised as anti-poverty efforts."[37] A massive welfare bureaucracy defeats the very purpose for which it

---

[34] West, 137.
[35] George Gilder, *Wealth and Poverty* (New York: Basic Books, 1981), 112.
[36] Ibid., 127.
[37] Ibid.

was created.

Second, self-perpetuation often handicaps welfare systems. Welfare "erodes work and family and thus keeps poor people poor," Gilder says, contending that men in welfare homes often rely on the subsidy their female relatives receive from the government.[38] Prolonged, excessive welfare programs kill the incentive to work.[39]

Third, nowhere does the Bible make government the dominant force in society. Welfare makes government all-important for many citizens.

Fourth, while government has the right to demand honor, financial support, military service, and respect for law from its citizens, the Bible never empowers it to demand love for neighbors. Only God may do that.

Lastly, a welfare state foreshadows socialism, which in my opinion betrays many biblical principles. When the state dominates the economy, its power is enormous. Personal incentive and the freedom to work for oneself are severely curtailed. But if one rejects social welfare, what can be done to help the poor? Gilder suggests:

> The goal of welfare should be to help people out of dire but temporary problems, not to treat temporary problems as if they were permanent ones, and thus make them so....[A] disciplined combination of emergency aid, austere in kind benefits, and child allowances—all at levels well below the returns of hard work—offers some promise of relieving poverty without creating a welfare culture that perpetuates it. That is the best that any welfare system can be expected to achieve.[40]

Gilder's view seems much more consistent with biblical values than does our current situation. Government should not demand charity of its citizens, nor should it usurp the

---

[38] Ibid., 114-15.
[39] Ronald J. Nash, *Social Justice & the Christian Church* (Milford, CT: Mott Media, 1983), 64.
[40] Gilder, 126-27.

role of the family and the (obedient) church as agents of compassion. Government is only an organi-zation, essentially impersonal and primarily a police agency. It cannot try to "institutionalize love."[41]

## A Christian's Responsibility to Government

*Upon Christians, as members of society, there falls the obligation of actually shaping the political community. This is not a matter of choice, for even doing nothing will still have an effect.*

Peter Hinchliff, *Holiness & Politics*[42]

*Duties owed Government*

### Supplication

1 Timothy 2:1-2 directs Christians to offer "entreaties, prayers, petitions and thanksgivings" for "kings and all in authority." The word "authority" implies preeminence or superiority of position.[43] All government leaders—whether at local, state, or national levels—merit our prayers because it is God who has placed them in their positions. Christians are called to pray for all officials, no matter how we feel about them. Why pray? So that government can keep social order and we might live peaceful and quiet lives (1 Timothy 2:2). As the government does its job, Christians will be able to spread the Gospel effectively (1 Timothy 2:3-4).

### Submission

Believers must subject themselves to the governing powers because God Himself ordains government (Romans 13:1). Peter tells believers to "submit for the Lord's sake to every human institution, whether to a king or to gover-nors" (1 Peter 2:13-14, NASB). While Nero was not perse-

---

[41] Thielicke, *Politics*, 289.
[42] Peter Hinchliff, *Holiness & Politics* (Grand Rapids: Eerdmans, 1982), 204.
[43] W.E. Vine and Merrill Unger, *Vine's Complete Expository Dictionary of Old and New Testament Words* (Ontario: Thomas Nelson, 1996), 89.
[44] Steven C. Mott, *Biblical Ethics and Social Change* (Oxford: Oxford University Press, 1983), 147.

cuting believers when Paul wrote to the Roman church,[44] the situation had changed by the time of Peter's letter.[45] It is pointless to argue that neither Paul or Peter would have urged submission to government had they known of coming persecution—God certainly knew, and yet he directed both men to write as they did.

Why should a believer submit to the state's authority? There are at least three reasons. The first is obedience, and Paul says to obey government is to avoid criminal punishment (Romans 13:3-4). A Christian who violates a proper civil law is not only rightly punished, but he brings dishonor to his Lord. God disciplines the criminal (Romans 13:2, 5). Believers should obey just laws in order to flee from God's anger against crime, which is also sin. Although Christ suffered in our place so that we could escape sin's eternal punishment, we are still subject to temporal discipline. God disciplines erring children, sometimes through government.

Second, obedience to the state honors God. The state is His agent (Romans 13:1-7). For His sake (1 Peter 2:13), we must obey its laws. Conscience judges our attitude toward government (Romans 13:5). Submission to state authority is right in God's sight.

Last, the Bible implies that our behavior toward government effects our testimony. Peter suggests that submission to government will help silence those who accuse Christians of promoting civil unrest (1 Peter 2:15). God is the not the author of confusion, says Paul, and His people are not to advocate revolution or anarchy. They shold live well-ordered, quiet lives (1 Timothy 2:2). Model citizenship is a vital ingredient of a good testimony.

These reasons for obedience are not absolute. There is extensive Scriptural evidence for civil disobedience.[46]

There is a difference between obedience and submis-

[45] David H. Wheaton, "1 Peter," *New Bible Commentary* (Downers Grave, IL: Inter-Varsity Press, 1994), 1236-37.
[46] Elsewhere I have written on the obligation of Christians to disobey government in certain instances. See H. Wayne House, "The Christian's Duty of Civil Disobedience to the Government" in *The Christian and American Law*, 139-174.

sion. Submission implies a willing subordination of oneself to another in general.[47] Obedience comes when you decide to submit. This is a logical sequence. Obedience is the *act* of submission. While Christians must always submit to governmental *authority,* times may come when they should not obey a governmental *decision.* Richard Foster writes that the great commandments to love God above everything and to love one's neighbor as oneself set the limits on submission to government. When submission becomes "destructive," he says—that is, it "becomes a denial of the law of love as taught by Jesus" and affronts "genuine biblical submission (Matthew 5-7 and especially 22:37-39)"—it must stop.[48] Only God is absolute, and obedience to family, government, employers, or anyone else depends upon the total obedience owed to God alone. In certain cases government *must* be disobeyed. Romans and 1 Peter teach that Christians are responsible to government and that governmental authorities are appointed by God. These letters are not complete expositions of the Christian's every response to the state. They deal with government as it should be—a minister of God's justice, helping those who do good while punishing criminals. Obviously not every government fulfills this role. Although I do believe Romans 13:2 and Daniel 4:17 imply that God's sovereign will establishes every governmental official, nowhere does the Bible hint that every state decision is faithful to God's Word. Neither Paul nor Peter intend to explain how we should respond at all times to a tyrannical government.[49]

Payment of Taxes

Paul instructs Christians to pay both the tribute-tax to Caesar and the revenue or customs tax (Romans 13:6-7). The tribute tax (also mentioned in Luke 20:22; 23:2) was levied annually on houses, persons, and lands.[50] It was collected to acknowledge the rule of Caesar. It was not a form

[47] Vine, 86-87
[48] R.J. Foster, *Celebration of Discipline* (New York: Harper & Row, 1978), 105.
[49] Mott, 149.
[50] J.H. Thayer, *Greek-English Lexicon of the New Testament* (Grand Rapids: Baker, 1977), 657.

of worship, but of respect, and was paid indirectly through Roman princes and governors and into the imperial treasury.[51] The revenue tax was an indirect levy on goods.[52] In Roman provinces (such as Galilee), the poll-tax went to the procurator of the Roman government. Other provinces sent the tax to local administrators (i.e., Herod of Judea).[53] Judea collected it through publicans, who were detested as extortioners.

Jesus' attitude toward taxation demands careful consideration. In Matthew 17:25, He asks Peter from whom earthly rulers receive both customs-taxes and tribute-taxes—i.e., their subjects. He then remarks that although the sons of kings are exempt, He and Peter should pay anyway, so as not to "cause them (the tax collectors who questioned Peter about Jesus' tax paying) to stumble." Peter went out, took a coin from the mouth of a fish, and paid the two drachma tax.[54] In the famous "render to Caesar" passages, Jesus does not directly state His position. *Jurisdiction,* not taxation as such, is His point in these passages. F.F. Bruce contends that the Pharisees asked Jesus about taxation because some Jews believed "it was unlawful to acknowledge the sovereignty of a Gentile ruler."[55] One answer would invite charges that Jesus was a seditionist who wanted to overthrow the yoke of Roman oppression; the other would be misrepresented to claim subservience to Caesar and disloyalty to God and country. The question was a ploy to discredit Him. With characterisitic incisiveness, Jesus replied that God and Caesar each have legitimate jurisdictions [God has absolute authority, and Caesar derived authority or jurisdiction], and that what belongs to each should be given to each. It should be clear that taxation is a valid function of government (Romans 13:6-7) and that Jesus Himself paid at least one tax (Matthew 17). His

[51] J. MacPherson, "Tribute in the New Testament," *A Dictionary of the Bible,* ed., James Hastings (New York: Charles Scribners, 1903), 813.
[52] Murray, 156.
[53] Vine, 263.
[54] A.N. Sherwin-White, *Roman Society and Roman Law in the New Testament* (Oxford, UK: Clarendon Press, 1965), 126.
[55] F.F. Bruce, *New Testament History* (New York: Galilee Trade, 1983), 96.

attitude toward taxation can be seen in His remark about not giving offense: as the children of God, the great King, we owe no government absolute allegiance, but in recognizing government's rightful place and to avoid the appearance of anarchy or rebellion, taxes should be paid. Even though taxes today are high and getting higher—and, by the way, Christians can use legal means to seek to lower them—we are still responsible to pay tax. F.C. Grant writes: "...the total taxation of the Jewish people in the time of Jesus, civil and religious combined, must have approached the intolerable proportion of between 30 and 40 percent; it may have been higher still."[56] Despite this unjust tax rate, Jesus urged payment.

What if, as James Boice has asked, "our taxes are being used for immoral evils; to support a gestapo, an unjust war, oppression of the disenfranchised by the rich and privileged, or other evils?"[57] The Bible does not answer directly. Some believe that paying a full share of tax pays for immoral activities (abortion is one good example; pacificist Christians resisting "war taxes" is another). They respond by calculating and withholding the percentage of tax spent on activities they see as evil, by refusing to pay taxes at all, or even by living below the poverty level to relieve themselves of any tax. I commend those who feel compelled to resist "immoral" taxation and wish all Christians showed the same vigor in their devotion to Christ. But I believe such action is improper.

Although the Roman government used some tax money for evil purposes, Christians were to pay anyway. No one praises Imperial Rome as a paragon of virtue: it supported an idolatrous religious system, maintained a huge slave labor force, and brutally oppressed those it conquered. Yet the New Testament is clear: give Caesar his due.

If everyone refused to pay part or all of his tax for ethical or religious reasons, government would grimly lurch from year to year under the pall of bankruptcy and anarchy.

---

[56] Ibid., 40.
[57] J.M. Boice, *God & History, Foundations of the Christian Faith*, Vol. 4 (Downers Grove: Inter-Varsity Press, 1981), 231.

Governments were ordained to keep order. Breaking the back of government through refusal to pay taxes is an illegitimate way to protest.

I do not suggest that if government should demand specific taxes to pay for racial genocide or some other horror that Christians should placidly submit. Unless thing change radically in the United States, however, that is not likely to happen. In this country, only *general* taxes—yearly umbrella taxes for all governmental activities—are collected.

Christians can take meaningful steps when they think taxes are unjust:

1. Pay
2. Pray that God will guide the government into righteous and biblically acceptable conduct
3. Write a letter with the tax payment respectfully requesting that none of the money be used for the item deemed objectionable, and that use of that payment to support the practice is deplored
4. Write to legislators, courts justices, and executive officers to try to change laws which support the evil
5. Actively participate in the political process by gathering petitions, making speeches, and (perhaps) even running for office!

The Roman government collapsed partly because of excessive taxation.[58] Christians should use law to advocate a just and efficient tax system and ensure proper use of tax dollars. But they should never—except in extreme cases—take the law into their own hands by refusing to pay.

Military Service

The New Testament does not spell out whether it is right for Christians to fight in a war. But it is remarkable that not one reference to converted soldiers (and there are several) contains a command to leave the army or to lay down arms. Luke 3:14 reports the instructions of John

[58] R.S. Lopez, T.H. Barnes, J. Blum, R. Cameron, *Civilizations: Western & World*, Vol. 1 (Boston: Little, Brown & Co., 1975), 102.

the Baptist to baptized soldiers: "Don't extort money and don't accuse people falsely—be content with your pay." Jesus did not order the Roman centurion of Matthew 8:5-13 to leave the army, but praised him for his trust in the Lord. Cornelius, the Roman centurion of Acts 10, was never advised to choose a different career, yet he became the catalyst through whom God showed Peter the need to preach the gospel to Gentiles. The jailer of Acts 16 repents and believes—again, with no mention of refusing to fight in the Roman army. While the passages cited do not directly relate to Christian military service, it seems important that although Jesus commanded repentant sinners to flee from materialism, adultery, and other sins, neither He nor His disciples required soldiers to leave the military, as if it were something of which to repent.

Much of the pacifist argument rests on two premises: the Christian must never kill, and the early church condemned Christian military service.

A better rendering of the command "Thou shalt not kill" is found in the *New International Version's* "You shall not murder." Evidently, God does not see all killing as murder since He used Israel to annihilate most of the Canaanites (Deuteronomy 20:10-20). Jesus' command to love enemies does not refer to national policy. The Sermon on the Mount was a list of Jesus' commands for the *personal* conduct of His disciples. Soldiers fighting against one another in warfare are not personal enemies. They represent national forces opposed to each other. If the Sermon on the Mount was truly intended to regulate international relations, why, then, does Paul give government the right to "bear the sword?" Someone within the state must exercise that power. I agree with R.E. Nixon, who, in commenting on Matthew 5:39 ("do not resist an evil person"), writes: "the context suggests that it is applicable to wrongs done to a person himself and not a prohibition of the defense of others."[59] *Defense* is the basis of the military—a valid, biblically-sanc-

---

[59] R.E. Nixon, "Matthew," *The New Bible Commentary*, ed. D. Guthrie, J.A. Motyer, A.M. Stibbs, D.J. Wiseman (Grand Rapids: Eerdmans, 1978), 824.

tioned function.

The second major argument—that the early church was largely pacifist—is supported by many of the early church fathers. Still, by A.D. 170 (roughly 75 years after the death of John, the last of the apostles), Christians composed much of Marcus Aurelius' "Thunderstruck Legion."[60] The argument that prior to this there were few Christians in the military is speculative. As pacifist Glenn Hinson writes, "we must be careful not to argue too much from silence, for Christians were few in number and often went unnoticed."[61] Church fathers urged Christians to avoid the military for two reasons: Christians should never fight and military service required idolatry. But only officers were required to sacrifice to the emperor, and in this case no Christian should have submitted. The only reason for abstaining from the officers' ranks was not killing, but idolatry.[62]

## Patriotism

Phrases like "love of country" are often so loaded that they mean considerably different things to different people. Before we try to construct a biblical basis for patriotism, it is important that we define some terms as I mean them.

Country: A country means the unique ideas, land, and heritage which are the common experience of a certain people within certain boundaries. Should we "love" and be thankful for all that is in a country? Our answer must be no at times. For example, abortion is an integral part of our national experience here in the United States, and, except when performed to save the life of the mother, it is grossly evil in the sight of God. The one who loves God will love what He loves and hate what He hates. He will view his country through Christlike eyes.

Patriotism: Patriotism is a love for the biblical ideals and

---

[60] E.J. Cadoux, *The Early Christian Attitude to War* (New York: Seabury, 1982), 229-31.
[61] E.G. Hinson, "Who Shall Suffer Injury at our Hands? Historical Christian Responses to War and Peace," *Waging Peace*, 148.
[62] Ibid., 147.

values which are the basis of a nation. One can legitimately love America because its Constitution splendidly embodies Judeo-Christian values, and because it has achieved many great things which sprang from those values. Our history, even checkered with its wrongs and errors, is one of the most pleasant and biblically consistent in human experience. For this we can be thankful. We ought to strive to make our nation ever more righteous in God's sight. But one must reject the "my country, right or wrong" mentality as idolatrous. No national loyalty can supercede loyalty to truth and proper values as taught to us by Jesus Christ. We must be careful to avoid excess in either direction. America's Constitution is remarkable. It has a firm Judeo-Christian base. America is the most free and democratic nation on earth, to my knowledge. The Bill of Rights grants Americans greater liberty than any people throughout history has ever experienced. The United States has been blessed by God with abundant natural resources, and our conduct as a member of world society generally has been commendable. But alongside these blessings there have been incidents of which we must be ashamed. Slavery, culminating in a war between the states, and slavery's parent, racism, have haunted our nation since its inception. Abortion-on-demand, the treatment of the American Indians in the 18th and 19th centuries, and selfish materialism are other dark blotches. Our blessings give us no right to ignore our national sins, nor should our national sins encourage a vicious anti-Americanism. The Bible does not speak about *love of country*. National Israel was to be humble—it was sovereignly chosen by God apart from any merit of its own (Deuteronomy 7:1-7). But the Hebrews loved their land, heritage, and culture. The mournful cry of Psalm 137:1, 4-6 pictures this:

> By the rivers of Babylon,
> There we sat down and wept,
> When we remembered Zion...
> How can we sign the Lord's song
> In a foreign land?

If I forget you, O Jerusalem,
May my right hand forget her skill.
May my tongue cleave to the roof of my mouth,
If I do not remember you,
If I do not exalt Jerusalem
Above my chief joy.

The New Testament demonstrates Jesus' love for Israel
(Luke 19:41), but it is based on God's love for His chosen
people, not on patriotic fervor. Giving thanks and praying
for rulers (1 Timothy 2:1-4) comes from respect for authority, the desire to live godly and quiet lives, and the hope
that everyone may be saved—not from love of country.
Honor and respect for governmental authority (Romans
3:7) are based on God's institution of government. They
are signs of submission to Him, and are not calls to patriotism. "Balance" should characterize our patriotic attitudes.
We can love our country by loving and worshipping God
alone, by loving our neighbors, and by being thankful for
those things in our national life that are compatible with
Scripture. We must avoid a patriotism which places country
ahead of God. We must also avoid a noisy disdain for our
nation and its leaders. The warning of Johathan Mayhew in
a 1750 sermon delivered in Boston is a fitting conclusion:
"There are those who strike at liberty under the term licen-
tiousness; there are others who aim at popularity under
the guise of patriotism. Be aware of both. Extremes are
dangerous."[63]

*Political Involvement*
    The dilemma: should Christians be involved in politics?
Many evangelicals have grave doubts. They view political
involvement with deep skepticism. In this portion, I will
present biblical examples of God's people in political life,
common reasons for non-involvement, and what Christians
can do to affect political change.
    Scripture is full of godly men and women who influ-

[63] F.P. Cole, ed. *They Preached Liberty* (Indianapolis: Liberty Press, 1977), 105.

enced society. Daniel was the prime minister of Babylon for
two different empires (Daniel 2:48, 6:28). Esther, queen of
Persia, used her office to save her people (Esther 4:1-5:8).
Joseph, as prime minister of Egypt, effectively governed his
nation and thereby saved his own land (and foreign lands)
from famine (Genesis 41:41-47). Joseph of Arimithea was a
member of the Sanhedrin, the Jewish ruling council, as was
Nicodemus (John 3:1, Mark 15:43). "Caesar's household"
(Philippians 4:22) may well have referred to civil administrators. In Jeremiah 29:7 the Lord tells Jeremiah to seek the
welfare of the city to which he was exiled so that "you will
have welfare." Mordecai "sought the good of his people...and
the welfare of his whole nation" as a ruler in Medo-Persia
(Esther 10:3).

Objection 1: "We should concentrate on saving souls, not
worry about social or political action."

A legitimate distaste for the classic "social gospel" (which
called for purely social change) is partly to blame for reactions like this. We must realize that God has placed His
people in the world as ministers of His grace. Those who
neglect social concern in the name of evangelistic zeal
are insensitive to the real physical and material needs of
others. The body is important—God made it! Someone
once questioned Lutheran commentator Dr. Oswald C.J.
Hoffmann, "Why should Christians be engaged in social
action?" Hoffmann replied, "Because they are Christians.
Next question please." When true revival stirs God's people,
social concern "is a fruit of repentence."[64] Why do many
Christians think they should let government take its
own "evil" course? Government is part of God's program;
the Bible speaks about it and so should we! Englishman
William Wilberforce, an outstanding soldier for Christ,
worked nearly a lifetime to abolish his country's slave
trade—and he finally succeeded. We should take heart
from his example. We must never forget that evangelism
is the top priority for Christians. But we must not there-

[64] F.E. Gaebelein, "How Paul Attacked Social Issues," *Eternity* (June 1974): 19.

fore neglect social action (including government involvement). Colossians 1:18 reminds us that Christ is Lord of all. "Christian commitment in this world had for its governing presupposition the lordship of Christ as the ruler of nature, the sovereign of the nations and the decisive center of history,"[65] said Carl Henry about the early Christians. As we obey Christ as Lord, we will work to implement His will for government, for justice, and the restraint of evil in society. To do less is sin.

Objection 2: "I don't know anything about politics."

All Christians have the "mind of Christ." They have been enabled to see things from His perspective as they know and apply biblical teachings. As they get to know God, they begin to see what concerns Him. This applies to society directly. Christians should rejoice in social righteousness and weep at social sin. Christians can learn about specific legislation, politicians, and issues. "Our inability to come to a perfect understanding of God's will on political matters does not serve as an excuse for silence," says Paul Henry.[66] On moral issues, we can know God's will, although it may be less clear on specific legislation. Several years ago intense debate raged over the Panama Canal Treaty. Christians were divided. What should they have done? By applying principles of government conduct (justice, honesty, restraint of national evil, defense against enemies), researching the issue, and reading statements from political leaders, they could decide responsibly. Conclusions may certainly have differed, but that is no excuse for failing to search Scripture, history, and legislation for answers.

Objection 3: "Politics is dirty."

If politics is dirty, we should strive to make it clean. Christians are responsible to help society and govern-

[65] C.F.H. Henry, *A Plea for Evangelical Demonstration* (Grand Rapids: Baker, 1971), 66.
[66] Paul B. Henry, *Politics for Evangelicals* (Grand Rapids: Baker, 1974), 79.

ment adhere to biblical ethics. Christians must contend for the principles of Scripture in public life. We should not seek to construct a society that denies freedom of religion or which tries to quash ideas. We should desire a society whose ethics is consistent with the Word of God. Edmund Burke once wrote that "the fate of good men who refuse to become involved in govenment is to be ruled by evil men." If we foolishly allow decisions which bind the entire country to be made by those without a firm commitment to Judeo-Christian principles, we can bid farewell to just govern-ment. This cannot be our choice.

Objection 4: "Christ is coming; why try to change a doomed world?"

Christians must oppose evil, whether it be social, govern-mental, or personal. The world is screeching toward destruction, but our eschatology should not keep us from working effectively in society. Quite the opposite! The doc-trine of the end times should motivate us to evangelize. Do not think that if we allow our society to embrace secu-lar values and our government to lose its ethical founda-tion, that we will be permitted to continue evangelizing. We would certainly lose that privilege. If for no other reason than evangelism, political engagement by Christians is imperative. The Reformation of the 16th and 17th centu-ries led to sweeping social changes. Had Luther been con-tent to merely "preach the word" and never challenge the Pope, history would have been different (and appallingly so). God is sovereign. All things are after the counsel of His will (Ephesians 1:11). Because some are elect, should we not evangelize? Because His will is irresistible, should we not pray? No thinking Christian would answer "yes." We are called to be faithful to the will of God. We will never usher in the millenium through our efforts, but that is not our purpose. We must work both for a just government that restrains sin *and* to evangelize the world. Faithfulness is our aim. We are to *occupy* until Jesus comes (Luke 19:3— *occupy* here does not mean 'to take up space'—it means 'keep busy'). Leaving politics to the devil is a resignation we can ill afford.

Objection 5: "One person cannot accomplish anything."

At the turn of this century, V.I. Lenin was an unknown political radical. By 1917, he had about 40,000 devoted followers who overthrew the Russian government and changed the course of Russian history. One man with an idea is enormously powerful. Whether we are victorious is immaterial. The key issue is that we are responsible. Political involvement under the Lordship of Christ is as spiritual as preaching a Sunday sermon.

The Bible "is concerned for society, but there is no such thing as a social gospel," writes A.N. Briton. "There is social law. There is also a gospel of salvation in Christ which has far-reaching repercussions in society when men who have entered into the experience of the gospel go to live it out."[68] What an excellent summary of this section! Theocracy will be the final form of the state when Christ returns to claim His rightful authority (Daniel 7:14, Revelation 11:15). Until that day, the sovereign God has delegated part of His authority to human institutions. As Christians and citizens of the state, let us participate in both church and state for the glory of God!

*How and when should Christians disobey the state?*

The great principle is most clearly seen in Peter's remark to the Sanhedrin (which had, under Rome, limited but active civil power): "We must obey God rather than men."[69] It is not insignificant that Paul wrote his last letter from a Roman jail (2 Timothy 4:6-8). He honored the Lord, not the will of men. Peter died for refusing to yield his trust in the Lord Jesus, the same trust which he declared early in

---

[68] A.N. Briton, *Whose World?* (London: InterVarsity Press, 1972), 182-83.
[69] Sherwin-White, 40.

his ministry: "Whether it is right in the sight of God to give heed to you rather than to God, you be the judge; for we cannot stop speaking what we have seen and heard" (Acts 4:19-20). Others in Scripture placed obedience to the will of God above the will of men. In Exodus 1:17-20, the Lord blessed Israel's midwives who hid the nation's newborn babies from Pharoah's slaughter. John the Baptist refused to keep silent regarding the sins of the king, and he paid for his opposition with his life (Matthew 14:1-12). While other examples exist, several principles can be gleaned from Scripture to guide the Christian in his response to government.

When the state makes laws amenable to God's revealed will, it should be obeyed. Condemnation of murder is *in keeping with* a law of God; it should be obeyed. City ordinances, in general, would *not violate* a law of God; we should submit to them.

We should disobey the state only when the state disobeys Scripture. When the law supports Scripture, we should support the law. In areas where the law may not have direct moral implications, we can disagree with it and work within legal means to change it, but we must obey it. Despite the inconvenience, Joseph and Mary registered for taxation (Luke 2:1). That governments should tax and that Christians should pay the taxes accords with Scripture (Romans 13:6-7). It is *not* a principle that going to one's hometown to register is the right way to do it. But because it did not *violate* God's law to register in one's hometown, Joseph and Mary faithfully suffered the inconvenience and obeyed. God honored their obedience by privileging them to become the parents of Israel's long-awaited Savior in the very city of David. God will honor *our* obedience to authority when it does not defy His Word. Daniel obeyed and administered the law of Babylon so well that "the king planned to appoint him over the entire kingdom" (Daniel 6:3). It was only when the government defied the Law of God that Daniel disobeyed (Daniel 6:10-11).

Christians should seek to resolve their disagreements with civil authorities. But when a government demands disobedience to Christ, the Christian cannot comply. He must explain his disobedience and should try to resolve the conflict without compromising his faith. Failing this, he must remain firm in his disobedience. The Bible calls believers to be reconcilers between God and man (2 Cor-inthians 5:20-21), and Christians should seek to make peace between themselves and the state. To live at peace with the state is desirable (2 Timothy 2:2), but to live in faithfulness to the Lord is imperative (Luke 9:23-24).

## CONCLUSION

Though Christians in this life are preparing for an eternal kingdom, the reality is that we are—during this life—in the kingdom of the world. God is concerned about how we relate to the worldly society in which we live, for He is the creator of both the physical and the spiritual worlds. Within this earthly existence He works out His will and reveals His glory. He established the home, then the religious community, and finally government as vehicles to express His will and to provide a context in which humans could carry on the daily operations of life. A theology of government is often ignored by theologians, but the Bible has a considerable repository of information on how the believer is to function within the human institution of the state. What one discovers is that whether relating to the family, the church, or the government, the duty and privilege of the Christian is to glorify God in everything.

# Socialism, Capitalism, and the Bible

Ronald H. Nash

## Introduction

Within the Christian church today, one can find a small but growing army of Protestants and Roman Catholics who have entered into an uncritical alliance with the political Left. The so-called liberation theologians not only promote a synthesis of Marxism and Christianity, but attempt to ground their recommended restrictions of economic and political freedom on their interpretation of the biblical ethic. A growing number of my own religious fellowship (those theologically conservative Protestants known as evangelicals) appear to stop just short of the more radical pronouncements of the liberation thinkers. These evangelicals of the Left are convinced that the biblical ethic obliges them to condemn capitalism and endorse the politics of statism and economics of socialism.

Many writings from the Christian Left illustrate what can be called the proof-text method. What these writers normally do is isolate some vague passage (usually one from the Old Testament) that pertains to an extinct cultural situation or practice. They then proceed to deduce some complex economic or political program from that text.

My approach to the subject rejects the proof-text method and proceeds via three main steps. First, a Christian should acquire a clear and complete picture of the Christian worldview. What basic views about God, humankind, morality, and society are taught or implied by Scripture? Second, he should put his best effort into discovering the truth about economic and political systems. He should try to clarify what capitalism and socialism really are (not what the propagandists say they are). He should try to discover how each system works or, as in the case of socialism, whether it can work. He should identify the strengths and weaknesses of each system. Third, he should compare his economic options to the standard of biblical morality, and ask which system is more consistent with the entire Christian worldview.

**Creator and Freedom, Morality and Sin**

We can begin, then, by noting several relevant aspects of the biblical worldview:

1. Certainly the biblical worldview implies that since God is the creator of all that exists, He ultimately is the rightful owner of all that exists. Whatever possessions a human being may acquire, he holds them temporarily as a steward of God and is ultimately accountable to God for how he uses them. However omnipresent greed may be in the human race, it is clearly incompatible with the moral demands of the biblical worldview.

2. The biblical worldview also contains important claims about human rights and liberties. All human beings have certain natural rights inherent in their created nature and have certain moral obligations to respect the rights of others. The possibility of human freedom is not a gift of government, but a gift from God. The Old Testament tended to focus on the economic and social dimensions of freedom. But gradually, as one moves into the New Testament, a more spiritual dimension of freedom

assumes dominance. Freedom in the New Testament is deliverance from bondage to sin and is available only to those who come to know God's truth through Christ and enter into a saving relationship with Christ. Some interesting parallels between the biblical account of spiritual freedom and political-economic freedom should be noted. For one thing, freedom always has God as its ultimate ground. For another, freedom must always exist in relationship to law. The moral law of God identifies definite limits beyond which human freedom under God should not pass. Liberty should never be turned into license.

3. The moral system of the Bible is another key element of the Christian worldview. While the Ten Commandments do not constitute the entire biblical ethic, they are a good place to begin. But it is important to notice other dimensions of the biblical ethic that have relevance for our subject. For example, Christians on the Left insist that the biblical ethic condemns individual actions and social structures that oppress people, harm people, and favor some at the expense of others. I agree. Where I disagree, however, is with the next step taken by the Leftists. They claim that capitalism inevitably and necessarily encourages individual actions and produces social structures that oppress and harm people. On this point, they are dead wrong. Fortunately, the question as to which system actually harms or helps different classes of people is an empirical, not a normative, matter. The Leftists simply have their facts wrong.

4. One final aspect of the Christian worldview must be mentioned: the inescapable fact of human sin and depravity. No economic or political system that assumes the essential goodness of human nature or holds out the dream of a perfect earthly society can possibly be consistent with the biblical worldview.

## Peaceful or Violent Exchange?

Now we must examine the three major economic systems that compete for attention: capitalism, socialism, and, somewhere between, the hybrid known as interventionism or the mixed economy.

One dominant feature of capitalism is economic freedom, the right of people to exchange things voluntarily and free from force, fraud, and theft. Socialism, on the other hand, seeks to replace the freedom of the market with a group of central planners who exercise control over essential market functions. While there are degrees of socialism, as there are degrees of capitalism in the real world, basic to any form of socialism is distrust of or contempt for the market process and the desire to replace the freedom of the market with some form of centralized control. Generally speaking, as one moves along the continuum of socialism to capitalism, one finds that the more freedom a socialist allows, the closer his position is to interventionism; the more freedom an interventionist allows, the closer his position is to capitalism. The crux is the extent to which human beings will be permitted to exercise their own choices in the economic sphere of life.

I will say nothing more about that deplorable economic system known as interventionism, a hopeless attempt to stop on a slippery slope where no stop is possible. The only way the half-hearted controls of the interventionist can work is if they become the total controls of the socialist. Anything less will result in the kind of troubled and self-damaging economy we have had for the past several decades in the United States.

I shall attempt to get a clearer fix on the real essence of capitalism and socialism, and then see which is more compatible with the biblical worldview. The best starting point for this comparison is a distinction made most recently by the American economist Walter Williams. According to Williams, there are two and only two ways in which something may be exchanged: the peaceful means of exchange and the violent means of exchange.

The peaceful means of exchange may be summed up in the phrase, "If you do something good for me, then I'll do something good for you." When capitalism is understood correctly, it epitomizes the peaceful means of exchange. The reason people exchange in a real market is because they believe the exchange is good for them. They take advantage of an opportunity to obtain something they want more in exchange for something they desire less. Capitalism then should be understood as a voluntary system of relationships that utilizes the peaceful means of exchange.

But exchange can also take place by means of force and violence. In this violent means of exchange, the basic rule is: "Unless you do something good for me, I'll do something bad to you." This turns out to be the controlling principle of socialism. Socialism means far more than centralized control of the economic process. It entails the introduction of coercion into economic exchange in order to facilitate the attainment of the goals of the elite who function as the central planners. One of the great ironies of Christian socialism is that in effect it demands that the State get out its weapons and force people to fulfill the obligations of Christian love. Even if we fail to notice any other contrast between capitalism and socialism, this already transgresses the biblical ethic. One system stresses voluntary, peaceful exchange while the other depends on coercion and violence.

Some Christian socialists object to the way I have set this up. They profess contempt for the more coercive forms of state-socialism on exhibit in communist countries. They would like us to believe that a more humane, non-coercive kind of socialism is possible. They would like us to believe that there is a form of socialism, not yet tried anywhere on earth, where the central ideas are cooperation and community and where coercion and dictatorship are precluded. But they provide very little information about the workings of this more utopian kind of socialism, and they ignore the fact that however humane and voluntary their socialism is supposed to become after it has been put into effect, it will take massive amounts of coercion and theft to get things started.

## Socialist Falsehood, Capitalist Facts

To that paradox, add one more: the fact that socialists need capitalism in order to survive. Unless socialists make allowance for some free markets which provide the pricing information that alone makes rational economic activity possible, socialist economies would have even more problems than those for which they are already notorious. Consequently, socialism is a gigantic fraud which attacks the market at the same time it is forced to utilize the market process.

But critics of the market try to shift attention away from their own embarrassing problems to claims that capitalism must be abolished or restricted because it is unjust or because it restricts important human freedoms. Capitalism is supposed to be unchristian because it allegedly gives a predominant place to greed and other unchristian values. It is alleged to increase poverty and the misery of the poor while, at the same time, making a few rich at the expense of the many. Socialism, on the other hand, is portrayed as the economic system of people who really care for the less fortunate members of society. Socialism is represented as the economics of compassion. Socialism is also recommended on the ground that it encourages other basic Christian values such as community.

If these claims were true, they would constitute a serious problem for anyone anxious to show that capitalism is compatible with the biblical ethic. But, of course, the claims are not true. People who make such charges have their facts wrong or are aiming at the wrong target. The "capitalism" they accuse of being inhumane is a caricature. The system that in fact produces the consequences they deplore turns out to be not capitalism, but interventionism.

Capitalism is not economic anarchy. It recognizes several necessary conditions for the kinds of voluntary relationships it recommends. One of these presuppositions is the existence of inherent human rights, such as the right to make decisions, the right to be free, the right to hold property, and the right to exchange what one owns for something else. Capitalism also presupposes a system of morality. Capitalism should be thought of as a system of voluntary relationships within a framework of laws which protect peoples' rights against force, fraud, theft, and violations of contracts. "Thou shalt not steal" and "Thou shalt not lie" are part of the underlying moral constraints of the system. Economic exchanges can hardly be voluntary if one participant is coerced, deceived, defrauded, or robbed.

## Allowing for Human Weakness

Once we grant that consistency with the biblical doctrine of sin is a legitimate test of political and economic systems, it is relatively easy to see how well democratic capitalism scores in this regard. The limited government willed to Americans by the Founding Fathers was influenced in large measure by biblical considerations about human sin. If one of the more effective ways of mitigating the effects of human sin in society is dispersing and decentralizing power, the conservative view of government is on the right track. So too is the conservative vision of economics.

The free market is consistent with the biblical view of human nature in another way. It recognizes the weaknesses of human nature and the limitations of human knowledge. No one can possibly know enough to manage a complex economy. No one should ever be trusted with this power. However, in order for socialism to work, socialism requires a class of omniscient planners to forecast the future, to set prices, and to control production. In the free market system, decisions are not made by an omniscient bureaucratic elite, but made across the entire economic system by countless economic agents.

At this point, of course, collectivists will raise another set of objections. Capitalism, they will counter, may make it difficult for economic power to be consolidated in the hands of the state, but it only makes it easier for vast concentrations of wealth and power to be vested in the hands of private individuals and companies. However, the truth turns out to be something quite different from this widely accepted myth. It is not the free market that produces monopolies—rather it is governmental intervention with the market that creates the conditions that encourage monopoly.

As for another old charge—that capitalism encourages greed—the truth is just the reverse. The mechanism of the market neutralizes greed as selfish individuals are forced to find ways of servicing the needs of those with whom they wish to exchange. As we know, various people often approach economic exchanges with motives and objectives that fall short of the biblical ideal. But no matter how base or selfish a person's motives may be, so long as the rights of the other parties are protected, the greed of the first individual cannot harm them. As long as greedy individuals are prohibited from introducing force, fraud, and theft into the exchange process, their greed must be channeled into the discovery of products or services for which people are willing to exchange their holdings. Every person in a market economy has to be other-directed.

## New Religion of the Left

Finally, some examples of the way in which attempts to ground American liberalism and interventionism or Latin American liberationism on the Bible involve serious distortions of the biblical message.

For instance, consider how radical American evangelicals on the Left abuse the biblical notion of justice. The basic idea in the Old Testament notion of justice is righteousness and fairness. But it is essential to the Leftist's cause that he read into biblical pronouncements about justice contemporary notions of distributive justice. When the Bible says that Noah was a just man, it does not mean that he would have voted the straight Democratic ticket. It means simply that he was a righteous man.

Likewise, many Christians on the Left seek to reinterpret Jesus' earthly mission in exclusively economic and political terms. In their view, Jesus came primarily to deliver those who were poor and oppressed in a material sense.

But every member of the human race is poor in the sense of being spiritually bankrupt. Jesus came to end our spiritual poverty by making available the righteousness that God demands and that only God can provide.

It is heresy to state that God's love for people varies in proportion to their wealth and social class. It is nonsense to suggest that all the poor are good and all the rich are evil.

Once we eliminate the semantic game-playing by which some refer to a non-coercive voluntary utopian type of socialism, it becomes clear that socialism is incompatible with a truly free society. Edmund Opitz has seen this clearly:

> As History's vice-regent, the Planner is forced to view men as mass; which is to deny their full stature as persons with rights endowed by the Creator, gifted with free will, possessing the capacity to order their own lives in terms of their convictions. The man who has the authority and the power to put the masses through their paces, and to punish nonconformists, must be ruthless enough to sacrifice a person to a principle...a commissar who believes that each person is a child of God will eventually yield to a commissar whose ideology is consonant with the demands of his job.

And so, Opitz concludes, "Socialism needs a secular religion to sanction its authoritarian politics, and it replaces the traditional moral order by a code which subordinates the individual to the collective." All of this is justified in the cause of improving economic well-being and in the name of compassion.

## The Choice I Make

I think I have said enough to allow me, at least, to make a reasoned choice between capitalism and socialism on the basis of each system's compatibility to the biblical worldview. The alternative to free exchange is violence. Capitalism is a mechanism that allows natural human desires to be satisfied in a nonviolent way. Little can be done to prevent human beings from wanting to be rich. But what capitalism does is channel that desire into peaceful means that benefit many besides those who wish to improve their own situation.

Which choice then should I, as a Christian, make in the selection between capitalism and socialism? Capitalism is quite simply the most moral system, the most effective system, and the most equitable system of economic exchange. When capitalism—the system of free economic exchange—is described fairly, there can be no question that it, rather than socialism or interventionism, comes closer to matching the demands of the biblical ethic.

# Responding to Richard Dawkins
## A Starter on the Atheist Ball Club

Michael Buratovich

## Introduction

British biologist and public commentator Richard Dawkins sports a worldview that is summarized in his many radio and television appearances, books, public lectures, and newspaper columns. Dawkins is a dyed-in-the-wool Neo-Darwinist who applies his highly reductionistic view of reality to all intellectual fields of inquiry, be they scientific or non-scientific. He withholds his most acerbic comments for Christianity and has highly derisive things to say about anyone who believes in a God that Dawkins cannot see, measure, or sense.

For Dawkins, organisms can be reduced to genes and genes to digital information. In his book, *River Out of Eden,* Dawkins writes that life is "...just bytes and bytes of digital information....Darwinism is now seen to be the survival of the survivors at the level of pure, digital code."[1] All social behavior, for Dawkins, is explainable by reference to W.D. Hamilton's theory of kin selection, whereby an organism

[1] Richard Dawkins, *River Out of Eden* (New York: Basic Books, 1995), 19.

behaves in a manner that enhances the reproductive capacity of another individual to which it is related, even when such behavior might deter its own reproductive success.[2] All life, even human life, is merely the result of mindless, meaningless forces and we must face this sad music and dance to it.

## The World According to Richard Dawkins

In his 1971 book *Necessity and Chance*, French molecular biologist and Nobel Prize winner Jacque Monod clearly defined the Neo-Darwinian worldview. Molecularly speaking, copying mistakes that occur during DNA replication—which we call mutations—occur spontaneously or through induction with mutagens in laboratory strains of mice, fruit flies, bacteria, viruses, and worms. These mutations can be detected phenotypically (by changing the appearance, development, or behavior of an organism) and even molecularly with modern recombinant DNA technologies. Therefore, it seems reasonable to predict that such mutations arise in nature and that huge quantities of them occurred during the course of geologic time—enough to drive the engines of organismal evolution. Thus, all organisms on the face of the earth that presently live or have ever lived are simply the result of blind chance (mutations) operating by means of the laws of nature (necessity).[3]

Dawkins' first book, *The Selfish Gene*, placed him squarely within the Neo-Darwinian tradition as defined by Monod. However, Dawkins took exception to the emphasis on chance in Monod's book. Instead, Dawkins championed natural selection as a highly deterministic, but ultimately

---

[2] William Hamilton, "The Genetical Evolution of Social Behaviour, I and II," *Journal of Theoretical Biology* 7 (1964): 1-52. Also see J.R. Lucas, S.R. Creel, and P.M. Waser, "How to measure inclusive fitness, revisited," *Animal Behaviour* 51 (1996): 225-228. The term "kin selection" was actually invented by John Maynard Smith. See John Maynard Smith, "Group Selection and Kin Selection," *Nature* 201 (1964): 1145-1147.

[3] Jacques Monod, *Chance and Necessity: An Essay on the Natural Philosophy of Modern Biology,* translated by Austryn Wainhouse (New York: Alfred A. Knopf, 1971).

mindless, force that sieves the mutations offered by random acts of nature by keeping those that increase survivability and discarding those that reduce survivability.

When Dawkins speaks of "genes," he largely employs the definition offered by George C. Williams, who wrote that any portion of a chromosome that lasts long enough to serve as a unit of selection is a gene.[4] This is not a perfect definition, but Dawkins adds to it the self-replicating nature of genes, since genes duplicate themselves by means of the reproductive process. Genes are identified with DNA and Williams suggested to Dawkins that DNA is the medium but not the message of selection. Genes are packets of information, not objects, and not all genes are of evolutionary significance. For Dawkins, those genes that cause phenotypic effects that promote their survival are the most successful, and are the winners throughout geologic history.

Are genes able to fight for their own existence? No, and Dawkins is somewhat careful to keep his discussion of the gene as the ultimate unit of selection above ground. Nevertheless, philosopher Margaret Midgley has criticized Dawkins for using anthropomorphisms that do not apply to genes. Genes, state Midgley, cannot be selfish or unselfish any more than they can be jealous or happy. To speak of selfish behavior only makes sense when one is speaking of organisms that are capable of behaviors, but not when speaking of molecules.[5] Dawkins has admitted as much, but insists that his use of such language is simply an analogy that communicates difficult concepts in an easily apprehended manner.[6] Dawkins has also honed his views on this subject. Organisms are containers for the genes and the most adaptively successful package of genes is most likely to be passed on. Dawkins suggests that organisms are a tool of the genes and not the other way around. Thus Dawkins constructed the concept of the "extended phenotype" in which the effects of genes are not limited to

[4] George C. Williams, *Adaptation and Natural Selection* (Princeton, NJ: Princeton University Press, 1966).
[5] Mary Midgley, "Gene Juggling," *Philosophy* 54 (1979): 439-458.
[6] Dawkins, "In Defense of Selfish Genes," *Philosophy* 56 (1981): 556-573.

the physical characteristics of individuals, but to their environment as well. For example, male bower birds construct an elaborate structure—a bower—on the forest floor from twigs, leaves, and moss. They then decorate the bower with colorful baubles, from feathers and pebbles to berries and shells. These bowers attract mates who visit their "bachelor pad" and mate with them. Species of bower birds with especially bright plumage tend to construct less elaborate bowers, while those with less attractive plumage compensate for this by fabricating more intricate structures. Therefore, the effects of genes on an individual are also influenced by interactions between those combinations of genes with the environment.[7]

Dawkins, however, does not merely bring his nuanced view of biological evolution to the lab bench and leave it there. Instead, Dawkins believes that Neo-Darwinism is a comprehensive worldview that can explain almost anything and everything. Instead of being a description of reality, it is an explanation of reality.[8]

According to this Neo-Darwinian view of the world, our world and even our existence is without ultimate purpose. In this regard, Dawkins follows closely in the footsteps of Monod's *Chance and Necessity*, which rejected any purpose within the cosmos. Monod criticized the views of his fellow Frenchmen Henri Bergson and Pierre Teilhard de Chardin, who had developed philosophies of life founded on evolution, but interpreted such life as having a kind of purpose. According to Monod, once the molecular basis of evolution was understood, it eliminated the notion of purpose altogether. There was a direction to the evolutionary process, but not a purpose or overall goal. There was no point in asking why things had happened; they just had.

Dawkins amplified these points and clarified them even further. The world may appear to have been designed, but this is an illusion that is easily explained by invoking chance mutations and the relentless process of natural selection. Dawkins believes that science is completely

[7] Dawkins, *The Extended Phenotype* (Oxford: Freeman, 1981), 199-200.
[8] Dawkins, *A Devil's Chaplain* (Boston: Houghton Mufflin, 2003), 78-90.

capable of answering the "why?" questions, since no other answer other than the Neo-Darwinian answer of natural selection is possible. We are here on no higher principle than natural selection. Our ancestors were able to increase the representation of their genes at the expense of others and there is no deeper or higher explanation than that.

While many might find the above account of our lives gloomy and depressing, Dawkins finds it liberating and exhilarating. We are a privileged people who have the capacity to research and discover how the world works. We need to "grow up and realize that there is no help for us outside our own efforts."[9]

Dawkins views humans as animals, even though he is critical of the designations used by Peter Singer ("speciesism"). However, he draws an interesting distinction between humans and animals in that human beings are not the prisoner of their genes, but are capable of rebelling against the "tyranny of the selfish replicators."[10] Thus despite his stalwart defense of natural selection and its wide-spread existence, Dawkins strongly believes that we should not endorse the ethical ramifications for natural selection despite its pervasive role in the life of humanity.

Finally, with regard to the concept of God, Dawkins possesses a deep hostility towards religious belief and views the existence of God as either impossible or highly improbable.

## Responding to Dawkins

There is much that we can say in response to Dawkins' appraisal of reality. First of all, the scientific method has neither the tools nor the language to address the problem of God. Distinguished scientists, like the head of the Human Genome Project, Francis Collins, argue that the natural sciences create a positive presumption of faith, while others, like the late Harvard paleontologist Stephen J. Gould, argue that the natural sciences have negative implications for

9 Dawkins, "Alternative Thought for the Day," BBC Radio 4, August 14, 2003.
10 Dawkins, *The Selfish Gene* (New York: Oxford University Press, 1989), 201.

theistic conclusions. Either way, the sciences prove nothing with regard to the God question.

Historically, "Darwin's Bulldog," T.H. Huxley, understood the limits of the natural sciences and was rather annoyed by scientists who made definitive statements about the existence of God. In 1880, Huxley coined the term "agnostic" to describe his ignorance on the matter.[11] Huxley's arguments are as valid today as they were in the past. Science drives one to agnosticism, and an individual conclusion of atheism or theism is derived by nonscientific means. In our day Stephen J. Gould has also addressed such illegitimate conclusions pronounced with the invocation of science.[12] Dawkins has even written that science cannot conclusively adjudicate the question of God's existence, but the matter of one's belief or disbelief in the existence of God is not a matter of personal inclination.[13] According to Dawkins, without a case for God's existence on the level of scientific proof, there is simply no good reason to believe in God, and therefore reasonable, educated people should believe no such thing.

However, Dawkins has merely sidestepped the issue this time. A belief in God is not a matter of personal inclination, but of reasoned, principled conclusions based on a variety of arguments in favor of the premise that God exists. To ignore this enormous corpus of literature is simply sloppy argumentation. The problem of God does not go away simply because one chooses to ignore it.

There is another problem with Dawkins's blithe dismissal of God's existence on the presumption that one cannot make a scientific case for it. Sometimes it is impossible to adjudicate between rival scientific theories precisely because they seem to offer equally good accounts of observations. Thus non-empirical factors tend to play a large role in the selection of one theory over another. A good example is the two rival schools of quantum mechanics, represented

[11] Alister McGrath, *Dawkins' God* (Malden, MA: Blackwell Publishing, 2005), 53-54.
[12] Stephen J. Gould, "Impeaching a Self-Appointed Judge," *Scientific American* 267 (1992): 118-121.
[13] *A Devil's Chaplain*, 149.

by the Copenhagen school (Niels Bohr and Werner Heisenberg) and the Bohm hypothesis (David Bohm). Today the Copenhagen school has achieved dominance because of historical exigencies. The Copenhagen School favors a universe that is essentially indeterminist in its functioning, but the Bohmian approach regards the universe as operating in a more deterministic fashion. Choices between these two schools cannot be made with conviction, since both models are equally elegant and simple, and consonant with the available data, but this has by no means prevented people from choosing between the two. If the scientific method cannot resolve an issue, it does not mean that all answers are equally valid or that we must abandon rationality to determine the best answer. Dawkins develops an argument for atheism that is non-scientific in nature, but claims a scientific imprimatur for it.

In several places, Dawkins argues that the concept of God is redundant and self-refuting. In his view, his "METHINKS IT IS A WEASEL" program, described in *The Blind Watchmaker*, explains the complexity of nature without reference to God or any other outside force.[14] Also, several times Dawkins refers to explanations that invoke God to account for the complexity in nature as self-defeating, because such arguments invoke a being that is much more complicated in order to explain the complexity of nature. In his mind, that simply pushes the question back one more step and fails to solve the original problem.[15]

These discussions are interesting, but Dawkins' solution to the problem contains its own problems. First, the "weasel words" program begins with something nonsensical and moves it toward a fixed goal.[16] This is exactly the way evolution does not work, since, according to Dawkins, it contains no goal or fixed final plan. Therefore, Dawkins' conclusions from this program are unwarranted. Additionally, even if the theory of random mutations culled by cumulative

---

[14] Dawkins, *The Blind Watchmaker* (New York: W.W. Norton, 1986), 46-51.
[15] Dawkins, *Climbing Mount Improbable* (New York: W.W. Norton, 1996), 77.
[16] See http://home.pacbell.net/s-max/scott/weasel.html for a web-based demonstration of this program.

natural selection explains the complexity of the biological world, it by no means sounds the death knell for Christianity, since Christian theologians have constructed systems whereby God works primarily through secondary causes. For example, Thomas Aquinas viewed God as the ultimate cause of all things, but saw God's causality as operating in several ways. God is certainly capable of doing things directly, but more often He delegates causal efficacy to the created order. Secondary causality is merely an extension of the primary causality of God and not an alternative to it. Thus the created order is completely open to inquiry from the natural sciences and these secondary causes are often known as the "laws of nature."[17] Christian scientists sometimes wish to explain the world *etsi Deus non daretur* (as if God were not given).[18] This view of God is compatible with Dawkins' views of the origins of biological complexity, but runs the risk of conceptually marginalizing God altogether. As noted by Pierre-Simon Laplace (1749-1827) in his extensive study of celestial mechanics, a self-sustaining mechanism effectively eliminated the need for God either as an explanatory hypothesis or as an active sustainer in cosmology. However, the alleged superfluity of God has no bearing on the question of his existence.

In *The Blind Watchmaker*, Dawkins spent the entire book addressing the arguments of William Paley (1743-1805). His conclusion: Contemporary Neo-Darwinism adequately explains biological complexity, and therefore there is no need to invoke a designer of any kind. In giving Paley a good trouncing, Dawkins is quite confident that he has completely undercut any foundational moorings Christianity might have. However, Dawkins seems completely unaware that while he refuted Paley, he has not refuted Christianity, since the two are not coextensive.

Paley's work comes in a long theological tradition called "natural theology." In the late seventeenth century, the rise of Deism challenged the intellectual integrity of the Chris-

---

[17] Etienne Gilson, *The Christian Philosophy of St. Thomas Aquinas* (Notre Dame, IL: University of Notre Dame Press, 1994).
[18] This is a phrase popularized by the Dutch jurist Hugo Grotius.

tian gospel. Many Christian thinkers, impressed with Sir Isaac Newton's demonstration of the mechanical regularity of the world, moved toward an appeal to the natural world as the basis for a defense of the Christian worldview. This appeal to nature fit nicely with the Christian intellectual tradition, since many Christian scholars studied the workings of nature as a means of appreciating the creativity and beauty of God. One of the most fundamental impulses that led to the development of the natural sciences in the 16th and 17th centuries was the belief that to study nature closely was to gain a deeper insight into and wonder for the wisdom of God.[19] Works like *The Wisdom of God Manifested in the Works of Creation* (1691) by John Ray (1628-1705) and others characterized this natural theology approach, and for a time, it was very fruitful. However, by the end of the 18th century, many saw that this postulated relationship between science and religion was a pyrrhic one, since a thorough-going Newtonian view of the world provided a self-sustaining universe that did not need God for its day-to-day operation.

Into this moribund view sprang Bishop William Paley. In his eyes, the Newtonian worldview would ride again. If nature worked like a watch, then God was the watchmaker. Paley's 1802 work *Natural Theology; or Evidences of the Existence and Attributes of the Deity Collected from the Appearances of Nature* was very popular and widely read. Nature, for Paley, was a "contrivance," like a watch that held the signs of design within it, since it possess a mechanistic technology. Despite Paley's popularity, his work was largely unoriginal and in many ways second rate. He depended a great deal on John Ray, even plagiarizing him to some extent. However, Paley was a powerful communicator and he brought the argument for design to a level that almost anyone could understand. Even Charles Darwin read Paley's work while a student at Cambridge and was very impressed and convinced by the arguments he found therein. Darwin's entire *Origin of Species* was fashioned as

[19] John Hedley Brooke, *Science and Religion: Some Historical Perspectives* (Cambridge: Cambridge University Press, 1991).

a response to Paley's arguments. In fact Darwin's tract on orchid pollination by insects was entitled "On the various contrivances by which British and foreign orchids are fertilized by insects." Darwin's use of the word "contrivances" was a direct criticism of Paley's work.

Despite Paley's success, many church intellectuals had serious misgivings about the entire argument from nature. John Henry Newman (1801-1890), in his 1852 lectures in Dublin on "the idea of a university," blasted the Paley's work and the entire argument from nature. Newman stated, "It has been taken out of place, has been put too prominently forward, and thereby has almost been used as an instrument against Christianity."[20] Thus seven years before Darwin wrote *Origin of Species*, Paley's view of Christianity was in its death roes. Once Darwin wrote his landmark book, others responded to it with fresh insights that attempted to unite the best of Darwin's approach with Christian thinking. This is well documented in James Moore's account of the Christian response to Darwinism.[21] Thus Paley must be viewed in his historical context and not as the undisputed champion of Christian thinking. Dawkins' rebuttal of Paley is just that and only that—a rebuttal of Paley, and not a rebuttal of Christianity *per se*.[22]

## Dawkins on Faith

On the subject of religious faith, Dawkins has much to say and none of it is good. In the first place, he defines faith as the great cop-out and an excuse to put off the hard work of evaluating evidence. He even goes so far as to say that faith is belief in spite of evidence, or even belief because of a lack of evidence.[23] In his prayer for his daughter in *A Devil's Chaplain*, Dawkins writes, "Next time somebody tells

[20] John Henry Newman, *The Idea of a University* (London: Longmans, 1907), 450-451.
[21] James Moore, *The Post-Darwinian Controversies* (Cambridge: Cambridge University Press, 1979).
[22] *Dawkins' God*, 69.
[23] *A Devil's Chaplain*, 117.

you that something is true, who not say to them: 'What kind of evidence is there for that?' And if they can't give you a good answer, I hope you'll think very carefully before you believe a word they say."[24]

Interestingly, Dawkins offers no defense of this otiose definition of faith. Despite his tendency to expatiate about faith, he never gets around to telling us where he found this definition and why he prefers it above all others. He has clearly never investigated the Christian definition of faith and appears not to care enough to do so.

A Christian definition of faith often refers to Hebrews 11:1, which states, "Now faith is the assurance of things hoped for and the conviction of things not seen." This verse tells us more about how we should view faith from the perspective of Christian practice, rather than actually rigorously defining what it is. W.H. Griffith-Thomas, former principle of Wycliffe Hall, Oxford, and a noted Anglican theologian, wrote that faith

> ...affects the whole of man's nature. It commences with the conviction of the mind based on adequate evidence; it continues with the confidence of the heart or emotions based on conviction, and it is crowned in the consent of the will, by means of which the conviction and confidence are expressed in conduct.[25]

This is a very good definition of faith and it bears little resemblance to the definition given by Richard Dawkins. Dawkins has repeatedly announced the importance of language and understanding how scientists use language.[26] Therefore it is extremely befuddling to see him use a definition of faith that is never used by Christian theologians. Having created a straw man and beaten it to a pulp, Dawkins thinks he has won without contest.

[24] Ibid., 248.
[25] W.H. Griffith-Thomas, *The Principles of Theology* (London: Longmans, Green, 1930), xviii.
[26] See *A Devil's Chaplain*, 91-103. Also see Dawkins' response to Margaret Midgley, "Philosophy," *Philosophy* 56 (1981): 556-573.

If faith in God is like the belief in Santa Claus or the Tooth Fairy, then once we "grow up" we should abandon this childish belief system. However, belief in God, at least in the Christian sense, bears no resemblance whatsoever to such a faith. Furthermore, Alister McGrath has shown in his book *The Twilight of Atheism* that people sometimes come to faith later in life after an earlier period of unbelief. Nowhere has anyone become persuaded of the existence of the Tooth Fairy or Santa Claus later in life. Clearly, growing up can consist of apprehending a belief in God. Furthermore, McGrath has also shown that people become atheists for all kinds of non-evidential reasons.[27] Therefore, Dawkins' grandstanding is beside the point, since his rabid atheism is probably derived from factors other than science.

When we come to a study of atheism, we must also keep in mind the effects of 20th century efforts to impose atheistic beliefs on people. In the Soviet Union, the Communist Party ordered an increased commitment to atheism in all its schools in July, 1954. An aggressive indoctrination program began, but the only thing this program achieved was a massive rebirth of belief in God after the collapse of the Soviet Union in the 1990s. According to Dawkins, a belief in God is imposed upon people from their childhood and, because of this horrific child indoctrination program, this belief persists in the modern world. However, in the case of the Soviet Union, an aggressive program to obliterate a belief in God completely backfired. If we were to apply Dawkins' logic to this historical scenario, then atheism is evil, immoral, and incredible. Children would not believe it unless it was forced upon them. The fact of the matter is that the institutional abuse of an idea does not discredit it.

The entire notion of believing something is rather interesting, since observational evidence can never, in principle, render a person's conclusion or interpretation certain—only probable. How probable would a conclusion or interpretation need to be in order for us to espouse a confident belief in it? Dawkins' simplistic model suggests either 0%, which

---

[27] Alister McGrath, *The Twilight of Atheism* (New York: Doubleday, 2004).

would be the case of blind faith, or 100% for scientific certainty. This dichotomy, however, flies in the face of reality. There are some conclusions of which the vast majority of scientists are very confident, since the probabilities of these interpretations are rather high. There are, however, other conclusions whose probabilities of being correct are not as high, and the conclusions are held with a great modicum of tentativeness. This is surely the way evolutionary biology works, since arguing for common ancestors is always probabilistic assessment with more or less confidence.[28] What, therefore, is the probability that God does not exist, according to Dawkins? He never presents an argument in this case and seems wholly uninterested in pursuing one, completely content to bask in his typical rhetorical exaggerations.

Dawkins' tenacious avowal of atheism sometimes begs the question, "Is science a religion?" Having been asked this over and over, Dawkins' answer is an emphatic no, since science has all the positive aspects of religious belief (evokes a sense of wonder and offers humanity inspiration), and none of the negative aspects of religion (immune from the blind acceptance of articles of belief). Therefore the only option for any thinking person in today's world is atheism. This sounds simple and final, but upon closer examination it completely falls apart. The definition of faith is all wrong, and Dawkins holds to that definition blindly despite evidence to the contrary.

This might lead us to ask if atheism itself is a faith of a religious stripe. According to Dawkins, agnosticism is, like faith, an intellectual "cop out." He views it in this manner because there are an infinite number of hypothetical possibilities which we can't positively disprove but are nevertheless highly improbable. Dawkins even uses the late Bertrand Russell's notion that one cannot conclusively prove that the sun is not being orbited by a teapot, and therefore, one is required by intellectual honesty to remain agnostic about this obviously absurd notion.[29]

---

[28] Elliot Sober, "Modus Darwin," *Philosophy* 14 (1999): 253-278.
[29] *A Devil's Chaplain*, 149.

Clearly Dawkins has made an important point, but he has also omitted some vital aforementioned points. We have good reasons not to believe that a teapot is orbiting the sun. How did a teapot—a man-made artifact—achieve escape velocity from the Earth, and, if it did, how did it stay in one piece while it achieved orbit? Given the huge mass and therefore gravitational disparity between the teapot and the sun and other planets, it would not remain in orbit for very long. The fragility of the teapot virtually guarantees that it would have been smashed to bits within a few minutes by interstellar dust and debris. Therefore the probability that a teapot is in orbit around the Sun is exceedingly low and we can say with a high degree of confidence that there is no teapot in an elliptical orbit around the Sun.

The question of the existence of God is not so easily solved. In the first place, Darwinism neither proves nor disproves the existence of God. R.A. Fisher, the population geneticist who provided the mathematical foundation for Darwinian evolution and one of the architects of the Neo-Darwinian synthesis, was a devout Anglican lay preacher. Asa Gray, Darwin's American colleague and supporter, was also a devout Christian. Darwin's bulldog, T.H. Huxley, was an agnostic and lambasted scientists who made confident pronouncements about the existence of God in the name of science. In our modern day, Stephen J. Gould has said essentially the same as Huxley. Thus a principled agnosticism that declares that the evidence is insufficient to allow a safe conclusion on the matter is possible.

However, this will not do for Dawkins. In *Climbing Mount Improbable*, Dawkins states that the concept of a "designing God" is intellectually self-defeating:

> Any designer capable of constructing the dazzling array of living things would have to be intelligent and complicated beyond all imagining. And complicated is just another word for improbable—and therefore demanding of explanation...Either your god is capable of designing worlds and doing all the other god-

like things, in which case he needs an explanation in his own right. Or he is not, in which
case he cannot provide an explanation.[30]

This passage drips with unjustified assertions. Why
would a designer who made all things have to be just as
complicated as the creation itself? This works to refute the
view of William Paley, but as we have said prior to this discussion, being a Christian does not automatically commit
oneself to Paley's view of God and nature. Also, Dawkins
relates "complicated" with "improbable." These are not
the same thing and the connection of these two concepts
in Dawkins' mind is a leap of faith. Furthermore, even if
God is improbable, *Climbing Mount Improbable* is all about
accounting for improbable entities that constitute life itself.
Additionally, one could just as easily assert that God is
one of these foundational elements in science that must be
taken for granted. As philosopher of science Philip Kitcher
states, "Science advances our understanding of nature by
showing us how to derive descriptions of many phenomena, using the same pattern of derivation again and again,
and in demonstrating this, it teaches us how to reduce the
number of facts we have to accept as ultimate."[31] Thus we
could require God as one of those "ultimate" concepts that
is amenable to description but not necessarily explanation.

In summary, in all of the written material where
Dawkins asserts his atheism, one of the most puzzling
features is the confidence with which he asserts it, since
inference is never a very exact science. However, when it
comes to his atheism, Dawkins is rock-solid confident, even
though his case for atheism is clearly not publicly persuasive despite his crowing to the contrary.

---

[30] *Climbing Mount Improbable*, 68.
[31] Philip Kitcher, "Explanatory Unification and the Causal Structure of the
World," *Scientific Explanation*, edited by P. Kitcher and W. Salmon (Minneapolis:
University of Minnesota Press, 1990), 410-505.

## Dawkins Does Theology, Badly

When it comes to discussions of Christian theology, Dawkins quotes classical theologians with disastrous results. For example, in *A Devil's Chaplain*, he quotes the early Church Father Tertullian (ca. 160-ca. 225), "An extreme symptom of 'mystery is a virtue' infection is Tertullian's '*Certum est quia impossible est*' (it is certain because is it impossible). That way madness lies."[32] In the first place, Dawkins has not properly quoted the text of Tertullian. Secondly, his poor understanding of this passage shows that he never even deigned to access the voluminous literature on Tertullian—given his misquotation, he is almost certainly quoting from a secondary source. Tertullian's complete set of words are as follows:

| Latin original[33] | English Translation[34] |
|---|---|
| Crucifixus est dei filius; non pudet, quia pudendum est. | The Son of God was crucified: I am not ashamed, because it is shameful. |
| Et mortuus est dei filius; credible prorsus est, quia ineptum est. | The Son of God died: it is immediately credible, because it is clumsy. |
| Et sepultus resurrexit; certum est quia impossible | He was buried, and rose again: it is certain because it is impossible |

In this passage, Tertullian utilizes ideas from Aristotle. He uses exaggeration and paradox to convey the truth he wishes to bring. The gospel of the Christian faith is counter-cultural and even counter-intuitive, and Tertullian uses a passage from Aristotle's *Rhetoric*, which argues that an extraordinary claim might be true simply because it is so outlandish that no one would make up such a tale. This passage was meant as a rhetorical joke for those who were familiar with Aristotle. In the words of Tertullian scholar James Moffat, "The phrase is often misquoted, and more

---

[32] *A Devil's Chaplain*, 139.
[33] Tertullian, *De Carne Christi* V, 4. Freely available on line at http://www.thelatinlibrary.com/tertullian/tertullian.carne.shtm.
[34] Translation is from McGrath, *Dawkins' God*, 100.

often it is supposed to crystallize an irrational prejudice in his mind, as if he scorned and spurned the intelligence in religion—a supposition which will not survive any first hand acquaintance with the writings of the African father."[35] Tertullian's attitude toward scholarship is better accounted by the following quotation, "For reason is a property of God's, since there is nothing which God, the creator of all things, has not foreseen, arranged, and determined by reason. Furthermore, there is nothing God does not wish to be investigated and understood by reason."[36] Thus there are no limits to those things that can be "investigated and understood by reason." However, that does not stop Dawkins from painting all religious believers with the same tawdry brush. This is horrifically sloppy scholarship and is reminiscent of the quote-mining for which he so vociferously lambastes Recent Creationists.

Finally, Dawkins endlessly recites the evils done in the name of religion as a means of beating it with a stick. His venomous essay "Time to Stand Up" is a recitation of grievances against religion for all the evils perpetuated in its name.[37] However, once again, the situation is not as simple as Dawkins would have us think. In the first place many studies (over 100 in fact) have examined the relationship between religion and human well-being. Of those studies, at least 79% have shown positive correlations between religious commitment and well-being, while only a measly 1% showed a negative association between religion and human well-being.[38] To this Dawkins might ask if we value truth over our health. However, because of his weak arguments for the non-existence of God, Dawkins has to supplement this poor argument with the provision that religion is bad for you. Here again the situation is not simple. Surely ter-

---

[35] James Moffat, "Tertullian and Aristotle," *Journal of Theological Studies* 17 (1916): 170-171.
[36] Tertullian, De *Paenitentia* I, 2. "Quippe res dei ratio quia dues omnium conditor nihil non ratione providit ordinavit, nihilque non ratione tractari intellegique voluit."
[37] *A Devil's Chaplain*, 156-161.
[38] Harold G. Koenig and Harvey J. Cohen, *The Link between Religion and Health: Psychoneuroimmunology and the Faith Factor* (Oxford: Oxford University Press, 2001).

rible evils have been done in the name of religion, but so has great good. If we wish to apply the same test to atheism, the final opening of the Soviet archives in the 1990s showed that the state-imposed atheism of the Soviet Union was anything but humanitarian, gentle, generous, or even gracious. *The Black Book of Communism*, which is based on those archives, details the crimes and excesses of Lenin and Stalin.[39] Here was an atheism that killed from 85 to 100 million people, which is far in excess of the tragedies caused by Nazism. What is good for the goose is good for the gander. Dawkins cannot have it both ways. He cannot lump Christianity in with everything else (there are distinct differences, which Dawkins ignores) and measure "religion" with one measuring stick, then throw that stick into the bin when it comes to his own atheism. This is nothing short of special pleading. The simple fact of the matter is that our belief systems inspire acts of great good and great evil, and ignoring one or the other is simply intellectually dishonest.

## Conclusion

Richard Dawkins continues to enjoy the status of celebrity scientist in his native England even though his arguments against Christianity are less than convincing and, at times, border on tantrums. Nevertheless, he has provided extensive ammunition to secularists and atheists in his day and will continue to do so. As long as the newspapers and British Broadcasting Corporation continue to give him a platform, Dawkins will almost certainly continue to blast away at Christianity in any way he can. For this reason we must construct a reasoned and cogent response to his arguments. The influence of this scientist should not be underestimated and he has shown no evidence of ceasing his inflammatory diatribes against Christianity any time soon.

---

[39] Stéphane Courtois, *The Black Book of Communism: Crimes, Terror, Repression* (Cambridge, MA: Harvard University Press, 1999).

# Creation or Evolution?
## Examining the Evidence

David and Mary Jo Nutting

## Introduction

There are really only two basic ideas about the origin and history of life on this planet—evolution and creation. Of course, there are many variations of these ideas, but at the base level the issue can be reduced to the question: Can the existence of the universe and the diversity of life best be explained by time, chance, and natural processes, or is the evidence better explained by the involvement of an intelligent designer?

Often our society has reduced this issue to a debate of "science vs. religion." In reality, both creation and evolution are philosophies. Both are equally religious in nature and neither can be "proven" scientifically, but we can evaluate the merit of each in the same way other events in the unobserved past are tested: by examination of circumstantial evidence, eyewitness reports, logical consistency, and correlation with observable facts.

How is it that two scientists looking at the same fossils and life forms can arrive at such different conclusions? The

data is the same for both creationists and evolutionists. Chemicals react the same way, rocks are just as hard, and organisms are the same for both. The debate is not really over the actual data, but rather over the interpretation of the data and the assumptions made in arriving at these interpretations.

While scientists attempt to be objective and unbiased, it is extremely difficult to separate oneself from one's worldview. If a scientist's worldview is based on natural-ism—that the material universe is all that exists—then all data must be interpreted within that worldview. Therefore, any explanation that includes a supernatural creator or events would automatically be dismissed. If, however, the scientist's worldview allows for the supernatural, the door is left open for a designer to exist. Thus, worldview plays heavily in the question of origins. George Wald, a 1971 Nobel Prize recipient who helped set the stage for what is currently being taught in biology, said:

"There are only two possible explanations as to how life arose: Spontaneous generation arising to evolution or a supernatural creative act of God...there is no other possibility. Spontaneous generation was scientifically disproved 120 years ago by Louis Pasteur and others, but that leaves us with only one other possibility...that life came as a supernatural act of creation of God, but I can't accept that philosophy because I do not want to believe in God. Therefore I choose to believe in that which is scientifically impossible, spontaneous generation leading to evolution."[1]

This bias against the supernatural has pervaded most classrooms, museums, and media around the world.

---

[1] George Wald, "The Origin of Life," *Scientific American*, Vol. 190: 46, 50

Though called a "theory," evolution is usually presented as fact and consequently students accept it as such. Having been educated and trained in the naturalistic, evolutionary worldview, we understand this bias. Both of us believed that evolution was a "proven" scientific fact—probably because that's all we were taught in school. It was not until we were teaching on the college level that we came across information questioning the theory of evolution. After studying the scientific evidence, we came to the conclusion that the evidence fits much better with a straightforward Biblical worldview, and we gave up our belief in evolution. In recent years, an increasing number of qualified scientists have been seriously investigating the evolutionary claims. Many have tured away from evolution and are opting for a worldview that includes intelligent design as a plausible scientific option.

In biology, the debate has centered primarily on the complexity of life and the lack of evidence of evolutionary

change occurring today. In paleontology, issues involve the abrupt appearance of fully developed life forms, the complexity of supposedly "early" life forms, and the lack of evidence of transitional forms. In geology, the focus has been around the rate of geologic processes, the age of the earth, and the reliability of dating methods. This chapter will focus on some of the most relevant data from biology. Some of the arguments used here have been around for a long time. In fact, we had read a book written in the mid 1950s refuting many of the arguments for evolution given in textbooks. The problem is, the evolutionary textbooks are still using the same outdated and false arguments, so we feel we still have to answer them today.

# Intelligent Design or Accidental Chance?

What is the origin of the complexity and diversity in living organisms? Can it be explained best by purely naturalistic processes, or does it point to the involvement of an intelligent designer? How would a person tell if something was designed? Does "science" even allow for a design interpretation?

Let's begin with the last question: Does science allow for a design interpretation? The answer to this question depends on the definition of science. At the root level, *science* just means "knowledge." Traditionally, according to Webster's dictionary, it has meant "systematized knowledge derived from observation, study, and experimentation."[2] However, in recent years *science* has been redefined by many to include only naturalistic explanations of physical phenomenon. In some state's science standards there has even been a lot of controversy when it was suggested that the words "naturalistic explanations" be removed. Thus, by the new definition, any potential interpretation of design by a supernatural designer would automatically be excluded from any "scientific" discussion. However, if science were viewed as a search for truth or knowledge regarding life and the physical universe, then an acceptable "scientific" interpretation of the data would include the proposal of an intelligent designer, if the data seems to point that direction. This really becomes a matter of semantics. Whoever makes the definition controls the classroom.

## Recognizing Design

How does a person recognize intelligent design versus something that is naturally occurring? Arrowheads are commonly distinguished from naturally occurring rock forms. Experience and observation tell us that rocks do not "naturally" take the form of an arrowhead, with precise symmetry and obvious chip marks. Similarly, observing a

2 Websters New Universal Unabridged Dictionary, 1983

pattern of sand grains on the beach in the form of "Susie loves Jimmy" would naturally lead one to conclude the presence of an intelligent author. Observation and experience tell us that sand grains do not "naturally" fall into this pattern, no matter how much time is allowed. Such conclusions seem almost intuitive, but are based on observation, experience, and logical inference. Our understanding of materials and natural processes helps us determine what is formed naturally and what has come about as the result of intelligence and design.

Some of the clues that lead us to conclude the presence of intelligent design are symmetry, purposeful-ness (form and function go together), complex inter-relationships of parts, and an understanding of how things "naturally" respond to outside forces (e.g. the way in which rocks normally chip or fracture and the way sand grains normally fall). We look for patterns "imposed" upon the natural materials—patterns that would not occur "naturally" because of the inherent qualities of the material. Several examples follow.

*Complex Language Systems*

Everyone knows that the placement of four letters such as STOP has significant meaning and indicates the presence of a language and an intelligence behind that language. We also know that computer programs don't just happen by accident. Our DNA is a very specialized computer code that is made up of combinations of four "letters" that spell specific instructions as well. This system, or language, is so complex and orderly that it taxes credulity to think it happened just by accident. Recent discoveries in genetic research are bringing to light even greater levels of complex-

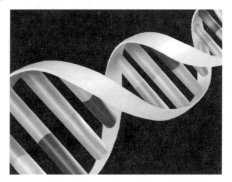

ity and order, compounding the problem for evolution. For example, it is now believed that the DNA "ladder" not only encodes in one direction, but also encodes another message when read in the opposite direction. This would be like writing a book which can be read forward or backward, each direction telling a different, but equally fascinating story—a seemingly impossible task even for a genius. But the complexity goes beyond just the linear order of "letters." DNA folds into a very specific three-dimensional structure based upon strategically placed connecting points. This folding is vitally important for proper functioning of the DNA. The case is getting worse for the atheist! (See *Genetic Entropy & the Mystery of the Genome* for details on these and other recent DNA studies).[3]

*Remarkably Specialized Systems*

Dolphins: Like all warm-blooded animals, dolphins need to maintain a relatively stable internal temperature. A thick layer of blubber acts like an insulating coat to keep them warm in cold water. However, this coat could cause serious overheating in warmer water or when a dolphin generates excess body heat during times of intense swimming. Fortunately, dolphins have a special 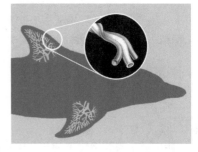 system of blood vessels in their dorsal fin that acts like a car's radiator to keep their blood at just the perfect temperature. If radiators can't happen by accident, neither did the dolphin's dorsal fin!

Bombardier Beetles: These unique insects have a highly effective defense: they mix special chemicals together within their abdomen to produce rapid-fire explosions that propel boiling liquids and gases into the face of an enemy. For this

3 J.C. Sanford, *Genetic Entropy and the Mystery of the Genome* (New York: Ivan Press, 2005)

to work, a multitude of components all need to work in unison: the chemicals, storage compartments, mixing chamber, firing tube, sets of valves, and the discernment to know when and on what to use it. Just imagine evolution trying to produce such a system by trial and error—

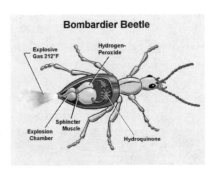

how many beetles blew themselves apart in the process? The whole system looks designed!

Woodpeckers: This little "living jack-hammer" hits its head against a tree hundreds of times a minute with a deceleration force of up to 1,000 times the force of gravity. Why doesn't it break its neck or knock itself silly? Why doesn't its beak fold up like an accordion or its eyes pop out of its skull? Woodpeckers have especially strong neck muscles and a special layer of cartilage in the skull that acts like a shock absorber. They also have extremely tough, chisel-shaped beaks and a special film that closes over the eye, keeping the eyeballs in and the wood chips out. What amazing design! But that's not all. Woodpeckers feed on insects that live in tunnels under the bark of trees. These insects would escape if woodpeckers didn't have long, sticky tongues. The tongue is actually 4.5 times longer than its skull! But this

poses another problem—what to do with the tongue when it's not in use. Fortunately, woodpeckers have a tongue storage compartment which wraps around the skull and attaches in the beak region. Which came first, the storage compartment or the long tongue? Without the tongue, the birds would starve; without the storage compartment they would choke on their long tongues. Do woodpeckers look like a product of chance and accident? No way! They clearly are designed by a master designer.

<u>The Mallee Fowl</u>: This "Incubator Bird" digs a huge hole in the ground, fills it with vegetation, buries it with sand, lays its eggs, and then covers them with more sand.

Although this may seem silly, as the vegetation rots, it produces heat which incubates the eggs. Using its specialized heat sensitive beak as a "thermometer," the bird then adds or removes sand to keep the nest temperature constant, despite changes in external temperature and solar radiation. How did this bird learn to do that? Looks like intelligent design!

## The Evolutionary Answer to Design

The above examples appear to be great evidence for creation by an intelligent designer. However, according to most proponents of naturalistic evolution, mutation and natural selection are the mechanisms which equip an animal for life in a particular environment. In other words, somehow the genetic information coding for these specialized structures has evolved from less highly specialized structures by changes in the genetic structure of the organism (mutations). Favorable mutations are then saved (or "selected") by natural selection, and passed on to the next generation. Thus, mutation and natural selection, taken together, are believed to be "creative" forces. Let's examine these processes in a little more detail.

Mutations are random changes in the genetic structure at the chromosomal level or within the genes themselves. They may impact chromosome structure or numbers, or they may affect the structure of proteins or other biologic molecules. They can occur in reproductive cells (egg or sperm) or in somatic (body) cells. Those occurring in reproductive cells could be passed on to the next generation, while those occurring in somatic cells might affect that particular individual, but would not be passed on. In order for mutations to be a creative force in evolution, there would need to be an abundance of beneficial, inheritable mutations producing something "new." However, research indicates that many mutations seem to be neutral with no immediate apparent effect on an organism's fitness. Of those mutations which have a "non-neutral" effect, most have been shown to be detrimental to the organism, causing disease, death, or some level of decreased fitness. Even the few that seem to have a "positive" effect in a very specialized situation appear to decrease overall fitness if the organism is placed in a more general environment. Thus, mutations do not appear to have what it takes to create the "new" traits and genetic information needed to drive evolution, at least not in the vast numbers needed to explain the diversity of life seen today.

Natural Selection, or "survival of the fittest," is the other mechanism proposed as an evolutionary force. It seems obvious that those organisms that are more "fit" in a particular environment or under particular conditions will be those that survive. However, by itself, natural selection has no power to "create" anything. At best, all it can do is "choose" between organisms that already exist. Thus, it has no power to explain the origin of a new trait. Furthermore, since survival depends upon a whole suite of traits, selection for only one particular specialized trait would be rare. In addition, observations have shown that highly specialized organisms may have an advantage in a very specialized environment, but are much less likely to survive in less specialized environments or under changing conditions. Thus, as an evolutionary force, natural selection does not seem able to explain the origin or diversity of the vast array of organisms observed on this planet.

In contrast, the creation model recognizes both mutation and natural selection, but doesn't rely on them as creative forces. Creationism proposes that a diverse array of living organisms was created with a diverse genetic structure. New "traits" arise primarily by normal genetic recombination of existing genes. Since the time of creation, mutational changes have occurred, most of which are harmful or have no immediate noticeable effect. (This would be expected since observation shows that random changes to a functional, ordered system normally do not produce something "better." For example, a two-year old typing randomly on this manuscript is quite unlikely to produce anything more intelligible. The fact that so many mutations have no noticeable effect is a tribute to the genius of the designer in producing systems that are self-correcting or have many "backups" to ensure survivability under changing conditions.)

Natural selection might be viewed primarily as a conservative mechanism—"weeding out" organisms which are less "fit" and preserving the fitness of the population as a whole. However, recent research is bringing into question the effectiveness of natural selection, showing statistically that it is not able to keep up with observed mutational rates and the build-up of harmful mutational load. This results in extinction over time rather than improvement.

Thus, mutation and natural selection cannot be the mechanisms so sorely needed by evolution. The evidence seems to fit better with the idea of original design by an intelligent designer. (Again, see *Genetic Entropy and the Mystery of the Genome* for more information relating to cutting-edge research on genetics, mutation, and natural selection.)

## Two Nails in the Evolutionary Coffin

Another observation in nature is a certain type of complex interrelationship of parts found in living organisms. Is this best explained by naturalistic evolution or intelligent design? Considerations include not only the "intuitive" arguments, but also more technical factors such as irreducible complexity and the laws of probability.

*Irreducible Complexity*

"Irreducible complexity" is a term coined by Michael Behe in his book, *Darwin's Black Box.*[4] It refers to a specific type of complexity in which highly integrated systems have multiple parts and reactions that work together only as a whole. Eliminating any one piece renders the entire system unworkable. (Behe uses a common mousetrap as an example.) Evolution supposedly operates by natural selection perfecting less-developed systems. However, in irreducibly complex systems, simpler systems don't work at all, indicating that mutation and natural selection could not have produced them. Three examples follow.

Blood Clotting System: This system clearly shows evidence of irreducible complexity. Fibrin forms the main clot, but if present in quantity it would produce spontaneous blood clots all over the body, causing death. So fibrin must

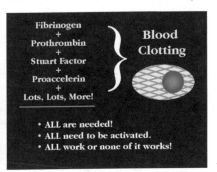

exist in an inactive form that needs to be activated. The activator plus many more critical chemicals must also exist in inactive forms; otherwise one would activate the other causing death from unwanted clots. Many crucial components are needed and all of them need to be activated to produce a blood clot. The whole system needs to be in place in the right order and working together or none of it works at all. This type of irreducibly complex system demands an Intelligent Designer![5]

Immune System: Our amazing immune system defies evolutionary origin. Blood antibodies, the heroes, are

[4] Michael J, Behe, *Darwin's Black Box: Biochemical Challenge to Evolution* (New York: The Free Press, 1996)
[5] Mary Jo Nutting, "Blood Clotting, Mousetraps, and Irreducible Complexity," *Think & Believe* Vol. 14, Num. 5.

equipped to (1) recognize and (2) destroy the antigens (germs) and still (3) tolerate the organism's own com-ponents. The only way antibodies can destroy the foe is to have a matching molecular structure. This requires a tremendous diversity of antibodies to fit the many shapes of anti-gens. Since it is an "all or nothing" system, evolution requires the simultaneous

development and operation of all of these critical factors before natural selection can preserve it. Also, when our immune system encounters something for which it has no matching molecular structure, it manufactures the precise structure, like a locksmith honing in on the right combina-tion. The immune system couldn't just happen![6]

Molecular Motors: If a bacterial cell could think, it would probably want to evolve an ability to propel itself to hunt food rather than wait for food to come to it. However, the mechanism that accomplishes this, called a molecular motor, defies evolutionary origins. Many parts resembling a complete motor—with bearing, shaft, and propeller—all work together in this one-celled organism, all at a molecu-lar level. If one part is missing or not functioning, none of it

works. The whole assembly has to be fully functional for there to be any evolutionary selective advantage for the cell. Evolution can't produce irreducibly com-plex systems like this, which are even more efficient than our best electric motors. They point to a master designer.[7]

6 Dave and Mary Jo Nutting, "The Incredible Immune Systen," *Think & Believe,* Vol. 15, Num. 1.
7 Kristy Dean, "Molecular Motors and Paddle Boats," *Think & Believe,* Vol. 15, Num. 6.

*The Laws of Probability*

All in all, the odds are enormously great against the successful occurrence of each of the myriads of needed evolutionary changes. Even the probability of 1 small protein occurring by accident is 1 chance out of $10^{260}$. (This can be compared to the odds of finding a blue marble in a universe filled with red marbles and doing it blindfolded three times in a row.) That is just not going to happen. Since we have thousands of even much larger proteins, it is even more inconceivable that they all happened by chance. Even then, proteins are not life. The probability of forming a living cell by chance was calculated by an atheist and an agnostic as 1 chance out of $10^{40,000}$. They stated that it would be more likely for a tornado to sweep through a junkyard and assemble a jet aircraft. They were actually quoted in the Seattle Times as saying "There must be a God." However, even though the evidence was inescapable, they said they were still looking for a way around their conclusions.[8] Dedication to naturalism has a strong grip on some people! Increasing the odds to include intricate structures like eyes, hearts, and lungs, the laws of probability scream out "Creation!"

## Design Conclusions

We believe that the evidence for an intelligent designer is overwhelming. Let us again emphasize that this is not an issue of science versus religion. Saying there was a designer involved in life's origin is no more or less religious than saying there was no designer involved (as dictated by the religion of atheism). Unless a person has a built-in bias against the supernatural, it seems that intelligent design is a much stronger interpretation of the actual data than chance evolutionary processes.

8 Dave Nutting, "Improbibility of Life by Chance," *Think & Belive,* Vol. 2, Num. 3.

## Examining Common "Proofs" of Evolution

Typically, textbooks, museums, zoos, and the media present a very one-sided, evolutionary approach to the question of origins, with no consideration of the possibility of creation by an intelligent designer. This section will show how data, which is usually interpreted as "proof" of evolution, can be interpreted through a different set of glasses. This evidence is grouped under four categories: change, similarities, supposed leftovers, and imperfection.

### Change

The evolutionary claim is that organisms change, thus proving evolution. Let's examine this claim. In the broadest sense, the term, evolution, just means "change," so at that level there is no contest. However, "evolution" as generally defined in the origins debate refers more specifically to the idea that the first "simple" cell arose spontaneously by natural processes sometime in the distant past, and that major changes have occurred naturally over time, producing the vast array of life we see today. This would obviously require the generation of tremendous amounts of new genetic information. Is there evidence for this magnitude of change?

Evolutionary textbooks often include evidences like the various beak forms in Darwin's famous Galapagos finches, color variations in peppered moths, antibiotic resistance in bacteria, and DDT resistance in insects. For each of these examples, it is necessary to determine the type and amount of change, and then see if this is adequate to explain the evolution of organisms from molecules to man simply by natural processes. In our experience, most evidences of change used to "prove" evolution in textbooks are relatively minor changes within the basic type of organism, not changes from one kind of organism to another. These examples are sometimes called "microevolution" or "adaptation," but finches are still finches, moths are still moths, and bacteria are still bacteria. Evolutionists may speculate that these minor changes could add up to become major changes, but it is just speculation, since there is no direct evidence that this is what has truly occurred.

On the other hand, creationists agree that organisms can undergo change, but this change is limited. The basic kinds of organisms were created distinctly at some time in the past, and there has been variation or diversification within those created kinds, but that one "kind" does not change into another "kind." This is consistent with the creation account in Genesis where the phrase "after its/their kind" occurs ten times. Thus, the creatures we see today are descendants of the originally created "kinds." Research is still needed to determine more accurately how to identify these kinds today, but they are generally thought to be at levels higher than the species level.

For example, consider the various dog breeds. Evolutionists and creationists both see change. The evolutionist would have to assume that all the traits for size, physical characteristics, and coloring were produced by mutations. Even the first real "dog" would have come from mutations of other animals. A creationist would point to the fact that most of the dog breeds have come into existence within the last several hundred years by selective breeding. Starting with "mutts" and repeatedly mating the puppies exhibiting a certain desired trait, the trait can be "favored" until Black Labs, Chihuahuas, or Dalmatians are produced.

Creationists would say this is not evolution in the broad sense, because the traits were already present in the original population. There is really no evidence of "new" genetic material—just a recombination of what was already there.

This holds true for the following "proofs" of evolution: finches, moths, and bacteria and insects.

Darwin's Finches: The finches found on the Galapagos Islands have differing sizes and shapes of beaks and are often cited as a positive evidence for evolution. However, it is now known that some of the different "species" interbreed, indicating they are the same species. Also different sizes and shapes of beaks really prove nothing. Think of all the different sizes and shapes of "beaks" (a.k.a. noses) in humans. Actually, the differences in beaks can be explained easily by variation within a created kind. Therefore, they don't "prove" evolution. Lately it has been shown that the variations in finch beaks correlate to changes in weather patterns from rainy to drought years. This throws an interesting twist on the topic.

<u>Peppered Moths</u>: After the industrial revolution in Great Britain, it was noticed that the peppered moth population shifted from predominantly light coloration to pre-

dominantly dark coloration. This was attributed to "natural selection" since the dark moths were better camouflaged on the soot-darkened trees, making them less likely prey for birds. This has been widely used as an example of evolution in action. While it might possibly be an example of natural selection, it certainly doesn't "prove" evolution, since both varieties of moth were present in the population in the first place, and moths are still moths. There is nothing new. This fits easily within the creation model of variation within a created kind. (It is interesting to note that the whole peppered moth story is now in question. See *Icons of Evolution*, by Jonathan Wells, for more information on peppered moths, Darwin's finches, and other common "proofs" of evolution.[9])

<u>Antibiotic Resistant Bacteria and DDT Resistant Insects</u>: These have been touted as proof of evolution in action. When antibiotics are first used on a population of bacteria, many die, but usually some survive and reproduce. This has produced seemingly stronger strains of bacteria (at least to that specific antibiotic). This does not prove evolution since there is no evidence of new genetic information. It merely underscores the fact that resistance was already present in the population. This can be shown from autop-

[9] Jonathan Wells, *Icons of Evolution* (New York: Regnary, 2000)

sies performed on explorers who tried to cross the Antarctic before the antibiotics were even being used. The explorers had antibiotic resistant bacteria in their stomachs.[10] Even if some antibiotic resistance could be proved to arise due to mutation, these changes are relatively minor. Bacteria are still bacteria. There is no evidence that this type of change can actually lead to the evolution of new kinds of organisms. Again, this evidence is easily explained by variation within a kind. A similar argument applies to DDT resistant insects.

*Similarities*

Another common textbook "evidence" for evolution is the similarity between various types of organisms. The similarity may be structural (e.g. bone structure in the forelimb of various animals), chemical (e.g. similar amino acid sequences in proteins or nucleotide sequences in DNA), or developmental (similar developmental sequences or structures). The claim is that similarity indicates common ancestry. If two organisms really *had* developed from a common ancestor, you would expect to find some similarities. However, you can't turn that logic around and expect it to hold true. Design by an intelligent designer would be another possible reason for similarity.

Structural Similarity: The forelimbs of various animals look somewhat similar, but evolutionary development from a common ancestor is not the only explanation—there are other reasons the similarities might occur. Similarity could be the result of design to perform a similar function (e.g. boats in the harbor have a similar basic structure because they were all designed to float on water). It could also be assumed that if a certain structure were optimal, then a master designer would make minor modifications of that optimal pattern for slightly different applications in other animals. Furthermore, similarity could be evidence of

[10] R. McGuire, "Eerie: Human Arctic Fossils Yield Resistant Bacteria," *Medical Tribune* (December 29, 1988): 1, 23

design by only one creator, not multiple creators. If structural homology really did result from common ancestry, you would expect this homology to be reflected in similar genes and developmental sequences. However, research has shown that this is not always the case. Sometimes structures that look outwardly similar have widely different genetic or developmental patterns. This seems more in line with origin from an intelligent designer, who feasibly could devise more than one way to arrive at the same structure.

Biochemical Similarity: Similarities in the amino acid sequence in proteins or the nucleotide sequence in DNA are often cited as evidence of an evolutionary relationship. However, closer observation shows many anomalies. The degree of similarity between different organisms varies according to which bio-chemicals are chosen. Clear relational patterns have not been found and attempts to construct clear "evolutionary trees" based on a wide variety of biochemicals have failed. Creationists would expect to find some similarities since

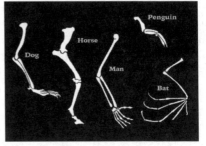

the whole language of DNA is based on only four possible choices in each location. Creationists also explain the differences based on the creator's unique design for the various kinds of creatures.

Embryological Similarity: Textbook pictures of human embryos often label certain structures as gill slits, a yolk sac, and a tail. They then say this proves we evolved from fish! This is just plain wrong and deceptive. These supposed leftovers from evolution are important in human development, but do not function as they are named. "Gill slits" are not gills. They do not function in oxygen transfer. Normally they are not even slits—they are pouches that grow into many structures of the neck and jaw. The "yolk sac" in humans doesn't contain yolk, but is a blood forming sac, used until the baby has long bones to manufacture its own blood. The "tail" is not a tail at all. Rather, it is an

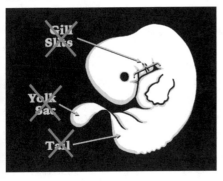

important part of human anatomy for muscle attachment for upright stance. Injure your coccyx and you will see how important it is! Why even call these structures by those names in a textbook unless someone is trying to make you think you evolved from fish?

The Biogenetic Law (Ontogeny Recapitulates Phylogeny or ORP): This so-called "law" taught that during prenatal development, a baby would repeat the stages of evolution in an accelerated manner. Ernst Haeckel's drawings of various embryos did much to advance this idea. However, it has been known for years that these drawings were fraudulent and the theory inaccurate. The differences are much greater than depicted in the drawings, and distinct features of various embryos are recognizable early in development. Some contend that this argument is not being used anymore. One Yale biology professor and writer stated, "Surely the biogenetic law is as dead as a doornail. It was finally exorcized from biology textbooks in the fifties. As a topic of serious theoretical inquiry it was extinct in the twenties..."[11] However, a review of textbooks published in the last few years showed that "modern" textbooks still contain the same "extinct" argument. Bad ideas sometimes die slowly.

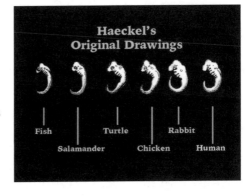

11 Keith Stewart Thomson, "Ontogeny and Phylogeny Recapitulated," *American Scientist*, Vol. 76: 273

Recently a revised notion of ORP has surfaced. Some say that the embryo skips the developmental stages that it doesn't need. For example, a mammal would not go through the stage where the embryo develops gill slits like a fish because it doesn't need gill slits. Thus, all unnecessary stages have been dropped off in the developmental process. This sounds very convenient, but what would be the mechanism for that? How does evolution have the brains to know what is not going to be needed? Keep in mind the argument tries to explain the noticeable absence of what has traditionally been expected and assumed to be there, but in reality is not. The evidence indicates that humans are human from the instant of conception, never passing through a "fish" stage or any other animal stage.

Another recent idea says that mutational changes in regulatory ("homeobox") genes can "turn on" a whole sequence of genes during development, resulting in the rapid appearance of new traits. However, this only begs the question: How did the complex sequence of genes evolve by accident in the first place—especially since none of the intermediate, unexpressed sequence would have any selective advantage until "turned on?" It is like imagining a whole house being wired with multiple lighting circuits by accident. Suddenly a main breaker is switched on and the whole system functions together. That is not likely!

Research shows a suite of extremely complex, interrelated events during development that defy chance evolutionary processes. The only logical explanation seems to be design by an extremely intelligent designer.

*Leftovers*

<u>Vestigial Organs</u>: Evolutionists predict that over the supposed millions of years of evolution there should be many "leftovers" (vestiges) from evolution that have no function today. Based upon that assumption, various lists of "vestigial organs" have been proposed. Included in the lists have been such crucial parts of our body as the pituitary gland, thymus, and parathyroid, which obviously have very

important functions. Even the appendix and the tonsils, which people still commonly state are useless leftovers, have now been demonstrated to function in immunity. Today virtually everything has been taken off of the list of "leftovers." (One might wonder how many cases of medical malpractice have occurred by removing truly useful organs because of wrong evolutionary thinking.) Creationists expect that further research will demonstrate functions for the few remaining organs. However, even if something really had lost function over time, that would not "prove" evolution. Loss of information or function fits easily within either model; it is the gain of information that is difficult to explain for evolution, as discussed above.

Junk DNA: Another form of "leftovers" from our supposed evolutionary past that is being tossed around today is "Junk DNA." In fact, up to 97% of the DNA has been classified by some evolutionists as "junk." Does this remind you of what happened with the so-called "vestigial organs?" We have contended for a long time that this DNA actually serves a very important function—we just don't know what it is yet—and that further research would demonstrate the function of these large segments of DNA. Recent findings are now confirming this prediction. According to Dr. John Sanford, noted Cornell University genetics researcher, "It is becoming increasingly clear that most, or all, of the genome is functional."[12]

*Imperfection*

Sometimes people will point to a structure that appears to them to be poorly designed. They think they could have designed it better. This argument from imperfection leads them to conclude that there must not be an intelligent designer and that evolution is true. This argument presupposes that we really do know better than the designer and that there was not a good reason for the form of the structure. It also ignores the fact that degenerative changes

[12] Sanford, *Genetic Entropy*, 39.

may have occurred since the original creation. Upon close inspection, however, it has usually been shown that the designer's way wins out over man's way.

A common example is the claim that the human eye is wired poorly. The claim is that we would be able to see farther and better in a dimly lit room if the nerve endings were at the side of the eye, rather than in the line of vision. However, if someone who thinks he can do better than the designer would try out his "improved" model, he would find himself blinded for up to 2 hours by a flash camera and likely totally blinded after venturing outside on a sunny day. Apparently, the designer knows best!

## Conclusion

In this brief chapter we have only scratched the surface of the biological aspects of the question of origins. We have seen that traditional evidences given for evolution do not hold up to scrutiny. We hope this will spur the reader to further study and contemplation. (For additional information on this topic and for resources dealing with geology, paleontology, and other topics relating to origins, please see our website: www.DiscoverCreation.org.)

Although the evidence for creation is very powerful, it doesn't say who that Creator is. It is our deep conviction that the Creator is the God of the Bible, and that true fulfillment in life is found only in Him, for now and for eternity. "For by Him all things were created that are in heaven and that are on earth, visible and invisible, whether thrones or dominions or principalities or powers. All things were created through Him and for Him. And He is before all things, and in Him all things consist." (Colossians 1:16,17 NKJV) "You are worthy, O Lord, to receive glory and honor and power; for You created all things, and by Your will they exist and were created." (Revelation 4:11 NKJV). To Him be the glory![13]

[13] Copyright Alpha Omega Institute, 2006. Used by permission.

We have tried to acknowledge original sources where we know them. However, over the years we have gleaned from many sources, processing, "digesting," and repackaging in ways that made sense to us. Thus, we gratefully acknowledge the faithful men and women who have "passed on" to us what they have learned. Much thanks goes to the Institute for Creation Research, Answers in Genesis, Summit Ministries, our colleagues at Alpha Omega Institute, and others too numerous to name. They have enriched our lives by sharing what they have learned. Likewise, we hope you will take what you have learned from us, combine it with what you have learned from others, and pass it on to others to do the same. "And the things that you have heard from me among many witnesses, commit these to faithful men who will be able to teach others also" (II Timothy 2:2 NKJV).

## Suggested Readings

Geoffrey Simons. *What Darwin Didn't Know.* Eugene, OR: Harvest House Publishers, 2004.

Geoffrey Simons. *Billions of Missing Links.* Eugene, OR: Harvest House Publishers, 2007.

Richard Milton. *Shattering the Myths of Darwinism.* Rochester, VT: Park Street Press, 1997.

Rodney Stark. *For the Glory of God.* Princeton, NJ: Princeton University Press, 2003, chapter 2.

Michael J. Behe. *Darwin's Black Box,* 10th anniversary edition. New York, NY: Free Press, 2006.

Jonathan Wells. *Icons of Evolution.* Washington, DC: Regnery Publishing, Inc., 2000.

Judith Hooper. *Of Moths and Men: The Untold Story of Science and the Peppered Moth.* New York, NY: W.W. Norton and Company, 2002.

Jobe Martin. *Evolution of a Creationist.* Rockwall, TX: Biblical Discipleship Publishers, 2002.

John C. Sanford. Genetic Entropy and the Mystery of the Genome. Lima, NY: Ivan Press, 2005.